DATE DUE

FEB 21 1997			
MAR 19 1997			
NOV 04 1997			
MAR 02 1998			
MAR 25 1999			
GAYLORD			PRINTED IN U.S.A.

The Pilgrims

The Pilgrims

Francis Dillon

(This is the revised edition of a book first published in
England under the title *A PLACE FOR HABITATION
The Pilgrim Fathers and Their Quest,* in 1973)

Doubleday & Company, Inc.   Garden City, New York   1975

Library of Congress Cataloging in Publication Data

Dillon, Francis.
The Pilgrims.

Rev. ed. of the author's A place for habitation,
first published in 1973.
Bibliography: p. 240
Includes index.
1. Pilgrim Fathers.   I. Title.
F68.D58   1975   973.2'2
ISBN 0-385-09594-5
Library of Congress Catalog Card Number 74–18792

973.2
D

For Kira

Preface

We do not know what the Pilgrims looked like: one portrait has
survived, but as in most seventeenth-century portraits we cannot
read the face; there is one description of a beard, but it has no
face at all; we know only the height and the color of hair of one
other man.

Except for some legal documents and court records, William
Bradford's chronicle *Of Plimouth Plantation* is the source of
nearly all that is known of the characters and behavior of the
Pilgrims; indeed, the form of the second half of this volume is in
the nature of a commentary on Bradford. But in spite of his vigorous writing, as men and women the Pilgrims are shadows. Nor
does he give us more than a word or two about the England he
and his companions left. It was in the time of James I, but most
of them had been born and lived their younger days as Elizabethans. They had habits of mind and were subject to social
pressures that did not change much over the forty years following the defeat of the Spanish Armada. In the air still hung the
echoes of that marvelous burst of vitality which produced
Spenser, Shakespeare, Raleigh, Sidney, Drake, and all the other
poets, pirates, and adventurers. At first sight it is difficult to see
the Pilgrims as heirs of the Elizabethan spirit, but their actions

prove that they were. It is worth remembering that after the first bitter weather in New England and half their number were dead, not one of the survivors wanted to be taken back to England on the *Mayflower*. Some idea, then, of the daily life of the later Elizabethans is essential to any understanding of what kind of people the Pilgrims were. At least it will provide a background that we miss in Bradford.

They left England because they sought freedom to worship in their own way; here again, to appreciate just what their religion meant to them we ought to know something of the history of the Reformation and of the forerunners of the brand of Separatism professed by the Pilgrims.

So this book begins with a light survey of Elizabethan England, continues with an outline of the Reformation, and ends with the story of the Pilgrims in Holland and New England.

My thanks are due to many people in England, Holland, and America, and particularly to L. D. Geller, who let me have the run of Pilgrim Hall Library, Plymouth, U.S.A., and to Arthur G. Pyle, late of Plimouth Plantation, for a mass of information unobtainable elsewhere.

Contents

Necessitie calling them to looke out for a place for habitation . . .

—Bradford: *History of Plimmoth Plantation*

When ye be come into the land of your habitations, which I give unto you . . .

—*Numbers* 15:2

The Pilgrims

1   England and the English

Up to the end of the fifteenth century, the Mediterranean was the center of the world both of civilization and of politics. England was on the outer fringe and of no great importance to anyone except herself. The closing of the overland road to the East by Mongols and Turks and the discovery of America put England into a dominant position in relation to the world, and the Mediterranean became a backwater, with its trade and influence in decline. This is a fact of geography and is still true today, with all the modern improvements in transport. The shortest route from the capital cities and the heavily populated industrialized areas of Europe to those of America is the great-circle route, and that route passes over the British Isles. Moreover, England's largest and busiest estuary, of the Thames, is directly opposite the estuary of the Rhine, and England's most important ports face west, to America. From America, England seems to be part of Europe, but Europe is much more "foreign" to the English than is America.

It took the English a long time to realize the change in their world position, and right up to Elizabeth's day they were extremely slow to cash in on their geographical advantage. One of the effects of their old comparative isolation was that both England and the English were thoroughly misunderstood by other nations. They did very little to improve their image; rather the contrary: they had a kind of "If you don't like us the hell with you anyway" attitude, which gave rise to several myths about England and the English still current today.

One of these lingering myths concerns the English weather and its effect on the English character. Coupled with the general is the particular myth that there has been a great change in the weather since Elizabeth's day, when oxen were roasted on the thick ice of the frozen Thames. But as an eminent geographer has pointed out, "If the Thames of the present day were allowed to flow almost unrestricted through banks very wide apart it would doubtless freeze over just as easily now as it did of old." When we describe the average English weather of today, we are describing the climate lived in by the Pilgrims.

Due to the influence of the Gulf Stream the British Isles have a milder climate than any other region in a corresponding latitude. The West of the land has a higher mean temperature in winter but is wetter; the East, including all East Anglia, is cooler and drier. In summer, rather more naturally, the East and the whole of the South are warmer. The dominant wind comes over the Atlantic from the southwest, but occasionally winds can blow from any point of the compass. Technically, the English weather, summer and winter, is determined by three main pressure systems, one over the Azores in the Atlantic, one around Iceland, and a third over the great land mass of northern Europe, and among them they play some intricate and unpredictable tricks too complicated to go into here. English weather, as a result, is the despair of forecasters, and long spells of hot weather are as rare as long spells of extreme cold.

Visitors to the island seldom complain of the very occasional heat waves in the summer or about cold spells in winter, but they very much resent rain and fog. Well, now more rain falls over Cape Cod than in most parts of England. Almost throughout the world, the British Isles are reputed fogbound through a good part of the year, but with all due respect to those who have been diverted from Heathrow Airport at one time or another, it is quite untrue. The old "pea-soup" fogs of London and other large towns have gone forever, we hope, with the ban on the burning of soft coal or, rather, the imperfect burning of cheap coal.

Of the weather especially, that saying by H. G. Wells is true: "The favorite topic of all intelligent Englishmen, is the adverse criticism of all things British." The Englishman even carps at the English spring, an exceedingly difficult thing to do, for it is the loveliest season of any in any land. Spring was even lovelier around the 1600s, for all England was becoming a garden except for the moorlands, the natural forests, and the wide stretches of water, and these have also figured in the joyous poetry of the age, at its sweetest when singing of the spring. The enclosure of thousands of acres of open fields, while it dispossessed many small peasant husbandmen, had allowed the new owners to put large amounts of capital into better methods of agriculture, and to set out those quick-set hedges that both kept in livestock and ornamented the countryside.

The geology of England, and it is the underlying geology of a country that dictates the landscape, is as varied though not as unpredictable as the weather. As Sir Dudley Stamp, the famous geographer, puts it, "It would be hard to find an area anywhere in the world of comparable size where wide variation in type of soil . . . give[s] such a wide variation in agricultural conditions as in Britain." The farmer of 1600 knew nothing of geology, but he knew good soil from bad, lime-poor from lime-rich, and the very peculiar shapes of most parishes are due to a sharing out of the good and bad land as equally as possible.

This great variety led to innumerable small communities who bothered only about their own affairs. The whole population was only about 4.5 million, but 80 per cent were countrymen. Each little group showed an intense affection for its own little area, and within a compass of a few miles each spoke its own dialect. The towns forced a kind of standard English on those who came to live in them, but the old country accents and some dialects have persisted, in a modified form, up to the present day. And this provincialism affected the character of the men, producing recognizably different types of behavior. The men of East Anglia were very independent, intolerant of authority, and less given to wandering than men in other parts. This is also true of Kent, but there the average income was higher and the contempt for other peoples rather more marked. Lincolnshire and Fenland people were hostile to all but their own kind. Sussex men were notoriously sly and seldom left their own county, which was the iron-working center and was rapidly eating up the vast oak forests of the Weald for charcoal. It is a pity they did not take their place in emigration to the New World, for they were some of the few expert axmen. On the whole, West Country people were amiable to strangers—except the Cornish, who even now regard all those outside the county boundary as foreigners; moreover, the East Cornish are not very fond of the West Cornish. The English of 1600 seemed to other nations an unfriendly lot, but they were not quarrelsome and were most unmilitary, although they made good soldiers. Above all, they were conscious of being English and they knew too that God was English. Typical is the comment of Peter Mundy, who after traveling in China, India, and Japan as well as all over Europe, said, "More to be enjoyed, more to be seen at home in our own land (take it in the general) than in any one country besides in the whole world both for conveniency and delight." Thomas Platter, a German writing in 1599, wrote, perhaps a little sourly, "The common people [of England] are still somewhat coarse and uncultured . . . so soon as they see a handsome man they say he is an Englishman or if they believe him to be a foreigner they say it is a pity he is not English."

The ordinary English left few records of the kind of people they were; they were frankly not interested in each other: there are no biographies whatsoever. What we know about them has had to be gleaned from assize records, a few diaries and letters, and their dialogue in plays, for the drama was the one art in which the English excelled until the Puritans clamped down on that outlet. The English had a curious lack of compassion; they were not quick-tempered, but showed a kind of calm violence in quarrel. They were serious-minded and very physically tough, because they were inured to hard work. Rough and exuberant games delighted them, as did music and dancing. As craftsmen, they were first-rate workers in wood, stone, and leather, but showed no great creative talents. Above all, they cannot be understood unless one realizes that they were deeply religious, and content with their station in life while keeping an eye open for a chance to move one step higher up.

2   Lords and Gentry

Modern historians insist that history is a continuous process with very few beginnings and no end, and that social, economic, and political history are so intertwined that any one of them in isolation makes nonsense. And the further we go back in time the greater the nonsense, because facts become increasingly sparse, and the outlines, which are all we have, are irritatingly simple.

But there is a popular response that says, "Yes, well never mind about all that, just tell us what it was like to live in Elizabethan England." Thousands of writers have tried to meet this innocent but fantastic demand, proving only that it cannot be done; a taste, a slant, a flash of scenery, some letters, a diary, some ballads and poetry, quite a lot of dialogue, all help, but at their most useful only assist the imagination, and perhaps the imagination of the skilled social historian is the best-informed. So these chapters are not history; they are aids to form pictures of life in England toward the end of the reign of the first Elizabeth, for although the first Pilgrims left England when James I had been on the throne for five years, they were Elizabethans and in many ways a new sort of English. One hundred years before, the great lords, each with a private army of retainers, had murdered each other in the Wars of the Roses; whole families had been exterminated. There were plenty of nobles left in the land but their power was gone. They had seats in the House of Lords but they were subject to the law even when put to them by a petty gentleman magistrate. At one time, and not so long before, they would have hanged the little gentleman out of hand for his impudence. Now it was the day of the small gentry. The old nobility struggled to keep some kind of prestige value, and in that they largely succeeded, but the castles and the great fortified houses were allowed to lapse into ruins, and smaller though still large houses built which could be warmed and lighted. Everyone with a large income or an estate to mortgage gave way to a mania for the new buildings. The noble still kept up a great estate, because he had not lost all his land, but as he was neither businessman nor farmer, he embarked on a process of selling off manors and parcels of land to waste on attendance at court, at jousts and masques and on entertainments he was still expected to furnish. We find that most of the ancient families who survived with a large estate intact did so by advantageous marriages with rich merchants' daughters, and the devotion of skilled lawyers.

Men still loved a lord but need no longer go in fear of him outside his own domain, unless he held an office under the crown, as in, say, the wild border lands of Cumberland and Northumberland, where the feudal power of the Percys and Nevilles had lately been broken and nobles loyal to the Queen put in control. Only force, not too nicely applied, could hold down the freebooting mosstroopers of those bleak valleys. There was no building of the new manor houses in those lands; men stuck to their castles and stone towers until well into the reign of James I, and the law was border law, not unlike western law in the U.S.A. around the late-nineteenth century. Until 1570, it was said in the border lands that there was no king but Percy.

Power in the rest of England outside the large towns was widely diffused through the gentry. On the continent of Europe the people were divided into noble and commoner; the nobles were still all-powerful and the peasants were serfs. In England all men were free, there were no serfs, and the division of the nation was between gentlemen, of whom the nobility were only a part, and those who did not qualify as gentlemen.

Much of our knowledge of Elizabethan times comes from *The Description of England* written by William Harrison in the 1570s, and he makes use of a greater antiquarian, William Camden (1551–1623), and, for his division of the English into classes, on Sir Thomas Smith, who died in 1577. After an extended disquisition on the attributes of nobility including exact details of dress proper to their orders, William Harrison defines the gentleman: "Whosoever studieth the laws of the realm, whoso abideth in the university giving his mind to his book or professeth physic and the liberal sciences, or beside his service in the room of a captain in the wars or good counsel given at home, whereby his commonwealth is benefited, and will bear the port charge and countenance of a gentleman he shall for money have a coat and arms bestowed on him by herald and be called Master, which is the title that men give to esquires and gentlemen, and reputed for a gentleman ever after."

We can best appreciate the condition of the ordinary laborer or small craftsman, from which class most of the Pilgrims came, by realizing the importance of the gentry in late-Elizabethan times, an importance that was to grow during the Stuart period. Of course the gentlemen—the gentry—came in widely differing sorts in education and wealth, but they all had the privilege of demanding satisfaction from any other gentleman, including earls and lords, in a duel. This was not quite so silly as it seems, for the new code of honor had taken the place of the "killing affray," in which an offended noble, with the assistance of a bunch of his retainers, would attack and kill a man. As late as the reign of James I, the Scottish Lord Sanquhar was executed for carrying out a "killing affray."

The whole countryside of England was held together by a web of country gentlemen—the squires. They had acquired wealth and power from two main sources, by easy purchase of church lands when the monasteries and chantries were broken up by Henry VIII, and by the new agricultural economy. Land given over to open fields since Saxon times was enclosed and made into cattle pastures or sheepwalks. When the fields were open, a man had a strip here and strips elsewhere and could do nothing but follow the rotation laid down for the village. Now the squire could grow on his land the crops best suited to it. There were still some open fields, indeed some persist to our own day, at Laxton for instance.

With the decay of the old feudal estates and the rise of the relatively small country-gentleman landlord, there came an amazing growth in the building of manor houses in every variety of style and size but usually modest mansions in the materials that lay to hand. In wooded country (country that was then wooded) oak frames were used, and as Harrison says, there was not "four six or nine inches between stud and stud," and a large number of the houses still stand in England as farmhouses or sometimes barns. Farther from the sources of good oak, only the principal parts of the frame were oak, with thin oak laths between, over which thick clay was plastered, the clay matted with chopped straw and finished off in lime and hair plaster. In Essex, overlapping boards were run over the frame, and this is the style that was taken to New England and still survives there, except that shingles are replacing the boards. On chalk land, flints and chalk were used, with sometimes the flint squared and showing a beautiful black face to the outside. But bricks were being used in some of the counties where the woods had long been cut down, and stone in places like the grassy downs of the Cotswolds, where the beautiful gold, gray, and rosy limestone had been handily deposited in layers easy to work. The very rich and ostentatious preferred stone and brick for their magnificent country palaces wherever they were situated, and some of the best of them, as Longleat, Hardwick Hall, Audley End, Montacute, and Haddon Hall are still showplaces today. But they were built to accommodate the hundreds of people who attended Queen Elizabeth in her progresses; the number can be judged by her luggage train—four hundred carts and twenty-four hundred horses. The fodder and stabling alone was a strain on any establishment.

But those vast structures were comparatively few and no concern of the country squire, whose house, however, was built to serve a large family. There was no standard house, and usually there were no plans, or plats as the term was. The mason or the master carpenter simply carried out the squire's ideas. They liked large rooms, because the Elizabethans "lived and enjoyed a very public life," though there were private rooms, or "lodgings," for members of the family and guests, and the pantry, kitchens, pastries, and so on were either partitioned off or, in the slightly larger houses, in separate buildings. The farmhouse and sheds were also separate. The manor house, then, was largely self-contained and self-supporting. *The Verney Memoirs* gives us a catalogue of the activities of a country squire and his wife:

[They] brewed and baked, churned and ground their meal; they bred, fed, and slew their own beeves and sheep at their own doors. Their horses were shod at home, their planks were sawn, their rough ironwork was forged and mended. Accordingly the mill-house, the slaughter-house, the blacksmith's, carpenter's and painter's shops, the malting and brewhouse, the woodyard full of large and small timber, the sawpit, the outhouses full of odds and ends of stone, iron, bits of marble, carved woodwork and logs cut for burning—the riding house, laundry, the dairy with a huge churn turned by a horse, the stalls and sties for all manner of cattle and pigs, the apple and root chamber show how complete was the idea of self supply and independence of trade of every kind in the country houses of the time. The stew ponds provided fish for fast days; a decoy provided a supply of wild fowl; hunting provided venison; and hawking game birds. Cattle were killed in the autumn and salted down for winter use. Much of the superintendence of this fell to the lot of the lord, save when he was absent at the wars, or attending to his country business; but the lady had much to do (all when her lord was away). The spinning of the wool and flax, the fine and coarse needlework, the embroidery, the cooking, the curing, the preserving, the distillery, were all superintended by the lady.

The size of house and estate indicated here was not unusual, but it called for a staff of up to twenty servants. The smaller the estate the less the lady superintended and the more she did with her own hands. There was still plenty of work for the maids, especially when only two or three were kept—something like the minimum for a squire. Nicholas Breton (1626) voices a maid's complaints:

I must serve the olde woman, I must learne to spinne, to reck, to carde, to knit, to wash buckes, and by hand, brew, bake, make Mault, reap, bind sheaves, weede in the Garden, milke, serve Hogges, make clene their houses, within doores make beddes, sweepe filthy houses, rubbe dirty ragges, beate out the old coverlets, drawe up olde holes: Then to the kitchin, turne the Spitte, although it was but seldome, for we had not roast meate often; then scoure Pottes, wash Dishes, fetch in Wood, make a fire, scalde milke Pannes, wash the Cherne and buter dishes, ring up a Cheese clout, set everything in good order.

The servants' routine began at 6 A.M. in summer, 7 A.M. in winter, and many households had a system of fines of one penny or twopence if the beds were unmade by 8 A.M. or the fireplaces not cleared or if the servants missed morning or evening prayers. These fines could add up to a heavy punishment when deducted from a wage that did not exceed five pounds a year.

The Elizabethans took great care of their gardens, as they had to do or go without fruit, vegetables, and herbs, for those they grew are just those which need almost constant attention: artichokes, cabbages, turnips (not for animal feed), broad beans, rounceval peas, pumpkins, skirrets ("the sweetest whitest and most pleasant of roots"—a kind of water parsnip, seldom grown today), radishes, carrots, parsnips, onions, garlic, leeks, endive, spinach, sorrel, lettuce, parsley, mustard, cress, sage, tarragon, fennel, thyme, mint, savory, rhubarb (used only as a drug), and a great number of other herbs. The modern gardener will notice that many of his most useful plants are missing from the Elizabethan list—asparagus, kidney and string beans, and, most familiar to us, potatoes. The herbs were very necessary; pepper and spices were imported and extremely expensive, and the herbs were used to make palatable the meat, which was salted down in the autumn. Few beasts could be fed through the winter, and there was of course no cold storage except the stone, north-facing larder. Other herbs were used for medicine, and out of them the housewife, who was her own druggist and doctor, made some nauseous-sounding nostrums, and also some delicious syrups and jellies.

Flowers too were grown as much for their medicinal value as

for their beauty. Saffron (a crocus—the powder comes from the stamens) was widely grown for the home as a flavoring and coloring, and it was also a good cash crop. Shakespeare mentions some twenty different fruits grown in his time, and Elizabethan cookbooks give some fascinating recipes for preserves, pastes, and candied fruits.

The gentry, says Harrison, took two meals a day, breakfast at 11 A.M., supper between five and six. Merchants dined at noon and supped at six. The poorer people "dine and sup when they may so to talk of the order of their repast it were a needless matter."

What kind of food each ate depended on the time of year, but foreigners were amazed at the vast quantities of food served in the halls of the rich. The queen normally sat down to twenty-four dishes, and a minimum of thirty when dining in state. At banquets arranged by courtiers one could expect extravagance, and up to one hundred and sixty dishes are mentioned. The still-enormous surplus was given to the poor. Civil servants in White-hall were used to seven dishes. Most of the gentry were more modest in their diet, but the calendar of the year called for many feasts as well as some traditional fasts. In Lent everyone by law ate fish, fresh near the coast and rivers, or perhaps fresh carp from the stews or pond, but some salt or smoked in dry uplands. But the law of supply also operated in Lent, for only the remnant of the bacon and the beef slaughtered in November was available, and it took a lot of spices to make it acceptable to a normal palate.

Before and after Lent, the countryman could usually find game, for the wastelands and woods swarmed with rabbits, hares, and all kinds of birds. It was estimated that of thirty-nine million acres of land in England one million were water, ten million were heaths, moors, and mountains, three were woods, three forests and common land. This estimate was made one hundred years after Elizabeth; in 1600, the woods, forests, and moors were much more extensive. April was the cruel month. Until then, that is from December through to the end of March, clouds of wildfowl were available in many parts of the country, particularly anywhere near the million acres of fen. After April there was buck venison and from October to December doe venison; these as a supplement to the farm animals slaughtered in midsummer. Most of the gentry were devoted to hunting, and even the smaller gentry kept a little pack of hounds. The richer preserved deer for hunting in their own parks, and it was an ambition among them to own a pack whose voices were matched like a peal of bells—"a tunable chiding of hounds" was the phrase. The smaller gentry trapped badgers, speared otters, and coursed hares, and all hunted the fox, both as a pest and for sport. Wildfowl were taken with hawk and net. The nets were arranged funnelwise over a stretch of water—a decoy, it was called —and the fowl lured in by all sorts of tricks. Sparrows, larks, and finches were lured by corn or bread, and, roasted, were much appreciated.

Hawking was a science with its own esoteric ritual and language. As to which kind of hawk any man should fly, exact class distinctions were laid down, although by late-Elizabethan times some of these distinctions were a little blurred in practice. But this was the order by law of falconry:

Gerfalcon for the king.
Falcon for a prince
    down to
Merlin for a lady
Hoby for a young man
Goshawk for a yeoman
Tercel (male hawk) for a poor man
Sparrowhawk for a priest
Musket (male sparrowhawk) for a holy-water clerk
Kestrel for a servant or laborer.

There was an old law still enforced which forbade the use of powder and shot in hunting or fowling, although of course the crossbow was freely used.

England was famous for its roast meats. Some authorities have surmised that the protein-rich diet of the Elizabethans was the source of their incredible vitality, but one cantankerous commentator suggests that the same diet took them to an early grave. The impression left by reading accounts of Elizabethan food is that all classes lived almost exclusively on joints of meat and whole birds, but in the ballads, the poetry, and the plays of the day we hear of "tarts and custards, creams and cakes, puddings, pies and pasties, fish and meat stews, brawn, and very frequently porage, or porridge, a name given to a wide variety of dishes made of oatmeal and other grain mixed with bits of meat, game, and such vegetables as peas. There was a plentiful supply of eggs, butter, and cheese both green and hard. Green was a kind of cottage cheese often buried in the earth for a few days to mature. The staple diet was bread, beef, and beer—good, wholesome home-brewed beer in two kinds, thick and rather sweet brown ale and a thinner, bitter ale lighter in color. The more prosperous gentry ate white bread of wheat flour that varied in quality. The queen's "manchet" was made from wheat grown at Heston in Middlesex, which Harrison says was the purest in many shires ("pure" may mean "fine"). The manchet was a flat, round loaf of half a pound weight that came out of the oven at six ounces. Even in the manor houses much bread was made from rye and barley, and, when corn was high in price or scarce, bread was made from peas, beans, oats, lentils, and even acorns. The subject of food is an endless one in every age; in short, we can say that at the end of the sixteenth and the beginning of the seventeenth centuries, food was plentiful and cheap for all classes though immensely more varied among the middle and upper classes.

The new furniture at the end of the queen's reign was hideous and got steadily worse. Many of the new houses were in shocking taste, but in the furniture a debased Italian style much coarsened by designers in the Low Countries was recklessly applied to (mostly imported) oak with knobs and bulges and every possible surface hacked over with crude carvings or weird figures and caricatures of the five basic orders of architecture. As the new rich in any period, they scorned the austere lines and restrained decoration of preceding ages exemplified in the lovely linen-fold paneling that country craftsmen were used to carrying out. Not that there was a falling off in the skills of craftsmen, who still made beautiful simple furniture for lesser folk than the parvenu squires; moreover, they took their skills to America to inspire that very pleasant Old Colonial style of furniture and household tools in New England. Fortunately, the late Elizabethans built few churches, although they contributed some vast and hideous tombs and monuments to the wonderful existing churches in every parish; stiff and ugly, mostly these tombs were surmounted by statues of the Elizabethans themselves with their families strung out in rows on each side.

It must be made clear that the country squires were not all Johnny-come-latelies; many families had acquired their position over many generations, but the growing importance of their class did sometimes bring out a certain pomposity in the newly created gentry, as the playwrights were fond of observing. The whole land was governed, or rather administered, by justices of the peace, and these were drawn from the gentry, who were, it is estimated, some sixteen thousand in number. As well as dispensing justice in their counties, they had to administer the poor law. (Their actual duties and responsibilities are the subject of a later chapter.)

Visitors to England were astonished at the custom among the gentry of sending out their younger sons into the wide world in search, one might say, of their fortunes. They were, as a first step, put as apprentices to merchants and craftsmen in the towns. London, with its population of 220,000, absorbed most of them. No other town exceeded ten thousand, except Bristol and Norwich.

Foreigners remarked on the affection the English gentry had for rural life. "Every gentleman," they wrote, "flieth into the country. Few inhabit cities and towns, few have any regard for them." In France and Italy, as elsewhere in Europe, it was the ambition of gentlemen to get a house in town, the bigger the house and the bigger the town the better.

The squires' daughters learned the whole gamut of housekeeping quite naturally from their mothers. They also learned to ride, handle the spindle and the needle, and usually enough music to read a song and fill in the chords on a lute. They were ready for marriage from fifteen years on, though many were married at thirteen, and at that age their partners were quite naturally selected for them by the parents. It was a question of estates and

settlements or dowries, although the field of possible partners seldom covered more than thirty miles in any direction. The squire
(more often, his wife) tried to pick from an estate a little higher
than their own, but if the daughter hung fire in the market, a
wealthy yeoman (who was not a gentleman) was quite often acceptable. There were of course a few love marriages, runaway
marriages, and refusals by the girls, but on the whole the system
was made to work.

Sir Thomas Overbury, in his *Characters*, is unusually sour
about the squire and stresses his provincialism:

> A country gentleman is a thing out of whose corruption the genera-
> tion of a justice of the peace is produced. [Overbury is referring to a
> pseudoscientific theory of the age that some precious materials were
> spontaneously generated out of a corrupt mass; it was also held to
> be true of worms.] He speaks statutes and husbandry well enough to
> make his neighbours think him a wise man; he is well skilled in
> arithmetic or rates; and hath eloquence enough to save his twopence.
> His conversation amongst his tenants is desperate; but amongst his
> equals full of doubt. His travel is seldom farther than the next
> market town and his inquisition is about the market price of corn;
> when he travelleth he will go ten mile out of the way to a cousin's
> house of his to save charges; and rewards the servants by taking
> them by the hand when he departs. Nothing under a sub-poena will
> draw him to London.

In fact, taken all together, they were the guardians of freedom
against encroachments by the crown, the court, and the higher
nobility, and many of them were, in the just and traditional
meaning of the word, gentlemen, and much more cultured and
assured than Overbury will admit.

3   The Merchant, the Yeoman, and the Laborer

Until quite recently, that is among people still living, no one engaged in trade could be considered a gentleman even if he had purchased an estate in the country and a knighthood. His son might qualify. In these matters your Victorian was even more choosy than the Elizabethan, whose rules William Harrison sets out:

> Citizens and burgesses have next place to gentlemen who be those that are free [men] within the cities and are of some likely substance [*wealthy enough*] to bear office in the same.

Grouped with the citizens

> are our merchants although they often change estate with gentlemen as gentlemen do with them,

which seems to mean that a gentleman could go into business, become a member of one of the great companies, but lose his gentility, whereas a rich merchant could buy a country estate, acquire a coat of arms, and be called gentleman. A certain James Howell protested against this particular snobbery:

Nor do I see how some of our country squires who sell calves and runts and their wives perhaps cheese and apples, should be held more genteel than the noble Merchant Adventurer, who sells silks and satins, tissues and cloth of gold, diamonds and pearl with silver and gold.

The rich merchants were organized into powerful trade associations, or guilds, some ninety of them surviving to modern times as livery companies, with not much left of their old power. The guilds originated in the Middle Ages and had within themselves an order of civic precedence. There were twelve "great" companies, as Mercers, Grocers, Drapers, Fishmongers, Goldsmiths, and so on, and a host of lesser companies, Dyers, Brewers, Butchers, et cetera. In the late-sixteenth century, they each dominated their particular trade, and by law no one not a member of the guild could carry on that trade, either as producer or as purveyor, that is neither manufacturer nor salesman. But trade was booming and trades were splitting into specialized units and, to escape the heavy hand of the guilds, industry and business houses began to be set up on the fringe of towns. The law pursued them without much success; in any case, they were small fish by the standards of the London companies.

The City of London was the merchants' stronghold, unchallenged by any other interest; neither the aristocracy, the court, nor the queen herself had any say in the government of the City; it was ruled by the mayor and his council of aldermen, and they were selected by the great companies. They commanded the only regular soldiers in England, the trainband of London; they directed the city churches into their own kind of religion, and that was Protestant with some leaning toward Puritanism. London was a state within a state and purely bourgeois. Outside the city boundaries lay the royal power, but those city boundaries enclosed a wide area up and down the River Thames. The merchants had their agents in most of the important mercantile cities in Europe. As we shall see in a later chapter, it was the London merchants who had the foresight and enterprise to finance expeditions to explore and open up markets in far-distant lands. They furnished ships to defeat the Spanish Armada and other ships to act as licensed pirates. They had the money; the state had none to spare. They were true Elizabethans and must not be thought of as a stolid, cautious body of tradesmen. They not only shared but fanned the excitement at the new discoveries, and were leaders in the Elizabethan spirit long held back by wars with France and Spain. In some sort they were poets, though you could have raised a laugh in the South Bank theaters by calling them such. Nevertheless, it took imagination to finance a forlorn hope like the Pilgrims.

All artisans and handcraftsmen were also organized into guilds, and to become a practicing member a man had first to serve a seven-year apprenticeship. The system of apprenticeship spread through every trade and calling. The younger sons of country squires were nearly always sent to a town, often to London, to be apprenticed to merchants and the better tradesmen, who were forbidden by the statute of apprentices to take anyone under the rank of yeoman's son. Another clause in this statute ordered that no one engaged in agriculture should be apprenticed to any ordinary craft in any town, which had the effect of keeping surplus population in country districts. It did not stop unemployed countrymen with no special skills outside agriculture from drifting into the towns and taking any one of the many low-grade, casual laboring jobs or joining the ranks of the beggars and vagrants, all grouped as "masterless men."

What has been said about London is broadly true of all the other towns in England, though some country towns were little more than villages.

The apprentice lived with his master, whose workshop was also his house, and when the seven years of board and service were over the apprentice could continue for wages as a journeyman or set up in business on his own account. Often enough to be the subject of ballads and quips in the theaters, the apprentice married his master's daughter and succeeded to his business. To set up as a merchant, a man needed seventy pounds' worth of stock and thirty pounds as a tradesman. (£70 = £2800 today, or $6,700.)

It is impossible even within the space of a small library to do more than brush lightly over the enormous variety of occupations in Elizabethan London, and we shall not attempt it. The place was bursting with all the activity of a newfound commercial prosperity, and every operation in industry was carried out by hand. Two thirds of all English trade and industry was centered on London. The London mob was easily aroused and the apprentices were happy to play a leading part in all uproars, quite a number of which were directed against foreigners, usually important visitors. It would seem like a town where a man could make his way and rise in the world, but the class system laid rigid barriers in the path of all without money or influence. As in any society, though, however rigid, there were always some few individuals whose talents, courage, skill, and downright effrontery made barriers useless. They were not always a town product.

It is a great pleasure to turn from the noisome, pullulating city streets to the sweet and fragrant air of the English countryside and to one who has always stood as the apotheosis of the sturdy reliable Englishman for some seven hundred years—the yeoman.

That same Sir Thomas Overbury who was sneering somewhat at the squire is all kindness and understanding when he paints the yeoman:

> His outside is an ancient yeoman of England, though his inside may give arms (with the best gentleman) and ne'er see the herald. There is no truer servant in the house than himself. Though he be master, he says not to his servants, "Go to field," but "Let us go"; and with his own eye doth both fatten his flock and set forward all manner of husbandry. He is taught by nature to be contented with a little; his own fold yields him both food and raiment; he is pleased with any nourishment God sends. . . . He is ne'er known to go to law; understanding to be law-bound among men is like to be hidebound among his beasts; they thrive not under it: . . . When he builds, no poor tenant's cottage hinders his prospect; they are indeed his alms-houses. . . . He never sits up late, but when he hunts the badger. . . . He allows of honest pastime and thinks not the bones of the dead anything bruised . . . though the country lasses dance in the churchyard after evensong. . . . He is lord paramount within himself. . . .

We feel inclined to say, "There ain't no such animal" or that he is a little too good to be true. But there must be some truth in the matter, for the yeomen of England have had a very good press for at least four hundred years. In the days of the longbow, which were just coming to an end with the development of the gun, the yeomen were the skilled and disciplined archers who dominated the battlefields of France in the Hundred Years' War, who shot down many times their own numbers with their arrows at Crécy and "filled the air as it were snow." Yeomen were peculiar to England; they did not exist in France and Italy, where men ranked either as upper class or peasant. Their number was estimated at about 180,000 families, of whom Sir Thomas Wilson (1600) says, ". . . about 10,000 in country villages are of wealth enough to mate with gentry." Technically, to be a yeoman a man must be able to spend forty shillings a year from his own freehold land, and this also qualified him to vote in parliamentary elections. He exercised this right very freely, and it was often his pleasure to vote on a side opposite to the squire. He was one of the main men to sit on juries. Nearly all yeomen were farmers, though a few were in business or industry. It should be noted that, in the towns, burgesses and merchants ranked before yeomen. John Stephens (1615) supplies one of the very few pieces of criticism to be written against the honest yeoman:

[He is] sufficiently book-read, nay a profound doctor, if he can search into the diseases of cattle: and to foretell rain by tokens makes him a miraculous astronomer. . . . The price of his housekeeping is a mess of cream, a pig, or a green goose; and if his servants can uncontrolled find the highway to the cupboard, it wins the name of a bountiful yeoman. Doubtless he would murmur against the Tribune's law, by which none could occupy more than five hundred acres, for he murmurs against himself, because he cannot purchase more. To purchase arms (if he emulates gentry) sets upon him like an ague and he can never be quiet till the herald hath given him the harrows, the cuckoo or some ridiculous emblem for his armoury. The bringing up and marriage of his eldest son is an ambition which afflicts him so soon as the boy is born, and the hope to see his son

superior, or placed above him, drives him to dote upon the boy in
his cradle.

This is the gentleman getting nasty about the newly rich, an attitude not unfamiliar even in our own day.

The houses of the yeomen naturally varied in size with their
wealth, but, since they seldom tried to rival the squires, on
average their houses were smaller but nearly always of timber
filled in with plaster and of a type common to most of northwest-
ern Europe. The timbers were exposed, and usually the upper
floor projected over the ground floor, cantilevered out by two or
three feet. Quite a number still survive in England and in
Europe; the style persisted into the eighteenth century. By 1600,
what had once been a single large room on the ground floor had
been partitioned off into smaller rooms. Thitherto, privacy had
not been unduly considered. These new houses had stone or
brick chimneys with an open fireplace for cooking, for smoking
meats, and of course for the only source of warmth in winter.

We have many records of the food the yeoman and his servants ate. The fare varied from county to county, but as a general rule he fed less delicately than the squire but ate larger
quantities: ". . . solid substantial food, no meats disguised with
strange sauces, but beef and mutton, bread, milk, oatmeal,
cheese, rabbits and chicken. Salt, sugar, spice only we buy." Like
any other extract from a diary, that leaves a lot of questions to
ask. And Goodman Fuller is talking of good times and favorable
seasons, for all classes lived as the crops in their seasons afforded,
and bad weather, poor crops, and diseases could easily bring a
local or even widespread famine, and inland transport was so
bad that it took a long time and great expense to get relief
supplies. Of course, the poor suffered most. In the three years
from 1607, there were famine conditions over the whole country
and again in 1623 and the three years to 1633. One form of insur-
ance against famine can be seen in the quite large number of
barns still standing in the English countryside—once the property of the gentry and the yeomen. They are not so massive as
the great stone-built tithe barns of the monasteries, which
housed the grain for the entire community, but fifty feet by

twenty feet is quite usual; they have massive doors to take a
loaded wagon, and the heavy oak roof timbers seen from inside
remind one of a cathedral.

The yeoman's furniture did not ape the fearful bulges, knobs,
and contorted carvings of the rich squire but was home- or
village made, large bed and all. He had several plain chests, a
heavy table, benches and stools and perhaps a chair with arms.
The host or husbandman sat in this chair at the head of the table
—the chairman, a word we still use in a slightly different sense.
Some beds had feather mattresses, but straw paillasses were in
most yeomen's bedrooms. Pewter dishes were common, and there
were occasional pieces of silver, but the yeoman ate from treen
(that is, wooden) bowls and platters. He drank from leathern
blackjacks, or mugs, but pewter and a little glass were coming
into general use. He no longer drew his dagger to cut his meat at
table, though the dagger came into use in the field for bread,
cheese, and fat bacon.

Very close to the yeoman in manner of living was the tenant
farmer and the peasant, who enjoyed "a secure tenure on a piece
of land at an unalterable rent"; indeed these three classes are
sometimes grouped under "yeomen," and all three might be
farming a large plot of enclosed land plus several strips in an
open field as well as running a flock of sheep. The very large,
open fields of grain not in strips were usually in the possession of
rich gentry.

Of tenant farmers there were probably fewer than there were
yeomen; we don't know the 1600 figures, but in 1696, when the
numbers of yeomen were declining, Gregory King's tables calcu-
lated that there were 150,000 tenant-farmer families to 160,000
yeomen.

Below the tenant farmers in class came the peasants, who
formed 85 per cent of the rural population and the artificers, or
artisans. "This fourth and last sort," as Harrison puts it, had neither voice nor authority but could hold minor offices as aleconners or headboroughs, but they were "to be ruled and not to
rule other" men. He then lumps into the fourth and lowest class
all those who have neither land, money, nor jobs, as well as the
cobbler, blacksmith, wheelwright, hostler, goldsmith, carpenter,

laborer, and the rest of those that a later age called "useful men." There is little evidence that the employed of this immense class, who were the majority of the population, ever bothered their heads about their position in society, even in the towns among the highly skilled craftsmen, except that they would certainly think of themselves as a cut above rogues and beggars. But all, peasants, artisans, and beggars, were aware and proud of the fact that unlike the peasant in Europe they were all free men. The absence of any political agitation, any sense of grievance among field laborers and artisans during the late-sixteenth and the early-seventeenth centuries has been a source of wonder to most historians. There had been a golden age for the peasant after the Black Death had halved the population and there was land to spare (to rent of course, not to own), but the enclosures of the open fields followed by changes from arable to pasture had turned small peasant farmers into laborers. (The process is much oversimplified in the preceding statement but that was the effect.)

The beginning of the sixteenth century saw a huge army of unemployed for whom no work could be found, but at the time with which this survey is concerned (that is, toward 1600), the industries of the towns had taken up the slack of unemployed and the very growth of the towns was demanding more bread, meat, and other foodstuffs. So the turnover to sheep and wool was halted and more of the land plowed. There was even in some counties a shortage of agricultural labor. Arable farming was a labor-intensive industry, or to put it in English, it took a lot of labor. But a good deal of the labor was seasonal: extra hands were needed at haying time, grain harvest, and shearing; in Kent and the fruit counties of the West, women and children were in great demand for apple, cherry, and hop picking.

This turnover of labor led to an astonishing mobility among the poorer classes. At one time it was supposed that in the eastern and southern counties the cloth trade, weaving, spinning, carding, and so on, all carried out in the cottages, kept the families busy and settled in one place, ready to lend a hand to the nearby farms at harvest. In fact, research has proved that large numbers of the laborers were on the move at all times of the year from one cloth center to another, from the little villages to the towns (not necessarily London). This was also true of the crafts-men—the carpenters, masons, and other skilled workmen—but in their case we can see the reason for their migrations, because new houses were being built all over England.

The general restlessness is something of a mystery. Of course everywhere in England there were farms and villages where the workers had stayed put for generation after generation, where the village crafts of leatherworker, smith, carpenter, et cetera, had been handed down from father to son and where in bad times the poor law made some slender provision to keep them there. The poor law of 1598 created no welfare state, but it was remarkable for its time and there was nothing like it elsewhere in Europe. But no parish wanted to help the poor of another parish; in fact, the law ordained that an unemployed person with no means of subsistence should be shunted from parish to parish until he got back to his place of origin.

Some counties were afflicted by swarms of Irish who had fled from famine conditions in their own country and were branded as rogues and sent back in shiploads, for they were reinforcing the hordes of rogues and vagabonds already wandering the roads and byways of England. A rogue and vagabond was simply one who had no means of subsistence and was begging or, quite likely, stealing. The Dutch and Flemings who fled the Spanish fury, and the Huguenots, were in a different case. Often they had some assets and were nearly always skilled in a branch of the cloth trade, and they came into areas such as East Anglia, Kent, and part of the West Country, where the cloth trade was flourishing. Similarly, few or none of the immigrant Jews ever made demands on the parish funds.

The myth is that the Flemings and Huguenots were made wel-come because they were Protestants, often Calvinists, and brought new skills with them, but the truth is that they were very largely resented as an influx of foreigners has always been resented by the English. The folk memory was and is of strange people who take over your job and eventually your land.

Of those fourth-class people who remained in one place, and it should be emphasized that they were the majority, the married men had usually their own small cottage, often of thin timbers, wattle, and daubed clay. There may have been two rooms but usually one, with a fireplace and no chimney: the smoke, when it did escape, went through a hole in the thatched roof. But brick chimneys were being built even by the cottagers. By law, each cottage had to have four acres of land, and we do not really know how often this law was ignored, but even on the impoverished soil of some areas a lot of food can be grown on four acres. The laborer had often access to common land to graze a cow or geese, and some knowledge of the ways of poor farm laborers in our own time suggests that the Elizabethan laborer had a hundred ways of getting additional food as well as firewood. In these little cottages, much of the elementary work of the cloth trade was carried on—spinning, carding, and weaving, especially of the coarser cloths. Some spun wool a clothier's chapman supplied and were paid by results on piecework; others, and the evidence is that there were many of them, bought their own wool and sold it as yarn "and made good profit thereof." As an instance of the division of labor, the flat, round caps almost universally worn, some of them known as Monmouth caps, ". . . first they are knit, then they mill them, then block them, then they work them with tassels, then they shear them," but "they" were different workmen for each process.

Many farm servants were indentured, that is hired, for so much a year, the farmer supplying food and lodging and often stipulated items of clothing, but the practice of paying by the day was on the increase.

Historians differ, as do their sources, as to how the poor sort fared. "Meat in plenty," says one; "pinched and hard fare," says another, but the balance of evidence points to a fairly unvarying diet of peas and oats porridge with such meat or tripes available thrown in and bread, cheese, onions, butter, and beer. The composition of the bread varied too, with what grain was at hand, but they baked no white bread. In Yorkshire a peck of peas to a bushel of rye "made a hearty bread." In the grain belt of East Anglia maslin flour was used, half wheat, half rye, and the West Country favored oats for their flour. Similarly, beer came in all sorts of qualities, flavors and colors. Harrison says, "Our malt bugs lug at ale pots like pigs at their dam's teats." In other words, the workmen liked their beer, and where orchards were they liked good rough cider and perry (made from pears). The ancient drink of mead, made from virgin honey, was now more often adulterated with water and herbs or spices into a kind of metheglin. On the whole, the English peasant had no head for strong ale, and when he got some at a wedding or a church-ale, he was prone to get "cupshotted."

A church-ale was only one of a whole calendar of holidays on which feasts were held, often in the churchyard. The Elizabethans were devoted to dancing, singing, and games of all sorts. Robert Herrick's well-known verses give a pleasant outline:

> For Sports, for Pagentrie, and Playes,
> Thou has thy Eves, and Holydayes:
> On which the young men and maids meet,
> To exercise their dancing feet:
> Tripping the comely country round,
> With Daffodils and Daisies crown'd.
> Thy Wakes, thy Quintals, here thou hast,
> Thy Maypoles, too, with Garlands grac't:
> Thy Morris-dance; thy Whitsun-ale;
> Thy Sheering-feast, which never faile.
> Thy Harvest-home; thy Wassaile bowle,
> That's tost up after Fox i' th' Hole.
> Thy Mummeries; thy Twelfth-tide Kings
> And Queenes; thy Christmas revellings:
> Thy Nut-Browne mirth; thy Russet wit;
> And no man payes too deare for it.

Some of the goings on were not quite so innocent as Herrick suggests, but they had not a hundredth part of the harm the Puritans imputed. One of the most popular games was football, against which the only moral objections raised were that it was usually played on holy days and Sundays and it encouraged hooliganism; a valid objection was that in the more boisterous forms broken bones were common. Rules varied from parish to parish, the main object of play being to carry, kick, or throw the ball past a fixed line, sometimes the parish boundary. Any

number could play, and hundreds at a time did. It was a time to
work off old grudges, whether the ball was being played or not.
The game still persists in some of the remoter country districts of
England.

Before the Puritans took hold, the fourth class of people in
England were extremely merry on a fair number of saints' days
in the year, and were famous throughout Europe for their dancing and singing. As a people, they are best and most accurately
seen in the plays of Shakespeare and his fellow poets and playwrights.

4   To Read, Write, and Obey the Law

> Now for learning with us this is all we go to school for: to read
> common prayers at church and set down common prices at markets;
> write a letter and make a bond; set down the day of our births, our
> marriage day, and make our wills when we are sick for the dispos-
> ing of our goods when we are dead. What more learning have we
> need of but that experience will teach us without book. If we live
> within the compass of the law, serve God and obey our King in our
> duties, and our prayers daily remember him, what need we more
> learning.—Breton's *Countryman*, 1618.

This is a yeoman or small farmer speaking, or it could be a
mason or a skilled craftsman: below that rank, very few of the
fourth class could read Common Prayer or write their own name.
When we read that the poor boy could progress from dame
school to grammar school or on to university, we have to inquire
about that word "poor." It usually means that the father of a boy
was at least a tradesman, as Shakespeare's father was a glover
and kept him at grammar school but not at university; Marlowe,
whose father was a shoemaker, got to university by hard work;
Ben Jonson, sent to Westminster School by his stepfather, a
master bricklayer, went on to Cambridge, but the money ran out
and he had to return to bricklaying. They would each have

begun their schooling by learning their letters at home. Nearly all children are quick to learn if the family atmosphere is favorable, but as most working families were themselves ignorant of letters and there was no compulsory education, the boy, if he went to a dame school, or "petty," left at eight or nine to help on the land, learn his father's craft with a view to an apprenticeship, or did a useful job at the spinning and carding or odd jobs at the loom. As Sir Thomas Wilson proudly wrote,

> Every child of six or seven years old is forced to some art whereby he gaineth his own living, something beside to help enrich his parents or master.

There is no record of any agricultural laborer ever being entered at a university in the reign of Elizabeth or James I, though there were always any number of poor boys there.

It is the pleasure of the Elizabethan and Jacobite playwrights to present their peasants, artificers, and rude mechanics as ignorant boors. Certainly they were not able to bandy classical allusions or to take part in the unending theological arguments of the day, except strongly to maintain the old religious myths and legends that had come down from the Middle Ages in folk tales, ballads, and carols. It is a great tragedy that we have lost most of these, buried under more meretricious learning, as we have lost a great number of the old skills. As late as the Second World War, a few of the ballads and some of the skills persisted in remote country districts in England. The tape recording has taken the one and machine tools the other. In 1942, Harry Cox of Wroxham, Norfolk, knew over three hundred old songs and sang them superbly; he could neither read nor write. Harry Rogers of Ironbridge built and used coracles for fishing on the Severn, as his ancestors, the Britons, had done. Kenzie, the wild-fowler of Sutton Bridge, could call hares and rabbits up to him and geese and ducks down to him from high in the air, and he painted wild fowl of all kinds very accurately; he could neither read nor write. At a slightly higher level, there were scores of now forgotten skills among the illiterate craftsmen of the sixteenth century; there had to be: the village cobbler made complete boots and shoes as well as saddlery; the blacksmith made anything at all from iron; the work and design of the village carpenter were of better quality than town-made furniture. There were no books of instruction, except one or two farming and brewing manuals; knowledge was passed down from master to apprentice by word of mouth and controlled experience.

In the early days of Elizabeth, schools were sparse; many had been closed after the dissolution of the monasteries and chantries. Then, about 1580, came a kind of surge in school building. There was a revival of interest in elementary education, an expansion of grammar schools, and a long-overdue clean-out of the universities of Oxford and Cambridge. At this time it was said, ". . . the cobbler will clout it till midnight, the porter will carry burdens till his bones crack again, the ploughman will pinch both back and belly to give his son learning." Hundreds of little primary schools, called "petties," were established, to which country children were sent at the age of six or thereabouts. These were no more than rooms, where space could be found, in a house or even in the church. Every one of the nine thousand parishes had at least one beautiful church, so many that very few churches were built in Elizabeth's day. In some places, the inhabitants of the village or little town built their own school, and the impetus for this came from Puritan or Church of England parsons who were determined to satisfy the new hunger for study of the Bible. The state did nothing much, but in the towns and cities rich merchants founded and endowed or in some cases refurbished grammar schools. Nearly always, the endowment was for the education of a stated number of poor scholars, and the impetus here was twofold: charitable in the first place, and in the second to help furnish a supply of employees who could read, write, and cast accounts.

Although every effort seems to have been made to get qualified, or at least competent, teachers for the petties, there are plenty of complaints about the ignorance of certain self-appointed instructors.

From the petties, the boy went on to grammar school if his education was to be taken beyond reading and writing, and there he was joined by boys who had been coached either by tutors at home or by a tutor to a group of the sons of gentry. Boys of every social class seem to have mixed in very happily together. The grammar-school masters were licensed by the bishop, who made sure that the master had no Romish or extreme-Puritan leanings. The Puritan was the one more likely to slip through the screening. The boys were aged from about eight to fourteen years. They were taught to read, write, and speak Latin, and some of the higher grades learned Greek. The disciplines of learning were extremely strict and mainly grammatical in the early years, going on by stages to Latin colloquies, double translation of Latin into English and back again, and great chunks of the classics learned by heart. In the last year, all conversation had to be conducted in Latin. It was, of course, a superb training for the mind, but as we can see by some of the English writings of the time it produced a somewhat stilted style replete with classical quotations. Yet, oddly enough, when these same classicists broke out into the vernacular tongue of ordinary people, they wrote good, vigorous, sinewy English. On the whole, though, English became more latinized.

Not until the mid-seventeenth century did the curriculum broaden to include geometry, European languages, and such science as there then was. But music was widely taught, and foreign visitors were astonished that so many men and girls and boys could read and sing a part and play an accompaniment on the cittern or the lute.

Only a fraction over 2 per cent of those who attended grammar schools went up to university: of those who left at fourteen or fifteen years of age, a large proportion were entered as apprentices; the younger sons of the gentry were put to the merchants of the great companies, the rest to tradesmen and craftsmen.

Talented boys of small or no means were freely subsidized to take them to Oxford and Cambridge; mayors and councilors, the colleges themselves, and prosperous citizens gave scholarships. Girls did not progress beyond the petties unless they had instruction at home, in which case they were either noble or gentle.

There were only two universities, Oxford and Cambridge. Oxford about 1620 had eighteen colleges and seven halls, with around 2,840 students; Cambridge had sixteen colleges with over three thousand students. It has been shown that the proportion of university students to population was many times greater than at the beginning of the nineteenth century.

Most of the students came up when they were sixteen or seventeen, a few were younger, and one or two older. They came to a more vigorous and more secular university than previous ages had seen. The large numbers of middle-aged clergymen who had lived in near idleness at Oxford and Cambridge had been packed off back to their parishes, and the medieval atmosphere had been dispelled. Nevertheless the teaching was still firmly based on the Latin and Greek classics, rhetoric was derived from Quintilian (born about A.D. 40), Cicero (106 B.C.) was the model for style, and the logic was that of Aristotle (384 B.C.) together with the accretion of dialectic that had grown around him during the Middle Ages. There were no modern subjects except the new theology, particularly that of Calvin, and that was not so much a matter of teaching as of students and sometimes tutors following their own bent.

There were no college tutors then, but the student or his parents arranged with one of the fellows of the college to act both as teacher and guardian, and each of these fellows had some half dozen pupils. Some fellows gave too much attention and liberty to the sons of rich gentlemen and neglected the poor, but on the whole the system worked fairly well. Harrison says, ". . . they ruffle and roist it out, exceeding in apparel and riotous company which draweth them from their books." There doesn't seem to be anything novel or even old-fashioned about that.

As in the outside world, the students were lodged and fed at several levels, though there was, naturally, a good deal of mixing of classes. At the top were the gentlemen commoners, who dined at high table with the fellows and had good, well-furnished rooms; some of these brought their own servants. The commoners were more numerous, and had part of their fees paid by scholarships, part by their parents. At the bottom of the heap were the battelers, on small scholarships and very little money of their own, who did various chores for the fellows—errands, waiting at table, fetching water, and so on. They had their food, their "battels," in the kitchen.

After four years of study, a bachelor of arts degree could be taken; the master of arts degree required three more years; advanced degrees in divinity, civil law, music, and medicine needed further study. Many of those who took advanced degrees stayed on as fellows and became teachers; others went on to the London College of Physicians or to the Inns of Court for further study in law or to take the bar examinations. The adventurous went to the German wars or entered the Dutch service to fight for the Protestant cause; most of these became professional soldiers, though not in England, which had no professional army. A few of the wealthy graduates went on a tour of Italy by way of France, and found for one thing that the international Latin tongue in which they were so fluent was almost incomprehensible to the Latinists of Europe. The English had developed a pronunciation peculiarly their own. Fortunately, some had acquired a smattering of modern languages at the university. In Italy they tended to acquire habits that their stay-at-home friends would denounce as foppish. Strangely, hardly one of the trippers paid any attention to the marvelous feast of paintings in Italy. England had no painters of her own with any touch of the spirit of the Renaissance, so that the English eye was completely untrained.

Most of the graduates who went to the Inns of Court (of which there were then twelve) to study common law did so as a preparation for their eventual selection as justices of the peace, which also implies that they were likely to be the eldest sons of the country gentry. The whole of local government was administered by these unpaid local magistrates. They were approved by the crown but thereafter functioned according to the law of the land and quite frequently in opposition to the crown when the crown threatened the ancient liberties of the subject. To the sovereign they owed neither income, lands, nor social esteem; this last came entirely from the goodwill of their neighbors. Nevertheless, until the Puritan revolution the majority upheld the sovereignty of the crown.

They were liable to be named sheriff of their county, but while they were extremely willing and proud of being magistrates they did their best to avoid the higher honor of sheriff and its heavy attendant expenses. The duties, too, were heavy. He issued the writs for Quarter Sessions and saw that juries were empaneled. He also carried out elections for knights of the shire, and here he was subjected to heavy pressure on behalf of rival candidates. He had to entertain the judges on circuit and could be almost ruined if the sovereign and his court descended on his county.

The justice of the peace could be chosen as one of the "quorum" at the higher courts, but in general he dealt with all the minor charges: drunkenness, breaking the sabbath, rioting—a host of petty offenses. More serious charges he referred to the Quarter Sessions. They checked that proper wages were paid and no more. They had control over alehouses and markets and weights and measures, but they were busiest in administering the poor law. For day-to-day duties the magistrate had various underlings: the petty constable, the churchwardens, and in minor posts such officials as aleconners and dogcatchers.

In theory the constable was a very important man in the administration of the village, but he was charged with so many duties that it is not surprising that he was not particularly effective in carrying out some of them. Every petty theft and misdemeanor had to be reported to him. He had not only to arrest criminals if he could find them but to take steps to prevent crime. At harvest time he had to round up additional labor, and he was the collector of various highly unpopular taxes. He could raise the hue and cry, bringing the able-bodied to arrest strangers or hound them out of the village. To the playwright he was a figure of fun, but in fact at an ordinary level of competence he was the only link between the common law and the people, about whom he knew more than anybody else. The penal system was extremely severe, and although large numbers of criminals escaped the law, of say a dozen thieves convicted eight would be sent to the gallows. It was cheaper to hang them than to keep them in prison. The prisons were foul and overcrowded and the length of a man's life there often depended on how much money he could afford to pay the jailer to ward off ill treatment and starvation.

Jailers often retired rich and sold their posts to the highest bidder.

The constable was, in matters outside the common law, inferior to the churchwardens, who were sometimes minor gentry and were responsible for the business affairs of the parish. Under the Catholics the life of the village had centered on the church and had been very highly organized by the priests and monks, who received considerable sums from all the parish and spent it, theoretically, for the common good, feeding and giving to the poor, repairing the church, and maintaining the very considerable properties that the church acquired from gifts and the wills of the devout. With the Reformation these good works fell to the two, four, or more churchwardens, whose resources were fewer.

In many parishes they had to levy property taxes, but they still had some church houses with rooms to let or to be used to bake bread and brew beer for the church-ales. These were a regular source of income in most parishes, and very jolly, not to say riotous, affairs they seem to have been. Various parishioners contributed meat, eggs, butter, and so on, and the maltster gave malt. To make sure plenty of ale was bought, the alehouses were closed for the day or sometimes four days, musicians were brought in, and the fun began, with dancing in the graveyard and the nave of the church, which by ancient right belonged to the people for their use. The Whitsun ale was commonly the most popular. The churchwarden worked closely with the overseer of the poor, and neither stinted charity to strangers who bore a voucher stating that they were not rogues and vagabonds but wounded soldiers or other men of good conduct passing through in search of work.

The churchwardens also paid for a number of nondescript officers: the dogcatcher, the keeper of the village common and woods, and the master of the pound—where stray animals were impounded and the owners fined.

The whole system sounds well organized and efficient; in fact it was not; it was loose and haphazard and held together only by the gentry as justices of the peace and by the poor laws as a kind of emollient.

No doubt among this mass of ordinary people there were some remarkable men and women, but in G. K. Chesterton's phrase, ". . . they have not spoken yet." There must have been a stirring of minds in the small towns and villages parallel with the great leap forward in the products of the grammar schools, the universities, and the Inns of Court.

The Renaissance came late to England, and its first effect on English literature was a pedantic, affected imitation of decadent Italian prose writing named after the prose romance of *Euphues*. Shakespeare satirizes it in *Love's Labour's Lost*. The style raged through the court like a plague. More suited to the native genius were the tales in pamphlet form by Greene and Nash. But in the middle of Elizabeth's reign literature burst into marvelous flower with Edmund Spenser's *Faerie Queene*. Poets came in brilliant clusters, and poetry was at the service of drama, because the ordinary people were all ballad lovers and it seemed natural to them that plays should be in verse. Kyd, Peele, Chettle, Nash, and Greene lead us to the splendid drama of Marlowe, on to the plateau of Ben Jonson, and up to the unsurpassable William Shakespeare. Prose, too, reached a perfection that few have since attained, notably that of Francis Bacon, whose essays are still models and whose *Novum Organum* groped after a scientific attitude.

All this gorgeous outburst may have been seeded by the Renaissance but it was nourished in the grammar schools and the reconditioned universities—plus Queen Elizabeth, perhaps the most fascinating figure in a fascinating time.

5   The Seas Around

Up to around the middle of the sixteenth century, a man's lifetime before the Pilgrims set off in the *Mayflower,* England ignored the New World and the great wonderland of India and far Cathay, and yet the mainland of America had been first discovered by a ship from Bristol. Columbus discovered the New World in 1492, but it was the island of Hispaniola he found, not the mainland. John Cabot, a Genoese naturalized in Venice and resident in Bristol, set out with two ships under letters patent from Henry VII of England and from a point in Newfoundland or Nova Scotia saw the coast of North America. He sailed down that coast in the year 1495, and returned in 1498 to sail down again as far as Florida. Both Columbus and Cabot believed they had been on the coast of China, or what they would know as Cathay. But Cabot brought back no gold or spices, and the canny Henry VII lost interest; moreover, he was busy with a rebellion in Cornwall, and nothing whatever was done by the English to follow up Cabot's great discovery.

The voyages of discovery had begun in Portugal, where Prince Henry the Navigator sat in Sagres in endless consultation with map makers, shipwrights, and sea captains working out longer and longer probes down the West Coast of Africa seeking a way

to the lands of gold, spices, silks, and jewels. The prince himself
never went to sea, but his shipwrights designed the caravel, long
and three-masted, able to face Atlantic weather and sail into the
wind, which the old, basin-shaped ships could not do. By 1487
the Cape of Good Hope had been discovered. In 1498 Vasco da
Gama had anchored at Calicut, in India. The cargo he brought
back repaid the cost of the voyage sixtyfold. The exploitation of
Portugal's empire in India and the Far East developed rapidly.

Henry VII of England died; Henry VIII busied himself with
wives, looting monasteries, and displaying himself on the Field
of the Cloth of Gold. Mary's short time on the throne earned her
the name of Bloody Mary and in her time no great voyages were
set forth, nor did anyone in England even set quill to parchment
about the new lands. Meanwhile, Balboa had sighted the Pacific
from Panama; in 1521, Cortés had conquered Mexico; Pizarro had
conquered Peru twelve years later, and gold and silver and
precious stones were pouring into the coffers of the King of Spain
to upset the economies of Europe and ultimately to ruin Spain
herself.

The New World, together with any lands or waters yet to be
discovered, had been neatly divided into two by a line drawn
down the globe, north to south, 370 leagues west of the Cape
Verde Islands: the eastern portion allotted to Portugal and the
western portion to Spain. The Pope who drew the magic line was
open to any bribe if large enough. He was Alexander VI, a busy
lecher with many illegitimate children, one who sold a record
number of benefices and distributed papal estates among his
family. Cesare Borgia was his son and Lucrezia Borgia his
daughter. At the time the line was drawn no one knew just how
much land there was in the New World or where it was but the
object was to keep everybody else out wherever it was or however much there was of it. However, no Protestant country accepted the division. In 1509, Sebastian Cabot, son of John, who
had been to Newfoundland as a boy with his father, took two
ships in search of a northwest sea passage through the ice to the
Pacific. Between 61° and 64°, which would put him in the
northern part of Baffin Bay, he found a strait that looked promis-
ing, but his crew threatened mutiny and he turned south down

the coast of North America to about 38° north, the latitude of
Virginia. He returned to Bristol and took service with Spain, but
in 1526 Bristol merchants again financed him to discover a passage through to the Pacific, this time south of the equator. Again
he was unsuccessful although he examined the coast of Brazil
and La Plata. Edward VI of England gave him a pension. In
1520 Ferdinand Magellan, a Portuguese in the pay of Spain,
sailed through the fearful straits named after him, from the Atlantic to the Pacific. Magellan himself died in the Philippines,
but his chief officer completed the voyage around the Cape of
Good Hope back to Spain, making the first circumnavigation of
the globe. It was fifty-seven years before Francis Drake followed
him, but Drake was not the first Englishman through the Straits
of Magellan, for there was an English gunner aboard Magellan's
ship.

In the 1530s Jacques Cartier of St. Malo was exploring the St.
Lawrence River. Meanwhile, the French established a colony in
Florida; in all, they sent three expeditions there. This was considered poaching if not piracy by Spain, who got the French to surrender on promise of safe conduct and promptly massacred every
one of them. Breton and Norman fisherman were already taking
cod on the Grand Bank of Newfoundland in the early years of
the century and were joined by English West Country boats.
There was cod for all; one fisherman said that he could walk the
waves on them, they were so prolific.

The news of Portugal's discoveries down the West Coast of
Africa soon reached Plymouth, that listening post for all matters
of the sea near and far, and in defiance of the declared monopoly
by Portugal, old William Hawkins, father of a great line of
seamen, opened up a trade in gold and ivory with the Negroes. It
was his son John who began the even more lucrative slave trade.
William made trading voyages to Brazil, but the North American
continent was still left fallow by the English.

At Bristol that strange man Sebastian Cabot held to his dream
of a way to Cathay through the northern ice. Rebuffed by the
spirits of the Northwest, he made plans for a voyage to the
Northeast around the rim of Europe past northern Russia and
Siberia to the Bering Straits, though no one knew those names

nor had any ship ever sailed those arctic seas. The Chinese may have known that there was a seaway between Asia and Alaska, but the Chinese were even more inscrutable then than they are now. Cabot became governor of the Muscovy Company and, financed by Bristol and London merchants, three ships set out from Deptford on the Thames on May 11, 1553, Sir Hugh Willoughby in command and Richard Chancellor second in command. Their ships were separated in a North Sea gale, and Willoughby with two ships discovered Novaya Zemlya and was driven to winter near the mouth of the River Varsina, where the men froze to death and were discovered by Laplanders in the spring of 1555. Chancellor, missing the agreed rendezvous, pushed on to the Dvina River and so to Archangel and on to Moscow, where he was well received by the czar. In all, he made three voyages to Moscow, but it was left to Anthony Jenkinson to make contact with the East, and this he did in the three years 1557–60 by way of the Volga to Astrakhan and the Caspian Sea and by camel caravan to Bokhara. He it was who opened up the profitable trade with Russia.

Elizabeth came to the throne in 1558, and there is a kind of legend that quite suddenly the whole mood of England changed, that there was a charge of electrifying energy newborn and increasing in intensity right up to the end of the century, by which time all her ancient enemies had been defeated, her people had spread to the ends of the earth, and the English language reached its highest development, as did English dramatic literature. The words Gloriana, Sea Dogs, Shakespeare, Merchant Adventurers, Raleigh, and one or two more are proper to this legend. The extraordinary thing is that the legend is firmly based on truth: the Elizabethan spirit really was a new one to England, but to regard it as a sudden explosion of energy coincident with the accession of Elizabeth is to telescope developments that grew over at least thirty years of her reign. And the trigger was not so much the wonderful queen but commerce, business, trade, the enterprise of English merchants, together with an accident of history in Flanders. It was Elizabeth's adroit maneuvers to ensure that England was never heavily committed to the wars in Europe while preserving an undercover freedom to be offensive in the

wider sense, and her clever cosseting of a spirit of religious tolerance, holding the extreme Protestants in check while keeping a
heavy hand free to put down Catholic power, that created a
climate in which business could flourish and wealth be created.

England's principal market in the early-sixteenth century was
Flanders, particularly Antwerp and Bruges. Those two cities
were the general trading focus of the world, and English trade
with them was alone worth two million pounds sterling. But the
struggle between religious factions was already making the merchants and craftsmen very uneasy, so much so that in 1560 Philip
of Spain was told that ten thousand of them had gone over to
England. Philip's reaction, through his cruel General Alva, was to
increase the severity of the Catholic persecution, which raised
the number of refugees to something like fifty thousand. They
brought with them to England an immense range of skills, particularly in the crafts to do with the finishing of cloth, and settled in
the areas where the English cloth trade was already established:
Kent, East Anglia, and parts of the West Country.

War broke out in the Low Countries and after the siege and
capture of Antwerp by the Spanish under the Duke of Parma,
London became the commercial center for world trade, ". . .
where the gold and sugar of the New World were found side by
side with the fine cottons of India, the silks of the East, and the
woollen stuffs of England itself." For the once fabulously rich
trading ports of Genoa and Venice had declined when the overland route to the East had been blocked by the Turks, and English fleets had begun to penetrate the Mediterranean. The trade
with the Baltic had been in the hands of the German Hanseatic
League; now it was English vessels that sailed to Scandinavia
and the northern German ports. New markets were sought, and
the talk of young men, scholars, merchants, and restless ship-
masters began to turn to dreams of strange lands heavy with
gold, and virgin to the plow.

Gold was the lure and particularly if the gold was in the hands
of the Spaniard; silver of course would do or any marketable
commodity from wine to Negro slaves. For there was among
Protestant seamen (to a man, they were firmly Protestant, even
Puritan) a bitter hatred of Spain well fanned by the atrocious

cruelties of the Inquisition, and, whether or not a state of war existed, letters of marque could be had for a ship to prey on enemy shipping—licensed piracy, in fact. If Elizabeth as a matter of policy clamped down on them, they hoisted the flag of the Huguenots or the Dutch. Most of these pirates, or sea dogs, were not in the least interested in settling in the New World; they wanted loot or trade and, above all, freedom to sail the seas of the world.

These things the Spanish and Portuguese denied them; nor did they permit any English ships to trade with the West Indies. Here they were acting against their own people, for the Spanish colonists were desperately short of labor. The native Indians, especially the Caribs, saw no point in working hard on plantations or in mines and simply gave up and died. There was therefore an open market for Negro slaves that John Hawkins and others were very willing to supply from the West African coast. However, by an act of treachery at San Juan de Allón, the Spanish wiped out a large fleet of English ships under Hawkins, and massacred or put to the Inquisition all the crews except some in the *Minion* and the *Judith,* who escaped with scarcely any food or water. Only fifteen of the *Minion* crew reached England. On the little *Judith* the captain was the young Francis Drake.

It was the end of any vaguely friendly attitude to Spain or her colonists on the part of the English, although at that point in time there was no war between Spain and England. Drake himself swore that he would spend his life in taking revenge. He did so, and the tales about him and his companions in their extraordinary and rather splendid forays—capturing towns for ransom, looting mule trains of gold and silver, voyaging around the world taking the Spanish treasure ship en route, to the final and one would have thought satisfying revenge of the defeat of the Spanish Armada—all have the glitter and some of the tragedy of great Elizabethan drama, lighted by the glow of immense treasure and the rare magic of Drake's personality. They are tales that lose their quality in synopsis and are simply mad echoes in the history of England and America.

By the time William Brewster and John Carver of the Pilgrim

Fathers were about four years old, that is in 1570, the Elizabethan spirit had gathered force and impetus. Two merchants of exceptional integrity and character, John Newberry and Ralph Fitch, had gone overland by way of the Syrian Desert and the Euphrates to India, where after incredible adventures, including great trouble with the Portuguese, they went to legendary Golconda and to the court of the Great Mogul at Agra. Fitch went on to the foothills of the Himalayas, to Burma, Siam, and along the Malay coast to Malacca. Ships were setting out to reconnoiter the Cape route to the East, but it was the end of the century before any real trading relations were established by English merchants, and these were made against fierce opposition by the Dutch.

No English colony was successfully established anywhere in the world during Elizabeth's reign. Most of the American voyages were made in fruitless quests for the Northwest Passage over Canada to Cathay. Sir Humphrey Gilbert and Adrian Gilbert were resolute backers of these desperate attempts to penetrate the arctic ice fields. Frobisher commanded three expeditions from 1576 to 1578, the last one with fifteen ships. They could not find the channel and were distracted by quantities of a black ore which they took aboard believing it to contain gold. Analysis proved it worthless, and no one sought the Northwest Passage for some years afterward. Then John Davis, a skilled and careful navigator, author of a very good seaman's manual, made voyages in 1585–86 and 1587, got as far as 73° north, and checked the geographical relation between Greenland and North America, but he was baffled by the mountainous ice. Henry Hudson reached Novaya Zemlya, later sailed across the Atlantic and explored the Hudson River, and on his next, and last, voyage entered Hudson Bay, where he wintered. The next year, his crew mutinied and set him adrift with his young son. Of the whole expedition only one seaman survived. There was a further attempt in the next century by William Baffin, but no one found a way through until the nineteenth century.

In the 1570s and '80s, the attitude to America began to change, and the idea of making a plantation there became an obsession with Sir Humphrey Gilbert, Sir Walter Raleigh, Sir Richard

Grenville, and some others who were intent on leading expeditions. Each of the three named died in the cause. There were also other groups who busied themselves with propaganda for the idea of expansion into the New World, and of these the most effective was Richard Hakluyt the younger. To him we owe almost everything we know of the American ventures; he was indefatigable in scouring the ports for survivors who could tell him of what happened on such and such an expedition—seamen, captains, anybody; he read everything published and any manuscripts he could get hold of, or as he said himself: "How many famous libraries I have researched into; what variety of ancient and modern writers I have perused; what a number of old records, patents, privileges, etc., I have redeemed from obscurity and perishing; into how manifold an acquaintance I have entered," and all to the making of the magnificent book *The Principal Navigations, Traffics, and Discoveries of the English Nation*, published in the year after the Spanish Armada was destroyed. The famous dedication to Walsingham, Elizabeth's Secretary of State, is written in the authentic ringing, almost flamboyant style of the true Elizabethan:

> For which of the Kings of this land before Her Majesty had their banners ever seen in the Caspian Sea? Which of them hath ever dealt with the Emperor of Persia, as Her Majesty hath done, and obtained for her merchants large and loving privileges? Who ever saw before this regimen an English lieger [subject] in the stately porch of the Grand Signior at Constantinople? Who ever found English consuls and agents at Tripolis in Syria, at Aleppo, at Babylon, at Basra, and what is more who ever heard of Englishmen at Goa before now?

He then recites the whole itinerary of Drake's voyage. It was a wonderful stimulant to the whole nation; in fact, reading the voyages still stirs the blood of those who can visualize what it was like to live in a world suddenly opened out to reveal magic vistas of fabulous lands, strange peoples, and wealth unlimited.

The reluctance of the English to begin their expansion overseas was not due to any shortage of ships and seamen; mostly it was preoccupation with the wars in Europe and with Spain, and a concentration on the immediate markets for woolen cloth. Once expansion began, there came a violent acceleration, and this was powered by the vast amount of shipping available. The training ground for seamen was, as with all maritime nations at that and at later periods, fishing.

Those of the population engaged in fishing, shipping, and all those trades based on the seas around the island exceeded in numbers those engaged in agriculture, the cloth trade, mining, and industry combined. Apart from the growth in commerce, which demanded more and larger ships, deep-sea fishing had increased in home waters, because the herring had quite suddenly moved from the Baltic to the North Sea. "Those herrings," wrote William Camden (1551-1623), "which in the time of our grandfathers swarmed only about Norway in our time, by the bounty of Providence, swim in great shoals round our coasts every year."

There were always plenty of cod in the seas around Iceland and nearer to England and in Scottish waters, but nothing like the vast numbers off Newfoundland. In New England waters the cod were larger, too large in fact for proper drying. Off Newfoundland the Basque, Breton, and Norman crews fished wet, that is they took their catch home to dry; the English fished dry, that is they took their catch ashore in Newfoundland to split and dry, which meant that it was deemed expedient for England to take possession of Newfoundland, which became England's first colony.

From the northern waters the English took their dried fish to Italy, Spain, Portugal, and any other available markets in Europe, and brought wine, olive oil, and fish oil to England. Most of the Newfoundland fishing fleet sailed from West Country ports—Plymouth, Falmouth, Dartmouth—where also the ships were built. But the larger and more modern ships were built on the Thames and at Bristol. Rye in Sussex specialized in fishing boats. But since London came to handle three or four times the commerce of her nearest rival, she also produced the most famous shipwrights, such as Matthew Baker and Phineas Pett, who built ships for the Navy and tall ships of three and four hundred tons for service in distant waters.

One curious sidelight on the men who manned these ships comes from a narrative published by the Hakluyt Society. The date is September 1607. Two ships, *Hester* (Captain Hawkins) and *Dragon* (Captain Keeling), on the way to India, anchored at Sierra Leone. On the thirtieth, Keeling notes, "Captain Hawkins dined with me where my companions acted King Richard the Second." The following day, "I invited Captain Keeling to a Fishe dinner, and had Hamlet acted aboard mee: which I permit to keep my people from idleness and unlawful games or sleep."

Elizabeth was dead, but for some years before she died the flame of the Elizabethan spirit, the exuberance, the reckless vitality had dimmed; a new race of men were about, serious, careful, sober in their manner, watchful in most things—the Puritans. They and their like planted the colonies.

In the first year of the reign of James I, peace was made with Spain. Attempts to found a colony in Virginia under war conditions had failed, partly because England's energies were being channeled into fighting at sea, in Ireland, and in the Low Countries, but now the great London companies of merchants could turn to the exploitation of the new lands. The motives were gain, profits, with not very much of the bright, intense patriotism of the Elizabethan heyday and the romance so eloquently expressed by Hakluyt. The Elizabethan adventures into Virginia and Guiana had been disastrous. Gilbert began his attempt on the mainland by formally taking possession of Newfoundland, but on leaving there his expedition foundered at sea, with the loss of his own life and a hundred men. Grenville took over Raleigh's expedition and successfully landed his contingent on Roanoke Island, but when he returned next year with supplies the colony had entirely disappeared. He had left fifteen men to hold the island until he could resettle a larger number, but when he came back the fifteen were dead; at least he found the bones of one of them and "all of the houses standing intact." These disasters drew from Raleigh some noble tributes to the courage and pertinacity of the Spaniards, "persisting in their enterprises with invincible constancy." Other small settlements were lost and Raleigh failed to settle Guiana or to find the fabulous city of gold, El Dorado, though he discovered the River Orinoco.

Under James I and the merchant companies a good deal of reconnaissance was done before three ships arrived in Chesapeake Bay to found Jamestown in Virginia. After a desperate and disease-ridden beginning, the colony would have collapsed but for the leadership of Captain John Smith. His is the name that should stand at the very head of the roll of honor of those who founded America. He was a skilled navigator, a firm and able administrator, and a brilliant propagandist for the settlement of New England. Moreover, he was a humane man with a lively sense of humor, which he was well able to express in his many writings, particularly his *Description of New England*, published in 1616.

6 The Book and the Clergy

The Reformation, the movement to reform the Church of Rome, had its logical end in a complete breakaway from any and all established churches by the Separatists, among whom the Pilgrim Fathers are the best known. But the movement was initiated from within the Church by men in holy orders and may be said to have had its explosive beginning with John Wycliffe, called the Morning Star of the Reformation. Wycliffe was, in William Bradford's words, "the first breaking out of the light of the Gospel in our Honourable Nation of England (which was the first of the nations whom the Lord adorned therewith) after that gross darkness of Popery which had covered and overspread the christian world."

The Church in England was by this time very rich and very corrupt. Monasteries of every order, even those once vowed to poverty, owned immense tracts of land; it was estimated that one third of the landed property was owned by the Church, and while this was probably an exaggeration, there was no doubt that the Church held very little waste or infertile land, and they ran vast flocks of the black-faced sheep whose fleece was so eagerly sought on the Continent. The monks conducted a busy traffic in pardons and indulgences and in fake relics of saints. But it would take an extremely long list to detail their sources of income; they had even swallowed up the tithes of the parish churches, so that the parish priests were very poor indeed and the churches themselves fallen into ruin.

We know little about the earlier years of John Wycliffe, except that he took his surname from a small village six miles from Richmond, Yorkshire, but we do know a great deal about him from the time when in his middle age he was appointed master of Balliol College, Oxford. The University of Paris had much decayed during the wars with England, whereas Oxford had been attracting some of the best minds in Europe, among whom Wycliffe was supreme. We hear of him pressing for reform in the Church, but at first he is protesting against various practices and not questioning doctrine. Then, around 1369, he wrote a treatise that challenged the whole authority claimed by Rome over the minds and souls of men. All power and dominion is of God, he declared; to the pope, He had granted dominion over the Church; to the king, dominion over the state, and each Christian owed obedience to priest and king, but—and this was for the time a revolutionary doctrine—each individual held dominion over himself direct from God. This cut away the function of the priest as the sole intermediary with God and destroyed the foundation on which the Roman Church was built. It followed that no man could be excommunicated by the pope unless "he were first excommunicated by himself." He issued tract after tract written not in the scholarly Latin of which he was a master, but in homely, colloquial English, if homely is the word for fierce, terse sentences, pointed sarcasm, and lucid arguments. He was the first to write in the common tongue, and the illiterate peasant could follow every word and every argument when it was read to him. He denied as useless and mere superstition all indulgences and pardons, all pilgrimages, and worship of images, relics, and saints. He went even further and denied the doctrine of transubstantiation, that miracle "by which the lowliest priest is raised high above princes, since only the priest can effect the miracle." This teaching and many more equally destructive were spread throughout England by a number of "simple priests," whom he had organized, wandering barefoot and vowed to poverty. These and his followers at Oxford were nicknamed "Lollards." Lollen, or lullen, meant to sing softly and also to babble, and the word seems to have come from the Netherlands and was first applied to Wycliffe's followers some three years after his death in 1384. They were vigorously persecuted not only for their heresies but because they attached themselves to any movement of revolt against the Church and the state. Moreover, there were Lollards everywhere, some in quite high places, and even after a hundred years of persecution there were Lollards awaiting the reformation which their movement had inspired. The single indestructible thread that sustained them was a belief in the Bible as the sole fount of religious truth. Lollardism was particularly strong in East Anglia among the weavers and the yeomen farmers, and there is no difficulty in tracing it out as one of the three influences on the characters of the original Pilgrims: first, the independence they inherited from the Northmen; second, their readiness to resist authority, shown in their leadership of the Peasants' Revolt; third, their appetite for religious dissent, shown in their assiduous harboring of Lollards.

Copies of Wycliffe's books were taken by some Bohemian servants of the Queen of Bohemia to the University of Prague, where John Huss was dean of the faculty of philosophy. In 1409 he was rector of the university. Prague was the capital of Bohemia, now the western section of Czechoslovakia. Bohemia is the country of the Czechs, or more strictly the lands of the crown of St. Wenceslas. In the early-fifteenth century it also included Moravia and Silesia but it did not include Slovakia, and it was rather loosely part of the Holy Roman Empire. (The towns of Bohemia were largely German, and so were nearly all the higher clergy, who owned over one third of the land.)

John Huss not only preached Wycliffe's tenets but in 1403 translated him into Czech. It should be remembered that neither Wycliffe nor Huss was a revolutionary. They did not want to abolish the Papacy, they wanted it to mend its ways. They were concerned to save Christendom from decay. Wycliffe was the original thinker, but Huss had a large, tough, and devoted peasant following. In 1414 John Huss was tricked into attending the Church Council of Constance, which condemned him on

thirty formal charges and handed him over to the secular power
as a heretic. He was burned at the stake in July 1415 and his
ashes were scattered into the River Rhine. The Hussites immediately raised a revolt, but after some success they came to terms
with the council of the Church. They remained a shadow over
the Church and an encouragement to reformers, although it must
be stressed that to most of the people of Europe they were
vicious heretics. As with Wycliffe, Huss was active before his
time had come, but the one sowed the seed and the other
nourished the plant that was to flower with Martin Luther. One
hundred years later, the first clouds of the storm of the Reformation were gathering over Germany and the earliest flicker of
lightning glared on the parchments Dr. Martin Luther nailed to
the doors of a church in Wittenburg, Germany, on October 31,
1517, All Saints' Eve.

Luther was prior of eleven friaries, district vicar of an Augus-
tinian order, and a professor at the university, intensely pious,
something of a masochist but extremely vigorous in mind and
speech. Wittenburg had its full share of medieval religious mal-
practices. The court church owned over five thousand relics of
saints, and on an appropriate payment these or some of them
could be shown and an indulgence given, that is, so many sins
forgiven for so much money. The immediate spur to Luther was
a proposition from Rome that eight-year indulgences should be
sold to help build St. Peter's there, half the cash for the pope,
half to the archbishop. Luther wrote to the Bishop of Branden-
burg: "Christ nowhere orders us to preach indulgences." The
bishop replied that no one could oppose the papal commissioner.
Said Luther, "Now, God willing, I will beat a hole in his drum,"
and proceeded to write and nail up his ninety-five theses as a
basis for a disputation or debate on the traffic in indulgences.
Some of these were

They talk nonsense who preach that with the clink of money in the
box the soul leaps into Heaven.

The indulgence is the net with which nowadays they fish for the
riches of mankind.

Christians should be taught that the Pope, if he knew of the extortions practiced by the preachers of indulgences, would prefer St. Peter's to be burned into ashes rather than it should be built with the skin, flesh and bones of his sheep.

Within a fortnight the ninety-five theses were printed and circulated throughout Germany and within a month throughout Europe. They were brought to England by the merchants of the wool towns of France, Germany, and the Netherlands, as were the powerful tracts Luther wrote that spread his message and incited revolt against the authority of the Church. At first he maintained that he had no quarrel with the pope himself, but he placed the Bible above the pope and began his translation of the Bible into German. Then, very soon, he issued a series of attacks on the Papacy itself and pretty well all its doctrines and rituals. He himself founded no Church, he was no martyr, and certainly no saint. His leadership came through the new art of printing, and the northern German princes gave him protection, for he, perhaps inadvertently, opened the way to the new nationalism—and later to bitter and bloody wars of religion.

Luther was no friend to the Renaissance and the New Learning. He despised reason and especially reason in religion as much as did the Papacy, and he substituted a dogma for which he claimed the same infallibility as did the Papacy for that of the Roman Church. His attitude is clear in his statement that "Man is enslaved by original sin and cannot by any efforts of his own discover truth or arrive at goodness"; a bleak prospect which seems to have been enthusiastically welcomed all over northern Europe, though not by the great minds of the New Learning in England—Colet, Thomas More, Tunstall, Pace, and others.

But, as J. R. Green says, "There was an England of which even More knew little," where the fire lit by Wycliffe, though damped by savage persecution, still smoldered. Luther fanned these embers of Lollardry in England and the flame was fed by William Tyndale.

William Tyndale made the first printed translation of the whole of the New Testament into English. At Cambridge he had first seen the Greek New Testament of Erasmus, and the rest of his life was spent in following a dream that every Englishman should read or hear the Bible in his own tongue. Yet he found no place in England free from persecution and restraint, where he could get his great work done and the result published.

Tyndale took refuge in Hamburg, went on a pilgrimage to Luther's town of Wittenberg, and finally printed and published his New Testament from Worms in 1526. Six thousand copies were sent or smuggled into England, joining the flow of Lutheran pamphlets, some of the most able and vitriolic written by Tyndale himself. They found a ready sale.

Tyndale's Testament was coldly received by the leaders of the New Learning, who were emphatically not Lutherans. It was sprinkled with Lutheran terms, "congregation" for "church," for instance, and "elder" for "priest." Henry VIII disliked it for the same reason, and the Church authorities denounced it as heretical. With this denunciation Sir Thomas More agreed. Tyndale was to be More's most dangerous opponent in a bitter war of pamphlets.

The Roman Church had not forbidden and had even encouraged translations of the Bible. The official Bible, the Vulgate, was itself a translation into Latin, which all educated men could read, and translations into many European languages had been authorized. But these were valuable and often very beautiful manuscripts. Printing was another matter, and might put copies into the hands of the vulgar—the people—and to this the Roman Church had very strong objections. What the Bible had to say must be told and interpreted to the people by their priests.

No real persecution was set afoot in England, because Henry VIII was involved in the preliminary stages of his first attempt to make the pope see eye to eye with his views on the sacrament of marriage. Henry wanted a male child to succeed him, and it was clear that his wife, Catherine, was now past childbearing. He had become infatuated with young Anne Boleyn, and he appealed to Clement VII to annul his marriage with Catherine.

Henry was both fortunate and unfortunate in his timing: fortunate because the Papacy was in a mess and needed help for which it might be expected to be grateful, and unfortunate because the pope was in fact a prisoner of the emperor, King

Charles V of Spain, whose aunt, Catherine of Aragon, was the wife Henry wanted to put away.

The pope had wanted Henry to present him with a *fait accompli* by a decision of Henry's own courts in England, but Wolsey advised against this course. Now, his advice proving bad and his intrigues with France also failing, Wolsey caught the full force of Henry's rage, was disgraced and charged with treason, and died. He was succeeded by Thomas Cromwell, an agent in Wolsey's employ. The great change that was to take place in the relations between Church and state and between the Papacy and England and in effect the making of the English Reformation was the work of this one man, Thomas Cromwell, who stage-managed the break with Rome and the dissolution of the monasteries. Although Henry remained a Catholic all his life, the break with papal authority was completed by the Act of Supremacy, by which all authority over the Church was vested in the king as the only supreme head on earth of the Church of England. To this act everyone of legal age had to swear allegiance. Another act made the bishops absolutely dependent on the king, who had to approve their election. The year 1534 saw the passing of the main laws establishing the new order. An Act in Restraint of Appeals forbade questions of wills, marriages, and tithes, which had thitherto been decided in Rome to the great profit of the Curia, to be taken any further than the Archbishop of Canterbury's court. This act was, Kenneth Pickthorn says, "the most important of the sixteenth century, if not of any century," for "it robbed Rome of all jurisdiction."

Cromwell was now home and foreign minister, vicar-general of the Church, and president of that equivalent of the Inquisition the dreaded Star Chamber. He had taken steps to supply the king's urgent need for money in 1535 by sending commissioners, or visitors, to all the monasteries, and in 1536 under act of Parliament monasteries with fewer than twelve monks were suppressed. This suppression of the smaller monastic houses had been no more than a dummy run, and Cromwell now moved against the great monasteries, which owned something like a sixth of some of the best agricultural land in England. By 1540 the whole "dissolution" was accomplished and the king's coffers had gained nearly two million pounds by the sale of monastic lands as well as by retention of lands by the crown worth a hundred thousand pounds a year. In modern money these are staggering sums. The lands were sold, often cheaply, to friends of the king and to various syndicates. There was a rush to buy, and by the time the speculators had sold parcels of land to smaller men a large new class had been created with a vested interest in the Reformation. No nice points of principle prevented the Catholic party from getting what share they could; in fact, the head of the party, the Duke of Norfolk, got one of the largest handouts of all. Many of the wealthy aristocrats of later centuries, some Catholic but mostly Protestant, trace their fortunes and their pretense to aristocracy back to the dissolution of the monasteries.

The dispossessed monks suffered very little hardship. Nearly all of them received a comfortable pension, some were appointed as parish clergy, and many settled down to a happy married life. But the monastic servants, much more numerous than the monks, got nothing. Henry to the end of his life conducted a kind of seesaw policy between Catholics and Protestants. He wanted unity of religion—for one thing as a check to civil war but also to maintain a balance that he could tip whichever way suited his foreign policy. To this end he contributed martyrs to both sides, burning Catholics for denying his supremacy and Protestants for denying the Mass.

When he died, in 1547, the council of regency he had established for his son Edward leaned out of balance to the Protestant side, though there were all the makings of a furious struggle for power, with each side ready to use religion as a destructive weapon.

Moreover, to the mass of people who were not yet much interested in religious dispute Henry had made available to everyone a veritable revolutionist's handbook—the Bible in English.

After a life of "poverty, exile, bitter absence from friends, hunger and thirst and cold, great dangers and innumerable other hard and sharp fightings," William Tyndale had completed his translation of the Bible to the end of Chronicles, when he was suddenly arrested in Antwerp and charged with heresy. Miles Coverdale, who had been his collaborator, continued the work, using several other sources for the Old Testament in German, Latin, and Swiss-German and printed the whole English Bible for the first time, in Antwerp in 1535. Tyndale was betrayed and burned at the stake in Vilvorde, near Brussels, in 1536.

The style and tone of this English Bible were set by Tyndale, but it is known by the name of his faithful collaborator, Miles Coverdale, who dedicated it to Henry VIII. Early in 1536 the clergy were instructed to place a Latin and an English Bible in the choir of every church. Of course not nearly enough had been printed, and a second edition was put in hand at Southwark, just over the river from London.

Then, in 1537, came Matthew's Bible, published in Antwerp by one of Tyndale's assistants; this was the Tyndale-Coverdale Bible with rather more of Tyndale's Old Testament. It was very quickly followed by the Great Bible, printed first under the direction of Cranmer in Paris and completed in London after the Paris clergy had raided the press and burned all the copies they could lay hands on. It is Coverdale's own revision of his 1535 Bible and is the one "of the larger size" ordered by royal proclamation to be placed in every parish church under penalty of forty shillings a month while the church remained without it. On the engraved title Henry VIII sits in, rather than on, a throne uncommonly like a large bed, handing out copies of the Bible, right hand to Cranmer, left hand to Cromwell. For this reason the Great Bible was often called Cranmer's and sometimes Cromwell's.

There is no doubt that Scripture had been curiously neglected in England. In other languages there had been numerous translations and printings, twenty in Germany alone in the fifty years to 1522, but it has been suggested that Lollardry and its revolutionary associations had scared the devout away from vernacular Bibles.

In some ways the common people may have been disappointed in the English Bible, in which the New Testament was firmly based on the four canonical Gospels. It included no part of the exotic junkyard of Gospels, Acts, and Apocalypses which as far as we know began to be compiled from the second century A.D. and included such inventions as the "boyhood of Jesus," the early life of Joseph and Mary, the Gospels of Peter, Thomas, and Nicodemus, and the later versions of "Falling Asleep of Mary," which contributed greatly to the cult of Mary worship. On this apocryphal literature many splendid mystery plays had been based, including the Coventry and Chester cycles, and also some lovely carols—the "Bitter Withy," for example.

In 1549 the first Act of Uniformity was passed, making the new Book of Common Prayer the only legal form of worship. It was a clever compilation by Cranmer and a panel of scholars of the New Learning. The language was English but the pattern of the Mass was kept. The prayers kept to Catholic doctrine although the wording made them acceptable to Protestants. The traditional vestments of the priest were kept, and so were some of the old rituals.

No one expected the sickly young Edward VI to live very long. He was himself a fanatical Protestant, and was easily persuaded by Warwick to set aside the Catholic Mary Tudor's right to the throne under the will of Henry VIII by making a will of his own naming Lady Jane Grey as his successor to the throne, but the country revolted and the council proclaimed Mary Tudor queen. Queen Mary rode into London through enthusiastic crowds cheering their welcome. Yet London too had been supposed largely Protestant. All the English now seemed to want was less-forcible feeding by the Protestant intellectuals and a return to the religious system of good King Harry the Eighth. This they believed was what Queen Mary stood for and, further, she stood as the legitimate successor to the Tudor dynasty, to which they were unswervingly loyal. What Mary saw was a populace repenting of their Protestant heresies and desperately anxious to return to the old and true religion.

The Spanish pride of caste that she inherited from Catherine of Aragon, her mother, would not allow her to marry an English subject. She would marry only the son of a king, and when Philip of Spain was suggested she at once agreed; indeed, he was probably the only one she had ever had in mind. There was a rebellion, notably among the Men of Kent, which was bloodily suppressed. Philip landed at Southampton and the marriage was solemnized. The next logical move, and Mary was an obdurately logical woman, was to end completely the schism with Rome. This stuck more largely in the parliamentary gullet, for it meant the end of all of Henry VIII's work and it threatened that the return of the loot from the dissolution of the monasteries might be demanded by Rome. Nevertheless, Rome and the English Church were united and Catholic doctrine was the religion of the state. Any Englishman who dissented from that doctrine or any part of it was a heretic and if brought to trial and convicted might be burned at the stake, and Mary was hunting for heretics to burn.

In February 1555 the burnings got under way with a number of leading churchmen each dealt with in his own town or city. In the next six months sixty more were put to death. In October Ridley and Latimer were led to the stake, and as the flames rose, Latimer, Protestant leader and splendid preacher, called out, "Play the man, Master Ridley, we shall this day light up such a candle by God's Grace in England as I trust shall never be put out." That candle burned brightly for centuries and still flickers here and there today, and so do the hundreds of tiny candles that were kept alight in the minds of the common people, for these little lights came from among them—weavers, tailors, laborers, women, a blind girl from Colchester; there were nearly three hundred of them, mostly from London and the London area, Sussex, Kent, and East Anglia.

We owe much of our knowledge about the Marian martyrs to *Acts and Monuments of These Latter and Perilous Days,* compiled and written by John Foxe, which in Elizabeth's day was a best seller popularly known as *The Book of Martyrs.* Some of the more gruesome martyrdoms of the early Christians are included, but the target is the Catholic Church under Bloody Mary. William Bradford was very familiar with *The Book of Martyrs,* and early in *Of Plimmoth Plantation* he writes:

Mr. Foxe records, how that beside those worthy martyrs and confessors which were burned in Queen Mary's days and otherwise tormented many (both students and others) fled out of the land to the number of 800 and became several congregations at Wesel, Frankfurt, Basle, Emden, Strasburg, Geneva, etc.

The London congregation seems to have been well organized, probably from abroad; at least, some ministers came back from exile to lead it, and this congregation may have preserved some of the records Foxe used. We don't know whether they followed the Edwardine Prayer Book, or, which is more likely, they had a simplified or extreme Protestant service, nearer the fanatically searched-for ideal of the early Church. What is certain is that the later Separatists claimed the London congregation as their forerunners. Their numbers varied from forty to two hundred, and although they continually changed their meeting place many were arrested and burned. William Bradford in his later writings refers to this London Christian congregation as some of the first Separatists.

The English exiles who were scattered among the Protestant cities of Europe were by no means a band of brothers in distress. For one thing, few of them were in any great financial straits, because the English merchants looked after them or invested in them; and for another, the various groups were chronically quarrelsome about Protestant doctrine. Gradually, the interpretation, or rather the theology, of John Calvin gained ground among the English exiles. John Calvin had fled from the persecutions under Francis I of France and got to Basel, where in 1535 he published his *Institutes of the Christian Religion.* This was something new, for not only did it set out a clear theory about what a Christian should believe and how he should serve God but it also drafted an organization for Protestants, based, it would seem, on the organization of the early Church.

In brief: every Christian man is called individually to Himself by God; every man is himself a priest; a group of Christian men formed a self-governing Church in which all are equal. The Church, that is the body of worshipers, elects lay elders and deacons, who, with the pastors already existing and with the approval of the Church, elect ministers. The minister preaches and directs religious instruction, and a group of such ministers decide on the interpretation of Scripture. A joint consistory of ministers and elders may admonish or excommunicate any member of the Church or it may bar the unworthy.

In 1536 Calvin was called to Geneva and became, when he

was only twenty-seven years of age, the spiritual leader of the Protestants there. For twenty-eight years he exerted a powerful influence over Protestant opinion and practice, an influence that is still felt today and in some places persists in its original purity and vigor. It was an austere doctrine, sometimes called gloomy, but it appealed to the Protestant exiles as "free from all dregs of obnoxious and superstitious ceremonies." But not to all of them. A large group at Frankfurt preferred to worship in accordance with the Edwardine Prayer Book and "to admit and use no other." Another Frankfurt group moved to Geneva "to build a Church of the Purity," and here may be the origin of the nickname "Puritans" applied to those who tried to reform the Church of England from within. This Geneva church made the metrical versions of the Psalms and produced the Geneva Bible of 1560, which had even greater popularity than the Great Bible. The Geneva was the Bible used by the Pilgrims.

In England the persecutions and the burnings went on to the end of Mary's life. For a long time, she had been in poor health; she was embittered by her failures: the loss of Calais, the departure of Philip, the hostility of the pope, and the growing support given to what she could only see as deadly heresy—a heresy she could not burn out of her people.

She died on November 17, 1558. At no time had she shown any understanding of the character of the English people, and her rigid bigotry had induced, even in some of the ardent Catholics among them, that strong aversion to Roman Catholic rule that was never to leave them.

7   The Right Worship of God

When Elizabeth heard that she had become Queen of England, she knelt and said, "It is the Lord's doing and it is marvellous in our eyes." It was indeed marvelous. It had been touch and go. Bloody Mary might have put her away, and did commit her to the Tower for a while, and the Tower was prelude to the headsman's block and there was always Mary Stuart hovering next in line with allies who were handy at hiring assassins. But now the immediate problem was the religious one. An Englishman of, say, twenty in 1534 had been brought up in the ancient religion of his forefathers, a religion he would have thought likely to last until the end of the world. In that year, 1534, he had the shock of learning that Henry VIII was now the head of the Church, and not the Holy Father. At thirty-five he had to become a Protestant and worship to the English Prayer Book. At thirty-nine he was back to being a Catholic or else he risked "going to the fire." And now, in 1558, at the age of forty-four, well might he ask: now what?

For it was very uncertain which way Elizabeth would go. Of course the persecutions stopped and the Protestant prisoners were released from prison, but Elizabeth was, if anything, a Catholic, or seemed to be. Did this first step mean some sort of religious toleration? In the event, it did. She declared that she would in no way meddle with the consciences of the people. They could have complete liberty of religious opinion, provided that they conformed to the national religion in worship. She rather cagily assumed the title of supreme governor and not head of the Church (although it had the same meaning), restored the Prayer Book in English of Edward VI with some slight alterations that were really concessions to the Catholics, and followed this by an Act of Uniformity forced through very much against the will of the bishops. England was now Protestant, although a traveler in England might have doubted whether the Act of Uniformity ran very far from London. The religious scene was thoroughly confused, and that was about how Elizabeth wanted it; at least there were not just two warring factions. She herself had faith in God but no liking for extremes in religion and a positive dislike for the bleaker Protestant church proceedings. But most of the people were Protestants in that they attended Church of England services simply because that was the state religion and everybody accepted that no state could have more than one form of religious service.

As for the beliefs, it has been estimated that in the early years of Elizabeth's reign two thirds of the people were still Catholic. They attended the parish church partly because the law insisted that they should and partly because the service was not violently dissimilar from the Catholic service, although it was conducted in English and not Latin. They continued to attend throughout Elizabeth's reign, and at the end they were pretty solid Church of England, although chevied a bit by the Puritans.

That is one view; another is quoted by A. Tindal Hart in *The Country Clergy:* "It has been estimated that at the end of Elizabeth's reign about 2 per cent of the population was ardently Puritan, 5 per cent Roman Catholic, 18 per cent zealous followers of the Establishment, and 75 per cent dull peasants utterly indifferent to any form of church government, provided it did not interfere too drastically with their own customs and superstitions."

Quite a large proportion of the Catholics were recusants in the early middle years of the reign; that is, they did not attend the

Protestant Church, because they were devout Catholics and heeded the Holy Father's injunction that they should, under pain of excommunication, stay away come fine or fire. The number of recusants dropped sharply after the Armada had come and gone.

The Puritans made a noise quite disproportionate to their numbers, but they willingly attended the state church, because they proposed to take it over. The Separatists did not attend the state church, and this was the only real distinction between Puritan and Separatist.

The clergy were required to subscribe to the royal supremacy (Elizabeth as governor of the Church), the Prayer Book (which contained the order of the service, the ceremonies, and much else), and the Thirty-Nine Articles of Religion (there was no great insistence on the whole thirty-nine), and there were injunctions that forbade images, relics, and miracles, and compelled the clergy to preach at least a quarterly sermon or read a homily and to catechize.

But even in the 1590s there were churches where no sermons had been preached for years. In the county of Norfolk in 1597 eight churches had no quarterly sermons, eighty-eight no monthly sermons, and in seventeen there were no homilies either.

There were constant complaints about clergymen who "haunted taverns, played at cards or dice, were fornicators, adulterers, dancers and brawlers"; others "hunted and hawked" and so on down a list of most possible sins. The Puritans were often the complainers, and by discounting some of their venom one gets the impression of a fair number of very lively parsons behaving very like their parishioners in the matter of Elizabethan fun and games. For this was the last period for many a long, gray year when the Englishman was famous in Europe for his singing and dancing, when the medieval games were still played, when the nave of the church was where the villagers held meetings and the churchyard was the place where feasts like church-ales were held. This was also the last of the time when the lovely old carols were sung as music to the dancers in the nave, for carol means a round dance, and at Christmas, for instance, the dance was around the crib of the Babe of Bethlehem. Some of these

carols survived in remote parts of England and were redis-
covered in the nineteenth century, which century, however, really preferred the damp and phony carols written by various
clergymen.

The pre-sixteenth-century carols had a direct folk poetry,
much nearer to "pure" religion, much more genuine in its feeling
for the Holy Family than any of the intellectual gymnastics of
the Calvinists, and much better tunes. And many of them had an
uninhibited gaiety that mightily offended the Puritans.

The populace was very loath to give up some of the old observances, and kept, often with the connivance of the parson, some
images of the Virgin, crucifixes, tabernacles, and old rituals. And
they hung on to their church music and their carols as long as
they could.

The medieval church had been a blaze of color, with the walls
painted with wonderful panoramas of life and death, some of
them very lightly based on Bible and Apocryphal stories, for they
were painted when the imagination of the artist was untram-
meled by the Bible itself. And the stained-glass windows glowed
with brilliant scenes and figures, as we can see by those few windows that escaped the hammers of the godly in such little
churches as Fairford and in mighty cathedrals such as York.
Modern technology has not been able to recover the secrets of
fourteenth-century stained glass.

When those who under Mary had been exiles returned to
England, they made a beeline for these "pagan" glories with ax
and hammer and whitewash brush. They were quickly checked
and, until they came to power in the next century, had to carry
out their task of rooting out "the marks of the Babylonian Beast"
rather more discreetly, though discreet is an odd word to use
about Calvinists.

The Puritans were most effective when they had converted the
gentry and were able to work through Parliament.

From the Puritan presses issued a barrage of abusive pamphlets, and these called forth from the government the first organized attempt at press censorship. Printing was restricted to
London and the two universities; every publication had to be

approved by the archbishop or the bishop of London; license to print was to be controlled by the Company of Stationers. These tight restrictions led to secret and illegal printing, notably of a savage series of libels under the name of "Martin Marprelate." After a long hunt the press was found by accident, hidden in a haycart, but neither printers nor writers were ever discovered. However, two suspects were arrested, and one of them, John Penry, was hanged; the other died in prison.

Another measure given to the commissioners to enforce forbade all preaching in private houses. This was held to include barns, open spaces, and woods, and struck hard at the very bottom layer of the religious pile—the Separatists, that sect of Calvinism whose history has been thoroughly researched because the Pilgrim Fathers, or as they called themselves, the Saints, were Separatists.

William Bradford, writing his First Dialogue, or "Conference," in 1648, tried to pass on some account of the origins and traditions of the Separated Church of Christ. Of the origins he says: "The true church and the proper government of the same is to be known by the scriptures, and to be measured only by that rule, the primitive pattern; which church and government of the same is sufficiently described and laid down in the writings of the apostles and evangelists."

The interpretation placed on these writings by the Separatists was that a church, that is a congregation, should choose its own pastor, elder, and other officers mentioned in the Scriptures; no bishop, whether acting for pope or king, had any say whatever in this matter of church officers; only the congregation speaking as a whole by common voice could depose its own officers, receive those worthy to become members, and excommunicate the unworthy. Says Bradford in his Third Dialogue: "It is not only an injury and damage to deprive them of this their right and liberty; but that it was no less than sacrilege and tyrannous usurpation in the lordly hierarchy so to do."

The English Separatist tradition, it is claimed, goes back to the reign of Mary. Bradford, in the First Dialogue, says: "In the days of Queen Elizabeth there was a Separated Church whereof Mr. Fitz was pastor; and another before that in the time of Queen

Mary of which Mr. Rough was pastor or teacher and Cudbert Simpson a deacon."

The documentation of the Separatist martyrs, as of other Protestant martyrs under Mary, is in Foxe's *Book of Martyrs,* always referred to by Bradford as "the acts and monuments of the Church," part of its original title. Foxe says that Rough and Simpson were arrested with others at the Saracens Head in Islington, then a village in the fields near London, where the congregation had met pretending they had come to see a play.

In spite of imprisonments and executions, the London congregation under Mary was never broken up; in fact, Foxe states that it grew in number toward the end of Bloody Mary's reign, and it is this congregation that the Separatists have fairly consistently claimed as the forerunners of their Church. They did not quite admit that these martyrs had found the true way to worship God, but they gave them credit for trying. John Barrow (of whom more later—he was hanged in 1593) wrote:

> The godly martyrs so lately escaped out of that smoky furnace of the popish church, could not so clearly discern, and suddenly enter into the heavenly and beautiful order of a true established church. It is more than a day's work to gather, to plant and establish a church aright.

We know very little about those early Elizabethan Separatist churches, but Bradford's Mr. Fitz (Richard Fitz) is mentioned in some documents cited by Dr. C. Burrage in his *Early English Dissenters.* One document sets out an order of worship and another a petition to the queen warning her that unless the marks of the Romish beast were cleansed from the Church of England "the Lord's wrath would surely break out over the whole realm" and concluding by complaining that six of their congregation, including Richard Fitz, had died in prison. (Here it should be noted that anyone kept in the insanely unwholesome prisons for any length of time was very likely to die.)

The Separatist who made the most noise in Elizabeth's day was Robert Browne. The label Brownist was attached to many of the congregations, including the Pilgrims, who repudiated

Browne as a "backslider." The whole Separatist movement is sometimes referred to as the Brownist Church, although it is quite clear that it began well before Browne came on the scene.

Robert Browne graduated from Corpus Christi College, Cambridge, in 1572, where he had mixed with extreme Puritans and it is likely that he came under the influence of Richard Cartwright, a learned and pious professor with revolutionary ideas. Cartwright preached that God had put the state below the Church, meaning the Calvinist, or Church of the Presbyters, and that the presbyters, or ministers, should have absolute control of doctrine, ceremony, and public morals. For the Church, his Church, he was claiming rather more authority than any pope had dared for the Church of Rome—and a stricter discipline. Those who differed from the Church were of course heretics and were to be put to death whether they repented or not. Understandably, he scared the moderate Puritans and checked those moderates in the Church of England who might have gone some way to meet the Puritans. The students naturally lapped it up, but authority just as naturally didn't and Cartwright was forced to quit Cambridge and then England.

When Robert Browne graduated from Cambridge he was a not very extreme Presbyterian Puritan. For a few years he taught school in Cambridge. He then decided to preach the Word of God, but also decided that he would not seek from the bishop the necessary license to preach. Authority told him he was not to preach. Sometime in 1581 he began to form a Separatist congregation who "took a covenant together and with the Lord." The Bishop of Norwich complained to the Privy Council and "the Lord called Robert Browne out of England"—to Middelburg, Zeeland. There he published several tracts expounding his theology, but the Middelburg congregation found him disruptive and Browne, with some loyal followers, joined the Presbyterians in Scotland. After a brief survey of his new Church he alleged that the whole discipline of Scotland was amiss. The Scots tossed him into jail. He came out after a short spell, got into some bother in England, and then in 1585 recognized the Church of England as a true church and promised to be a loyal member. He may have been, but it also seems likely that he encouraged some people to

Separatism. By 1591, though, he may be said to have forsaken Separatism, for he was instituted rector of Thorpe-cum-Achurch in Northamptonshire. "Troublechurch Browne," as he came to be called, died in October 1635—in Northampton jail.

Apart from odd spells in prison, Browne's relative immunity can be traced to no less a person than the queen's chief minister, Lord Burleigh, who was a distant kinsman. Two men who merely distributed some of Browne's writings were burned at the stake. There may be a dotty logic in this: Browne was not important, but his writings were. He was the first to set out a fully argued and consistent doctrine of the Separated Church.

There is no doubt that Browne had many disciples in London, but two leaders of the London congregation (of which Browne, too, had been a leader), John Greenwood and Henry Barrow, were, like the Pilgrims, at pains to deny that they were Brownists. Speaking from the Fleet Street prison, Barrow said, "We are no Brownists, neither were we instructed by him or baptised into his name until by such as you we were so termed." John Greenwood said, "You term us Brownists and Donatists whereas I never conversed with the men or their writings."

But the Brownist tab can be justified even if Barrowism did not derive from Brownism. There is only a hairline between them.

Greenwood was arrested in October 1587 with twenty others, and when Barrow went to visit him in the Clink in November he too was arrested. In 1592 Francis Johnston was chosen pastor, and Studley and Knifton were chosen elders of the London congregation. They were in a hot spot. There were already fifty-two men of the congregation in prison in 1590, and every few months saw additions to their number. There were also subtractions by death from jail fever: ten by 1590, another fifteen by 1596. In April 1593 Barrow and Greenwood were hanged. John Penry was hanged in May. (He was a late-comer to the Separatists, but recent scholars have suggested that he was the mysterious author of the Martin Marprelate tracts.)

These three were executed as a warning to all Separatists, but they were indicted under the useful Anti-Catholic Act of 1581, which made it a felony to write, publish, or distribute "any false, seditious and slanderous matter to the encouraging, stirring, or moving of any insurrection or rebellion within the realm." The Separatists always maintained they "meant no harm to the State" and if their "number were increased [they] meant it not but to the service of God," but since they advocated the overthrow of the Church, the suppression of the bishops, and the abolition of the Queen's supremacy, the prosecution had not many points to stretch to secure their conviction. Francis Johnson was also in jail at the time of the three executions, expecting that he too might be hanged. He was a son of a one-time mayor of Richmond in Yorkshire and had taken his B.A. at Christ's College, Cambridge, in 1582. His brother George took his in 1585. Francis got into trouble for preaching Puritan sermons and after a term in jail went over to Middelburg. There he became minister to the Congregation of English Merchant Adventurers, which was not a Separated Church, and neither was Johnson then a Separatist. His conversion makes a nice story in Bradford's First Dialogue (though there is some confusion of dates, which need not bother us). Johnson apparently had been asked by the English ambassador at The Hague to investigate the printing of some "scurrilous pamphlets" in Middelburg. He found a printer running off copies of Barrow's *A Plain Refutation* and had the whole printing seized and publicly burned. However, he rescued one or two copies from the flames and took them to his study so that he might confute the errors if the matter should come up. Then, says Bradford, "He began to turn over some pages of this book, and superficially to read some things here and there as his fancy led him. At length he met with something which began to work on his spirit, which wrought with him and drew him to the resolution, seriously to read over the whole book; the which he did once and again. In the end he was so taken, and his conscience was troubled so, as he would have no rest in himself until he crossed the seas and came to London to confer with the authors, who were then in prison, and shortly after executed."

He was elected pastor of the London, or Barrowist, Congregation, was arrested, and we left him awaiting sentence, which was delayed four years.

Meanwhile some, possibly fifty, of the congregation had taken the execution of the three leaders as a broad hint, and under bland official encouragement had emigrated to Amsterdam. In 1597 George and Francis Johnson were released after a petition to the Privy Council, and after some adventures at sea joined their congregation in Amsterdam, where Francis took up his position as pastor. The teacher was Henry Ainsworth, another Cambridge man and a student of Hebrew, whose versions of the psalms, "englished both in prose and metre," were sung by the Pilgrims in New Plimouth. Daniel Studley was an elder and so was George Knifton.

George Johnson was a bitter critic of his brother Francis, and their differences went back to London days. While still in the Clink, Francis had married Thomasine, widow of Edward Boys, a Fleet Street haberdasher and Separatist who had died of jail fever. She was much too attractive to be approved of by the uncompromising George, and she seems to have taken no pains to make herself plain and worthy. "A bouncing girl," says George, "who wore whalebones in her breast, an excessive deal of lace, and a showish hat." Scent and starched linen are mentioned. Starch was, of course, "the devil's liquor." Moreover, Francis was "blinded, bewitched and besotted" with his wife. Thomasine, according to George, disturbed others of the congregation, but he was the one who made the noise.

There was no scandal attached to the name of Francis Johnson; in fact, he appears to have judged the ordinary run of sins, including adultery, with a kind of innocent mind. But he had a sharp eye for certain theological or ecclesiological errors—those of the Dutch Reformed Church, for instance, which he pointed out in a series of letters. Some of the objectionable practices were that they baptized the children of non-members, used prayer books, did not follow exactly the disciplinary procedures in Matthew 18:15–17, worshiped in buildings that had once been Romish churches ("idol temples of Anti-Christ,") celebrated marriages as church ceremonies, observed Christmas Day, Easter Day, and Ascension Day, et cetera. The Dutch replies were civil but understandably cool.

Francis led his congregation for twenty-five years, and it came to be known as the First English Church of the Separation in

Amsterdam, or the "ancient church." It steadily grew in strength from about forty members in 1597 to "about three hundred communicants" when Bradford first met them, in 1609. This steady success can be traced to the able propaganda published by Francis and a few others and the quiet and persistent teaching of Henry Ainsworth. (It would be pleasant to feel that Ainsworth's music played a part.)

There is no doubt that George had a point when he accused his brother of encouraging Separatists in England, particularly preachers, to come to Amsterdam, where "they must fall to carding or weaving, there is no cure [for the preachers] to increase their studies"; and as a result the churches in England were weakened and Amsterdam strengthened. Against that view, Francis may have thought that there was not much of a future for Separatists in England anyway. Whichever was the just view, Francis made Amsterdam a magnet that eventually, or more exactly, initially, drew the Pilgrims.

The attraction of Amsterdam as a city of refuge for religious dissidents, or as Nicholas Brereton had it, "the Fair of all the Sects," rested on a decision of the States General in 1569 to allow liberty of conscience to both the Reformed and the Catholic Church, and in 1578 Amsterdam gave freedom of worship to all, even Anabaptists.

England moved no nearer to religious toleration of this order as the century and the life of Elizabeth began to fade. There were more convinced Protestants, a great many more Puritan clergymen, and swarms of what William Haller calls "articulate, voluble, opinionated men inclined to identify their own opinions with those of the Almighty," and of these Parliament had a full share.

Elizabeth died on March 24, 1603, and the age of the Renaissance died with her. The influence of both remained: England was in the forefront of European powers, and the English people as a whole were less insular than before, and they were more intelligent and knowledgeable and a great deal wealthier. They had not yet absorbed all the riches of the Renaissance, but they were as forward as any nation in their relentless study of the Bible.

The Catholics had high hopes of Elizabeth's successor, James I, the Sixth of Scotland. Had he not been negotiating with the Papacy? Did he not denounce the Dutch as rebels against their Spanish king? Equally hopeful were the Puritans: Was he not a Calvinist Presbyterian?

8   Their Native Soil

James I came to London in May 1603. His big head, rickety legs, complete lack of personal dignity, and a thick lazy tongue mouthing the coarsest speech gave Londoners a shock. The Puritans got their shock at Hampton Court in answer to a petition they had presented as soon as James crossed the border. James was, in the words of the French King, "the wisest fool in Christendom," and particularly he was a heavy pedant with a great taste for theological dispute. The Puritans overlooked the fact that James had had a bellyful of Presbyterian obstruction in Scotland. He accused the Puritans of trying to establish a presbytery "where Jack and Tom and Will and Dick shall meet, and at their pleasure censure me and my Council and all their proceedings." (New to England, he does not seem to have realized that Parliament might do just that.) He ended with a threat to the Puritans that flattened all their hopes of Church reform. "I will make them conform or I will harry them out of the land, or else do worse."

Some conciliatory noises were made to the Catholics and the recusancy fines were remitted, but the number of recusants grew so rapidly in the North that all of the Elizabethan restrictions and penalties were reimposed; sick and disappointed, some desperate Catholics including Guy Fawkes hatched the Gunpowder Plot, which, discovered in 1605, did their cause no good, nor anyone else except the modern fireworks manufacturers.

And at the same time, away from all these stirring affairs, heeding not at all the dire threats of James, a few friends went on with their private prayer meetings at Gainsborough in Lincolnshire, and Babworth and Scrooby in Nottinghamshire. In William Bradford's words:

> Whenas by the travail and diligence of some godly and zealous preachers, and God's blessings on their labours, as in other places in the land, so in the North parts many became enlightened by the word of God and had their ignorance and sins discovered unto them, and began by His grace to reform their lives and make conscience of their ways.

The godly preachers, like most of the Separatist leaders, whether at large in England, hanged, imprisoned, or in Amsterdam, were Cambridge men, and one is tempted to say that the Pilgrim movement began not in Marian London or Gainsborough or Babworth but at Cambridge University (more than once denounced as "a vile cesspool of sedition").

John Smyth, sometime fellow of Christ's College, Cambridge, began a Separatist congregation at Gainsborough, but Edward Arber calls this only an accidental help and insists that the Pilgrim movement began in the rectory and church of Babworth. In fact, the root of the movement has several fangs. The rector of Babworth was Richard Clifton, who became pastor of Scrooby congregation in 1606, with John Robinson as his assistant. These two had apparently been holding meetings on Separatist principles for some little time before. Clifton had held extreme Puritan views for years. William Brewster too had been holding or assisting at meetings before the establishment of a Separated Church.

Clifton, Robinson, and Brewster were all Cambridge University men, and so was Francis Johnson, and this gives another fang to the root. B. R. White, in *The English Separatist Tradition*, says: "As far as possible the "Gainsborough-Scrooby congregation were organised as replicas of Johnson's congregation in Amsterdam."

John Smyth had been tutored by Francis Johnson at Christ's College. (He was later to assist in the disintegration of the Amsterdam "ancient brethren.") In 1594 he was elected a fellow of his college, after he had been ordained, and he was soon in trouble with his bishop for making public objections to parts of the Anglican service. Nothing much is heard of him until 1600, when he is known as a loyal member of the Established Church. In 1602 he was dismissed from a lectureship to the Corporation of Lincoln as a "factious man." In 1603 he was given license to preach in any part of the Province of Canterbury. His bishop protested at once, the license was revoked, and revocation of the license was published at morning prayer in all the churches of Lincoln. He moved to Gainsborough and was in trouble for preaching there and also for "practising physic without license." He then organized a Separatist congregation on the principles of Barrow and Johnson, but there is no clear evidence as to the exact date. It could not have been before March 1606, when a letter to the bishop said that in preaching in Gainsborough Church on March 2 (which he was not licensed to do) "there did not pass from him one word tending to the disturbance of the present estate of the Church." Smyth has been called the first Pilgrim pastor, but the claim is doubtful. He did influence Robinson to become a Separatist, and he was at least at the beginning of the Pilgrim movement.

Of Richard Clifton we know very little before 1586, and not much between then and 1605 except that he was rector of Babworth, where his services were nearer Puritan than Establishment. He was, according to Bradford, "a grave and reverend preacher, who by his pains and diligence had done much good and under God had been a means of the conversion of many";— to Separatism we may suppose, which together with his appointment as pastor to the Scrooby congregation makes him at least a main fang in the root of the Pilgrim movement. In 1606 he was over fifty years of age, "with a great white beard," the only glimpse we have of the physical appearance of any of the Pilgrim Church except Edward Winslow, of whom a portrait in oils has survived. (To those with a slight knowledge of the whole Pilgrim story it may be necessary to say here that Miles Standish, "Captain Shrimp," was never a member of the Church.)

The Reverend John Robinson, "that famous and worthy man," was born in 1576 and went to Corpus Christi, Cambridge, to which he was elected fellow in 1597. He became a minister at St. Andrews, Norwich, in 1603–4, but was one of those clergymen who refused to subscribe to the complete Thirty-nine Articles of Religion and were dismissed. Most historians say some three hundred clergymen were dismissed, but a recent (1962) survey by Dr. S. B. Babbage reveals only ninety, of whom some were reappointed. Up to 1604, clergymen had only to subscribe to those articles concerning the faith and the sacraments. Bancroft, the new Archbishop of Canterbury, moved and had made law a rigid conformity to all thirty-nine. This made the final breach between the extreme Puritans and the Established Church. Bancroft had shown himself a bitter enemy of Puritans as long ago as 1588, when he preached "A warning against Puritans" at St. Paul's Cross. He was at that time Bishop of London.

Robinson saw no future in what he viewed as a corrupt Church and retired to his birthplace, Sturton-le-Steeple, which may also have been the native village of John Smyth. Robinson married Bridget White of Fenton, a village less than half a mile away. Very soon after, Robinson joined with Brewster and Clifton in meetings at either Babworth or Scrooby, and together they formed the Separatist/Pilgrim Church at Scrooby in 1606.

William Brewster was the son of John Brewster, postmaster at Scrooby. The Great North Road ran through the village, but like all other roads in Elizabethan England it could be traveled for any distance only on horseback. There was no metaling and practically no maintenance, but at least the Great North Road was not overgrown, was distinguishably a track heading in the right direction, and had posts where fresh horses could be hired. The postmaster also ran an inn for bed and meals. As well as postmaster, John Brewster was bailiff and receiver for the extensive lands and rights of the manor of Scrooby, and caretaker *ex officio* for the manor house, in which he lived. There were a number of small houses, a granary, and a collection of outbuildings all

enclosed within a moat. Just which buildings held his stables or
served as the inn we don't know. The moat is now dry and the
manor house is a medium-sized house incorporating perhaps
one wall of the old building. The original building was really a
minor palace of the Archbishop of York. Of half-timbered con-
struction, it had in its heyday some forty rooms and was impressive enough to have attracted the presence of Henry VII's daughter Margaret on her way north to marry James IV of Scotland,
Cardinal Wolsey when he was reduced to the See of York, and
Henry VIII himself. Both Elizabeth and James I cast an acquisi-
tive eye on Scrooby manor house as a possible hunting lodge, but
the pass in each case was adroitly parried.

John Brewster held the manor for Samuel Sandys, whose father Edwin, Archbishop of York, had granted him a lease, that is,
Samuel received the moneys Brewster collected. The Sandyses
took very good care of each other, and some of the family could
be found wherever there was money to be got or influence to be
exerted or used. (Later, another son, Sir Edwin Sandys, was to
be a useful contact for the Pilgrims.)

John Brewster sent his son William to Cambridge in 1580,
where he entered Peterhouse but left without a degree, to be
taken into the service of Sir William Davison, one of the ministers to Queen Elizabeth. This was a splendid opportunity for an
ambitious lad; he had no definite post, and he certainly was not
Davison's secretary, but he was in close attendance on him during a mission to the Low Countries, close enough to be entrusted
with the keys of the town of Flushing, held as token security.
Brewster in after years said he kept the keys "under my pillow on
which I slept the first night."

William Brewster saw something of court life when Davison
became assistant to Sir Francis Walsingham, Secretary of State,
but his wagon thus hitched to a star, when the star fell, down
came he. Davison had signed the warrant for Mary Stuart's execution, and in her revulsion from the decision that Mary should
die, whether Elizabeth actually took it or not, she made Davison
a scapegoat. He was sent to the Tower, where he was kept for
two years, Brewster performing "many faithful offices of service
in the time of his troubles." His loyalty may have yielded one

dividend, for it is likely that Davison used his influence to beat off some court intrigues for the lucrative job of postmaster at Scrooby and secure it for William in succession to his father, who died in 1590.

There remains one other to complete the cast of those from around Scrooby who were to play leading parts in the Pilgrim drama: William Bradford, but he was a juvenile with a walk-on part for many years, though in America he held the lead for most of the lifetime of the Plymouth Colony, and without his history *Of Plimmoth Plantation* the Pilgrim story would have been a hazy patch in history and American literature would have lost one of its masterpieces.

He was born in 1589 in Austerfield in Yorkshire but only three miles north of Scrooby, Nottinghamshire, and on the same side of the River Idle, with the market town and river port of Bawtry between them. He was the son of a prosperous yeoman farmer who died soon after William was born. His mother remarried and William Bradford lived first with his grandfather and then with two uncles, who put him "like his ancestors into the affairs of husbandry."

He took to reading the Bible very assiduously at an early age; this would have been the Geneva Bible, whose rubrics were a Calvinist manual. He and another twelve-year-old would walk on Sundays the ten miles to Babworth to hear Richard Clifton. And quite possibly he began to point out to his uncles and others the error of their ways in attending the purely Anglican church, and they in turn told him what they thought, which affected him not at all, "nor could the wrath of his uncles, nor the scoff of his neighbours now turned on him as one of the Puritans divert him from his pious inclinations." They gave him up as a bad job and allowed William Brewster to take him under his wing at Scrooby. There is evidence that Brewster and young Bradford went together to Babworth to worship.

Gainsborough, Scrooby, Babworth, and Sturton-le-Steeple lay within a ten-mile circle. From Scrooby, Gainsborough was ten miles due east, Babworth seven miles nearly due south, and Sturton-le-Steeple ten miles southeast as the crow flies. Robinson probably went up the Roman road to Wheatley and cut over the hill to Babworth and on to Scrooby, just about fifteen miles.

Scrooby, Babworth, and Sturton are in Nottinghamshire and Gainsborough just in Lincolnshire by the width of the River Trent, which explains Edward Arber's insistence that the Pilgrim movement was a Nottinghamshire movement. Blyth and Harworth are also in Notts, each about five miles from Scrooby and each contributing Pilgrims to the Plantation in America. Blyth has one of the finest Norman churches in England and is altogether a lovely village. Francis Cooke, one of the *Mayflower* Pilgrims, came from Blyth. He was a wool comber and had married a Walloon refugee, who must have been useful when they got to Holland.

Ten miles east of Gainsborough, Ermine Street, one of the most ancient roads in Britain, ran straight as a ruled line due north from Lincoln to York. Once, it was good firm going from London to Hadrian's Wall on the frontier of Roman Britain, but in the days of the Pilgrims it was, like the Great North Road and every other road, almost impassable in wet weather and hellishly dusty in fine. From Ermine Street another Roman road ran northwest to Bawtry, near Scrooby.

The members of the Scrooby congregation may never have seen Ermine Street but they were aware of the River Trent, the "Roaring Trent," because it was a dominant feature of the landscape. In length it is the third river in England; for pollution it is the first, a fast, foul, and rumbuctious river with spring tides running forty miles upstream. When the spring tides meet the flow of the river, a five-foot wall of water, the Bore, or Aegir, comes swinging upriver. Gainsborough's use as a port was much diminished by the coming of the railway, though 120-ton barges are still towed sixty-odd miles up to Nottingham, passing through the mast-high detergent foam of Cromwell lock. In Smyth's and the Pilgrims' time, Gainsborough was a very busy port, a link with Hull and the Midlands. The River Idle, which passed close to Scrooby, and made of Bawtry a small river port, enters the Trent below Gainsborough at West Stockwith, where there was a shipyard.

So, tiny village as it was, Scrooby was by no means cut off from the bustling world. Nowadays it is; the railway and the main road bypass it and there is no traffic on the River Idle.

The land around the group of villages that sent godly members to the Scrooby congregation was good arable land and, being well watered, was good pasture for cattle. There would have been sheepwalks on the low range of hills between the Trent and the Great North Road and to the west of the road, but no massive flocks. North of a line from Gainsborough to Bawtry, that is, a few miles from Scrooby, the fenland ran up to the Isle of Axholme and to Hatfield, full of wild duck, goose, swan, waders, and bitterns (butterbumps, the Pilgrims would have called them), and sometimes the sky would have been darkened with flights of fowl. There were plenty of fat eels, and there were deer in the woods. This was the stretch of country that suggested to Elizabeth I and James I that Scrooby Manor would make a handy hunting lodge, and even in the 1600s it was an easy place for a man to find food. One can tell by the number of village names ending in "-by" (village) that the Scandinavians had settled around this part of Nottinghamshire; they had come up the Trent in their longships, and there are Danish characteristics in the people, particularly those most prized by the savage Northmen, Danes, or Scandinavians—generosity, loyalty, courage; to which should be added independence and a certain pigheadedness.

We do not know how well peopled the area was in 1608, perhaps slightly above rural average, but there was plenty of room for every house to have its statutory four acres of land. The whole population of England was only about four and a half million, 80 per cent of whom lived south of a line from the Wash to Bristol. (These figures are, of course, estimates. There were no reliable population statistics before 1800.)

Until 1606 there had been much to-ing and fro-ing between Gainsborough congregation and those at Scrooby and Babworth, until (and all future quotations will be from Bradford unless otherwise identified):

These people became two distinct bodies or churches; for they were of sundry towns and villages. In one of these churches (besides others of note) was Mr. John Smyth, a man of able gifts and a good preacher; who afterwards was chosen their pastor.

That was the Gainsborough church, and Bradford goes on to anticipate later troubles in Holland: "But these afterwards falling into some errors in the Low Countries, there (for the most part) buried themselves and their names." (And that was that, as far as Bradford was concerned and he has very little more to say about John Smyth and his fellows, but in due course we shall have to disinter them and say what happened, for there were some very rummy goings on in Amsterdam.) He continues with the Scrooby congregation—the second church—under Richard Clifton, his assistant or teacher John Robinson, and William Brewster:

> They could not long continue in any peaceable condition; but were hunted and persecuted on every side, so as their former afflictions were but as flea-bitings in comparison of those which now came upon them. For some were taken and clapped into prison, others had their houses besett and watched day and night, and the most were inclined to leave their houses and habitations, and the means of their livelihood.

Gervaise Neville, grandson of the High Sheriff of Nottinghamshire and three others from Worksop, a town about nine miles from Babworth, all of whom might have been members of one or other of the two churches, were arrested and so was Brewster and they were each fined twenty pounds for being members of an illicit congregation, but that is the sum of what we can now find out about the persecutions Bradford mentions. It is more than likely that some of the "besetting and watching" was done by neighbors who found them obnoxious. The authorities at any rate do not seem to have bothered them much. We don't know, but

> By a joint consent they resolved to go into the Low Countries where they heard was freedom of religion for all men; as also how sundry from London and other parts of the land had been exiled and persecuted for the same cause, and were gone thither and lived in Amsterdam and in other places of the land.

By the Low Countries Bradford really means Holland and Zeeland; the Low Countries south of the Scheldt had been overrun and devasted by the Spaniards, and large numbers of Walloons had fled to Holland and Zeeland. Those from London were of course Francis Johnson's London congregation, or the "ancient brethren." "The others" include Smyth's congregation, some of whom had already gone from Gainsborough to Amsterdam.

> Being now constrained to leave their native soil and country, their lands and livings and all their friends and familiar acquaintances it was much, and thought marvellous by many. But to go into a country they knew not (but by hearsay) where they must learn a new language, and get their living they knew not how, it being a dear place, and subject to the miseries of war it was by many thought an adventure almost desperate, a case intolerable and a misery worse than death. Especially seeing they were not acquainted with trades nor commerce but had only been used to a plain country life and the innocent trade of husbandry.

Bradford is writing some time after 1630, and here he is piling on the misery. They, that is Smyth and Robinson, had been in touch with Francis Johnson, who was very unlikely to have painted such a discouraging picture. Bradford's piece should be read as a device to get more power into the next passage:

> But these things did not dismay them for their desires were set the ways of God, and to enjoy His ordinances, but they rested on His providence and knew whom they had believed.

(The reference here is to II Timothy, 1:12: ". . . for I know whom I have believed.")

What they were up against in trying to leave the country was an order of the Privy Council, reciting an ancient statute, forbidding any except soldiers, merchants, etc., to leave the kingdom without special license. However,

> They were fain to seek secret means of conveyance, and to bribe and fee the mariners and give extraordinary rates for their passages.

In possibly November 1607 they arranged for a ship to pick them up at Boston, to which town they made their way on foot according to one reading, but this is improbable. Boston is fifty-three miles as the crow flies and about seventy miles across country. By boat on the Idle and the Trent to Gainsborough and then continuing upriver to Torksey by Foss Dyke (the canal the Romans made, the way the Danes came from the Humber to Lincoln), across to Lincoln, and so down to Boston by the River Witham seems more likely. After they had been kept hanging about at the rendezvous for a day or two, the hired ship put in after dark and took them aboard.

> But when he [the captain] had them and their goods aboard he be-trayed them, having beforehand plotted with the searchers and other officers so to do.

The Pilgrims were never slow in finding little defects in a man's character and would pounce very quickly on minor sins, but were continually being foxed by major rogues. Perhaps they suffered from moral myopia caused by staring too hard at the Whore of Babylon. The ship's captain, like a fair proportion of his fellows in the coastal trade, was a villain, and so too were most of the port petty officials; to them the Pilgrims were mugs it would have been unnatural not to rob. They put them off the ship into small boats "and there rifled and ransacked them searching them to their shirts for money." Then, as loyal subjects of the crown, they turned the wretched people over to the magistrates, who, Bradford says, used them courteously but kept them imprisoned for a month until they heard from the Privy Council. All but seven were released and told to go home. The seven, including Brewster, were held pending trial, but as no charge was preferred they too were released. Since Brewster had already resigned or sold his postmastership, and presumably the others had sold their homes, their condition must have been tricky over the winter months. It is reasonable to suppose that they sheltered with Separatists or sympathizers who were staying put.

> The next spring after, there was another attempt made by some of these and others to get over at another place. And so it fell out that

they chanced on a Dutchman at Hull, having a ship of his own belonging to Zeeland; they made agreement with him and acquainted him with their condition, hoping to find more faithfulness in him than in the former of their own nation; he bade them not fear, for he would do well enough.

But affairs seldom went according to plan for the Pilgrims, and this adventure was no exception. It began well enough. They agreed with the captain that he should pick them up on the shore between Grimsby and Hull, well away from any town, which seemed wise. The original group, less a few who had had quite enough adventure at Boston, sailed down the Idle to West Stockwith, where the men went ashore to cross the Trent to the east bank to walk the forty or so miles, crossing Ermine Street, to the rendezvous, and the women, children, and baggage went on downriver on a small bark with the sensible idea of arriving a day early. Or it would have been sensible had not the sea been very choppy and the women and children too seasick to remain hove to, tossing up and down, all night. They persuaded the crew to put in to a small creek and wait for the Dutch ship to appear. Again a sensible thing to do, but they ran aground on a shoal and were not likely to get off before noon the next day. Early next morning, the Dutch ship arrived and began to take off the men who had arrived on the shore near the stranded bark. One boatload had got aboard when

"The master espied a great company (both horse and foot) with pikes and guns and other weapons (for the country was raised to take them). The Dutchman seeing that, swore (his countrie's oath) Sacremente, and having the wind fair weighed his anchor, hoisted sail, and away."

The Dutchman (who judging by his oath had come under multilingual influences) bore away for Holland but ran into a violent North Sea gale that raged for well over a week and drove him near the Norwegian coast. The Pilgrims prayed, says Bradford, and the storm abated, but the mariners too would have prayed, for all men in that time were pious, and sailors it was said more pious than landsmen, though Bradford has no doubt that the Pilgrim prayers were the more effective. After fourteen days (for a two-day sail) the battered and penniless Pilgrims, heavy with anxiety for their families, put in to Amsterdam, "where the people came flocking admiring their deliverance the storm having been so long and so sore."

Those they had left behind were apprehended by the formidable-sounding troop or mob of horse and foot (who probably thought they were Catholics anyway), "but not all of the Pilgrims abode their question."

> The rest of the men that were in greatest danger made shift to escape away before the troop could surprise them; those only staying that best might, to be of assistance to the women.

The women were understandably in great distress, wondering what would happen to them. So were the authorities who moved them from place to place, from one parish to another. They were, in fact, treated as vagrants and not as lawbreakers and were given the standard poor-law treatment, being moved on so that they would not remain as a charge on the parish funds. Two paragraphs from Bradford close this part of the Pilgrim story:

> To be short, after they had been thus turmoiled a good while, and conveyed from one constable to another they were glad to be rid of them in the end upon any terms, for all were wearied and tired with them;

and

> They all gat over at length, some at one time and some at another, and some in one place and some in another, and met together again according to their desires, with no small rejoicing.

Not all the Scrooby congregation stayed the course and got to Amsterdam, and those that did may not have numbered more than thirty and possibly nearer twenty. We do not know; Dexter puts the figure at "not less than one hundred and twenty-five," but that must include Gainsborough and some late arrivals.

9 Amsterdam, the Fair of All the Sects

The Pilgrims had arrived in Amsterdam at the beginning of a Golden Age for the Dutch Republic, which was to rise to extraordinary power and influence throughout the first part of the seventeenth century and decline slowly toward the end. The rise from beneath the heel of Spain began only in 1572, when a group of Calvinist seamen calling themselves the Sea Beggars captured the town of Brill to use as a base of operations against the Spaniards. It was the signal for Calvinist risings in many towns of Holland and Zeeland, and though several years of bitter fighting followed, Spanish might, money, and utter ruthlessness never again subdued the Nederlander north of the western Scheldt. In 1579, seven provinces including Holland united to defend their civil and religious liberty and two years later declared themselves independent of Spain. England and France signed a treaty of alliance, and in 1609 Spain agreed to a twelve-year truce. The Spanish infantry, then the best in the world, could not fight effectively against a people who used water as a weapon and operated from hundreds of small ships. South of the western Scheldt, in Flanders, Hainault, Brabant and Liège (the Low Countries), the Duke of Alva and his Blood Council held the land under a reign of terror. Spain was deliberately conducting a war of religion. Calvinists from this area fled to Holland.

But the Dutch had been fighting for freedom and liberty of conscience and were prepared to extend both to everyone. At the union of the provinces, in 1579, it was laid down that "every citizen should remain free in his religion, and no man be molested or questioned on the subject of divine worship," and this confirmed a liberty already established in Amsterdam.

But when the republic was firmly established "on a legal and orderly basis," naturally the Calvinists, who had been the more active rebels, more or less monopolized the public offices. A not unexpected change in the balance between the two main religions took place. In Holland in 1587 nine tenths of the population were Catholic; by the time the Pilgrims arrived, in 1608, the numbers of Protestant and Catholic were about equal; by the time the Pilgrims left, in 1620, only a quarter of the population were Catholic, although that quarter included some of the richest and most influential in Holland. Maybe they had been converted by those typical Calvinist virtues of industry, enterprise, sobriety, and a care for public order so essential to commercial success.

Most European powers had sought to achieve greatness by military power and aggression; not so the Dutch, although in the Scots phrase, with which Middelburg was familiar, they were "bonny fechters." However, from now on they showed a tendency to use mercenary soldiers, diverting some part of the enormous wealth they were creating by trade to an occupation that had never shown much profit, and in which they were not interested unless as freedom fighters, and even then they usually hired auxiliaries.

Water was their element, and where ships could go the Dutch went, armed of course. With their continually expanding and improving merchant fleet, they exploited the whole known world, and into Amsterdam flowed all kinds of merchandise, from the timber and pitch of the Baltic to the spices and silks of the East Indies. Amsterdam's great days came when the Spaniards crippled the port of Antwerp. Jews driven by the Inquisition from Portugal had established Amsterdam as the world's diamond-cutting and -dealing center. Flemings driven from Antwerp were both cloth merchants and financiers, and Jews, Flemings, and Dutch, but mostly Flemings, pioneered national banks, chartered companies, a stock exchange, and all the intricate machinery of large-scale capitalism. The Dutch Republic was the most solvent state in Europe, and its solid prosperity arose out of the tolerance it had extended to refugees from outside its own frontiers.

As well as religious toleration, the Dutch had established freedom of the press. Most other countries had a strict censorship. Puritan books and pamphlets were burned in England but freely published in Holland. So were newspapers, which were usually propaganda sheets like the *Gazette d'Holland* banned but circulated in France. Many manuscripts of books by advanced thinkers were smuggled out of other European countries and first published by a Dutch press. As Joseph Scaliger observed at the time, in one of his self-righteous judgments, "In this country everything is allowed, providing that nothing is done or said against the Government. There are good people in Holland but there is not another country in the world in greater need of Divine Chastisement." When foreign ambassadors complained of some particularly vicious publication, the Dutch Government sometimes took action if it wanted to please the country concerned, but as a rule it went through motions resembling action but did nothing to inhibit the press.

There are two contemporary reports from shrewd observers that temper Amsterdam's reputation for solid prosperity. Sir William Brereton, in his *Travels,* writes: "A most flourishing city yet the air so corrupt and unwholesome especially in winter time, when most part of the country round about overflowed. Here no fresh water, no water to brew but what is fetched from six English miles distant. Hence they have much beer but no water to wash withal but rain water; little fire except turf, the most of the wood burnt here brought out of Denmark and Norway; the coals come from Newcastle." And Sir Thomas Overbury: "No one is extraordinarily rich and few are very poor." This last does not quite square with the records we have of some extraordinarily rich merchants and financiers, but maybe they used the kind of camouflage that comes naturally to such people in uncertain times. As for the very poor, their number was to be augmented a little; as Bradford points out in a most vivid passage,

> They saw many goodly and fortified cities walled and guarded by troops of armed men. Also they heard a strange and uncouth language, and beheld the different manners, and customs of the people, with their strange fashions and attire, all so far different from that of their plain country villages (wherein they were bred and had so long lived) as it seemed they were come into a new world. But these were not the things they much looked on or long took up their thoughts, for they had other work on hand and another kind of war to wage and maintaine. For though they saw fair and beautiful cities flowing with abundance of all sorts of wealth and riches, yet it was not long before they saw the grim and grisly face of poverty coming upon them like an armed man, with whom they must prepare for action, and from whom they could not fly, but they were armed with faith and patience against him and all his encounters, and though they were sometimes foiled yet by God's assistance they prevailed and got the victory.

This piece has an inspiring end but it lacks all the hard facts we most want to know, such as how much money had they among them, where did they lodge, and exactly what jobs did they get? Some of these facts were dug out in the past eighty years by painful research on the part of, mostly, American scholars.

The Pilgrims stayed in Amsterdam for about a year and then moved on to Leyden, and Bradford gives the reasons for their move in one paragraph, stating that the "flames of contention were like to break out in the ancient church" and they wanted no part in it. In fact all hell broke out, first around that godly man John Smyth, lately pastor at Gainsborough and now pastor of the Second English Church of Amsterdam. His restless mind began to question some of the settled beliefs of the Separatist Church and he affirmed that he had good cause to reconstitute the Church, its ministry, and its baptism. To the Separatists the points raised by Smyth were very disturbing. The vaguely unreligious student in our own time finds the constant Calvinist bickering over delicate shades of theological coloring either boring or exasperating, but in the sixteenth century all educated men were intensely interested in theology, and once they had grasped and held what they thought was an aspect of the Divine truth they were ready to go to the stake for it (and a great many did), for only by following the true path without the slightest deviation could they hope to find salvation and a life after death. No one really believed that there was no life after death.

But Smyth was a bit much even for the sixteenth century; both Robinson and Brewster found his "instability and wantonness of wit" something of a bore. They agreed with him when he insisted, in one of his frequent pamphlets, that "God's word doth absolutely describe unto us the only true shape of a true visible church" and further that "there is only one true shape and portraiture of a true visible Church for there is only one faith and truth in everything," but they were quite sure that the true shape, et cetera, had been revealed to them and were not prepared to be bothered by Smyth's doubts and discoveries.

Quite soon after he and his congregation had arrived in Amsterdam to found the Second English Church, Smyth began a controversy on three issues. The first concerned the nature of the covenant between God and the church members; Smyth's definition was ambiguous but also seemed to be heading straight back to Browne, and moreover he was contradicting a series of statements he had made in a previous pamphlet, *Principles and Inferences*. In response to protests he blithely said: "It is our covenant with God to forsake every evil way whether in opinion or practice that shall be manifested to us at any time," which is at least as much a stopper as the famous "to change is to improve and to change often is to achieve perfection." The second issue he brought up was the position of the ministry, which he said had no power that the congregation could not take away, and furthermore that the pastor, the teacher, and the ruling elder should be replaced by one having the functions of all three. Third, it was quite clear from the Gospels that each church should be solely responsible for the needy among them and should refuse relief from outside. This last was a crack at Francis Johnson, who had accepted money from the Dutch Reformed Church.

Johnson, Ainsworth, and Clifton spent some time confuting these opinions, but Smyth was only firing ranging shots from his battery. He proceeded to shatter his own congregation by denouncing the use of the English Bible as a sin; God could not have spoken in English; in Hebrew he might have and possibly Greek, but translations into other tongues must be corrupt and impure. As a compromise, the English Bible was kept for reference but banished from the service.

The real uproar began when Smyth declared that none of the Separatists was a Christian, since they had been baptized as infants, and he denied that an infant could make a covenant with the Lord. So—the church must be disbanded and each member be baptized into the Christian faith in the name of the Father, the Son, and the Holy Ghost, and the Church made whole again. But how to begin?—for an unbaptized person could not very well baptize others. However, since John the Baptist himself had not been baptized Smyth decided that it was up to him to solve the problem by first baptizing himself and then proceeding in proper form to baptize the others. A shock wave swept through the Anglican as well as throughout the Separatist churches generated by a mixture of doubt and horror. It subsided in time, leaving the word se-baptist, or self-baptizer, to mark Smyth's place in history.

There remained for Smyth the serious problem of infants who were due for hell if they died unbaptized, and since he was a good Christian he resolved this by stating his belief that "either they are all saved . . . or that they are one of God's secrets, and not to be searched into."

His congregation might still have held together had Smyth not taken another of his unpredictable leaps, this time backward, and declared that his self-baptism had been "a damnable error." The split, or compound fracturing, of his congregation was hastened by two other developments in Smyth's intricate theology. One was that Smyth and Helwys (he it was who had organized the exodus of the Gainsborough church) both declared that the Mennonite sect was a true church. The Mennonites were followers of Simons Menno of Friesland and were a mellowed version of the Anabaptists, who did not believe in infant baptism either but who pursued this and other doctrines with an extreme fanaticism that made them unpopular everywhere, even in Amsterdam. Then Smyth and Helwys took sides in the theological controversy begun by Jacobus Harmensen, or Arminius, of Leyden which was tearing all Calvinist Holland apart. In short, the Arminians held that God grants forgiveness and eternal life to all who repent and believe; that He wills all men to be saved; that predestination is founded on God's foreknowledge.

Smyth's congregation dissolved. Helwys and about a dozen others who still believed in adults-only baptism returned to England and were the forerunners of the English General Baptists; another group, formed later (1630s), reverted to a stricter Calvinist discipline and became the English Particular Baptists. John Smyth, with a band of loyalists who may not have quite understood where he was taking them but who would have followed him anywhere, approached the Mennonites with a confession of his se-baptist error and asked to be baptized into their Church, for they now belonged to no church at all. Only after they had thoroughly sniffed them over did the Mennonite Anabaptists consent to receive the group, in 1612, and by then John Smyth had died of tuberculosis, a disease associated with all kinds of hardship and deprivation. He was a good man with a good if erratic mind who deserves to be better remembered in the annals of the Pilgrims.

The Scrooby congregation had moved to Leyden (today we spell it Leiden) in May 1609, because Francis Johnson was already reacting to Smyth's Anabaptism, and what with that and Smyth himself and one or two other things, Robinson and Brewster saw trouble ahead. Richard Clifton, the Scrooby pastor, defected to the "ancient brethren," a move he was to regret. It seems to have been an individual decision by Clifton, for no others of his congregation followed him; in fact he was boarding a sinking ship, for when Robinson applied to the burgomaster of Leyden for a permit he spoke of his Church "to the number of one hundred souls," which meant that a large number of the "ancient church" were joining Scrooby, and possibly, although there is no other evidence to go on, some of Smyth's congregation too had joined them.

The break-up of Francis Johnson's First English Church of the
Separation in Amsterdam began in December 1610, when a
group of thirty or so led by the gentle Ainsworth formed a separate Church. There had been a year of bickering over changes in
Johnson's theology. One major difference between them lay in
the interpretation of Matthew 18:17, "tell it unto the church,"
which Johnson now held to mean "tell the elders" and not the
whole congregation. This was the reading that George Johnson
and Thomas White so violently objected to as removing all
power from the congregation. Another shift due to Johnson's
hatred of Anabaptists (and he does not appear to have taken
much notice of them before Smyth leaned their way) was to the
opinion that Rome must be considered a true church, that baptism of infants by that Church must stand, otherwise you are
hand in hand with the vile Anabaptists. There was also the dis-
reputable Elder Studley, who stuck in a few gullets. Johnson per-
sistently supported him and so did Clifton when he became pastor
in Ainsworth's place, but in 1612 Studley confessed to his past
misdeeds with many an ingenious gloss on his various fornica-
tions and attempted seductions, and with what he apparently
thought was the perfect answer to his accusers: he had repented
and reformed in 1610. But he had to go, though not before several had left for the English Reformed Church on his account.

After Ainsworth and his group split off or were excommunicated by Johnson, there was a sordid lawsuit over the ownership of the meeting house in the Bruinestengange, which Johnson had seized as his own. Ainsworth's group won the case, and
Johnson's church moved to Emden. Ainsworth's church in Amsterdam kept in brotherly touch with Leyden, but two years after
the Pilgrims sailed for America Ainsworth died and his congregation gradually drifted to the English Reformed Church, whose
pastor was John Paget. This Church was very close in most
religious beliefs and observances to the Dutch Reformed Church,
and in consequence it was much in favor with authority.

Over Francis Johnson's church a kind of disenchantment had
fallen; members left, some for England, and in 1616 the venerable Richard Clifton died. He had been very unhappy in his last
days. Perhaps his thoughts went back to his valiant single-

minded fight against the Church of England; back to the lovely church of Babworth and to the noble tower of Scrooby; he had been too old to leave his village to preach in an Amsterdam alley and he had been very silly to forsake his old Scrooby friends for Johnson's contentious company.

Francis Johnson died in 1617, and the year after his death his congregation took ship for Virginia on a voyage that ended in a terrible tragedy, which cast a chilling shadow over the hearts and the plans of the congregation at Leyden.

10 The Fair and Beautiful City of Leyden

They removed to Leyden, a fair and beautiful city and of a sweet situation but made more famous by the university wherewith it is adorned, in which (of late) had been so many learned men. But wanting that traffic by sea which Amsterdam enjoys, it was not so beneficial for their outward means of living and estates. But being now here pitched they fell to such trades and employments as they best could; valueing peace and their spiritual comfort above any other riches whatsoever. And at length they came to raise a competent and comfortable living but with hard and continued labour.

It is still a beautiful city, and so is Amsterdam, the architectural attraction of each dating back to the seventeenth century, but in 1609 Leyden would have been the preference of the Pilgrims quite apart from the impending unpleasantness among the First and Second Churches of the Separation, for it was a smaller, more compact town, about a third of the size of Amsterdam, and the people were agreeable, hard-working, and made them welcome as they did all "honest men." Only later did the Pilgrims have to pull long faces at the Leydeners' zest for taverns, song, dancing, and excessive frivolity on the Sabbath.

Leyden was shield-shaped within strong high walls, and the

waters of the Old Rhine flowed around the walls as a moat and were also led through the town in broad channels, meeting the New Rhine with many linking canals. Outside the walls were extensive orchards and nursery gardens, and inside, although the houses were closely packed, they were mostly built around central gardens. Even as they do today, the Dutch used every scrap of unoccupied ground to grow something.

Naturally, it being 1609, there were some dark alleys leading from the main streets, which were broad straight avenues across the top of the shield from dexter to sinister chief, and a hatchwork of short streets from the flanks and across from waterway to waterway to the center. Conspicuous on a map of the time are two great churches, and an ancient burgh, keep, or fort on a raised mound.

Out of these packed houses came the clacking of looms, the snipping of scissors, all the noisy symphony of the cloth trade when it was a domestic industry and the power used was the power of the human muscle, for Leyden was a center for the cloth trade. Even England sent cloth there to be finished. And there were the numerous ancillary trades: fullers, combers and carders of wool, ribbon makers, felters, tailors, drapers, and among them the merchants in large houses and the enormous variety of occupations peculiar to an almost self-sufficient town of the seventeenth century. Self-sufficient, that is, outside the exigencies of trade. One would have thought that there was plenty of work for all, and so there was, but the Pilgrims, unskilled in any industrial work (except for Francis Cooke, the wool comber, and a few others), had to take menial, backbreaking jobs, since all the better and more highly paid ones were reserved to guild members and the guilds were as tightly organized as modern trade unions, of which they were the ancestors. A man had to be admitted as a citizen of Leyden before he could become a member of a guild.

The Dexters, father and son, spent long years digging up such traces as the Pilgrims had left in the records of Leyden, and they published their findings at the turn of the last and the beginning of this century. No one now is likely to add much to their results. They found fifty-seven different occupations distributed among those who were Pilgrims or connected with them, and most of the jobs were in or on the fringe of the wool trade. Bradford himself is described as a fustian maker (and that cannot be said of his prose). The Dexters also made a careful check on the number of Pilgrims in Leyden, and at first sight the number is surprising. From 1609 to 1620 there must have been between four and five hundred, or on breakdown: known or presumable Pilgrims, 298; those more or less loosely associated with them, 281; which gives a total of 579; but 106 names occur in both lists, so the whole Pilgrim colony equaled 473 men, women, and children. Thirty of them became citizens of Leyden before 1620.

For some years after their arrival, we don't know much about what they did or where they lived, but they seem to have clustered together in the maze of lanes and alleys around the Pieterskerk—St. Peter's Church—in the southwestern part of the city. St. Peter's itself stood in a large open space used then and now as a market. We do know that Brewster's house was in Stincksteeg, or Smelly Alley. In 1611 the congregation bought a large old house in the Klooksteeg, or Bell Alley, off St. Peter's Square, as we may call it. Behind the house was a garden and a piece of ground set about by three walls like a squash-racket's court with a canal on the serving side, and on this ground were built a number of houses for the less-well-off members of the congregation. The large house, called the Green Gate—or Groenepoort—served as meeting house and parsonage, and the Robinsons, John and his wife Bridget, three children, and a maid, moved in. Here you would say they were all nicely settled, and we first begin to hear of Robinson making his mark at the University of Leyden.

The university had been founded in 1575 to honor the stubborn defense put up by the Leydeners against the Spanish, their ferocity sharpened by the knowledge that if the city had been taken by the Spaniard those of their number who were not slaughtered out of hand would have been handed over to the racks and fires of the Inquisition. Sir William Brereton, in his *Travels,* published some fourteen years after the Pilgrims left, writes of Leyden University: "Here be only two colleges; in one about thirty students of Divinity, who have their diets and twenty guilders apiece, a square uniform little court or quadrangle; in the other twenty students of Divinity who have therein their diets and fifty guilders apiece; these only go in the habit of scholars, so is here no face nor presence of a university."

Brereton became a successful military commander, and he seems to be assessing the university with the eye of a billeting officer. It may have been small, but twenty years before Brereton saw it Leyden University was already famous and students came from all Protestant Europe. It was considered pre-eminent in philosophy, political science, and natural philosophy. With Utrecht and Groningen, Leyden produced a greater number than any other country of the leading philosophers, theologians, and scientists in Europe. Robinson matriculated there in September 1615—in theology, of course, and this gave him certain privileges, including an allowance of beer and wine, but he had to teach his subject three times a week and Brewster taught English mostly to Danes and Germans at the university "by reason he had the Latin tongue," says Bradford, but then all scholars had. The point seems to be that Brewster was an excellent grammarian in spite of not having taken his degree at Cambridge. But theology was the raging subject in those times, and Robinson soon got drawn into the great debate begun by Arminius of Leyden, which debate spread through Calvinist Europe but was pursued most vehemently in Holland. Robinson, says Bradford, "began to be terrible to the Arminians." A professor had put up some theses (in the manner of Luther, but a common practice), which he would defend against all comers. Some other professors urged Robinson to dispute, but he was, being a comparative stranger, rather shy. But, said the professors, "such is the ability and nimbleness of the adversary that the truth would suffer if he did not help them." So . . . "he prepared himself against the time, and when the day came, the Lord did so help him to defend the truth, and foil the adversary, as he put him to an apparent nonplus in this great public audience. And the like he did two or three times upon such like occasions."

Protestantism from its very beginning has shown itself as naturally fissiparous, able to go on splitting itself indefinitely into sects, each of which is the sole custodian of the true light, though some sects admit that certain others possess a gleam or two. Arminianism was a refutation of both parts of a split in Calvinism. Calvin maintained that predestination was a mystery, that the elect were to be saved and the damned damned and that was that. But two sets of Calvinist theologians began to pick this thesis to pieces. One set argued that God had predestined some men to be of the elect and the rest were damned from the beginning. The other set argued that God had made his selection only after Adam's fall from grace. Arminius said "boo" to both these arguments, and maintained that God desired the salvation of all men, who may accept or reject His grace, and this rather noble, agreeable, and generous if not downright cheerful view is what Robinson got all the kudos for denying. The Dutch States General wanted the argument settled. Too much time and energy were being spent not only in the universities but in the market places, the streets and houses, and probably up and down the canals as well; it was affecting business. So the States General convened a synod at Dort, in Holland (1618–19), to which Calvinist theologians came from Switzerland, Germany, and England, but for some reason not Scotland, and they had either to agree with the Arminians or throw them out. They threw them out, and no doubt a good time was had by all. Two hundred of the Arminian clergy were deprived of their livings by decree, though in the tolerant Dutch way the decree was soon withdrawn and the argument went on and on in a muted kind of way.

By this time, that is by the time Robinson was sorting out the professors at Leyden, the division of Europe into Catholic and Protestant spheres had, very roughly, formed the pattern it was to keep for a long time, win or lose a state here or there, the Catholic Church on balance a winner. The Protestants were divided into two main confessions, Lutheranism and Calvinism. Lutheranism was the vaguer, less conclusive in its theology, and so gave ample scope for argument and dissension. Saxony, Hesse, and a good part of southern Germany and some of the Baltic States were Lutheran, as well as Scandinavia, Finland, and Iceland. Calvinism, being a more logical and consistent system with a firm discipline (the Arminians were heretics), captured some parts of Germany, and had made of Geneva, in the words of John Knox, "the most perfect school of Christ that ever was on earth since the days of the Apostles." Scotland was firmly Calvinist, as were Hungary, the Netherlands, and parts, large parts, of France, where the Calvinist Huguenots had about eight hundred congregations (due to be reduced by massacre and persecution). Before the end of the century, France became a country of one religion, Catholicism, although being France she had her own, national brand of Catholicism.

The Jesuits, the brilliant spiritual soldiers of the advance guard of the Counter Reformation, had penetrated and occupied Poland. That country, which had tolerated Jews, Hussites, Calvinists, Lutherans, and many other sects, was now almost totally Catholic, and the Protestants were a small, persecuted minority. The Jews held some ground against fearful odds. Lithuania and parts of White Russia were Catholic.

Southern Europe below the Alps and the Pyrenees was completely Catholic, with the exception of Venice. All opposition had been wiped out. Spain was the powerful secular arm of the Vatican, ready with the Inquisition to carry God's work forward into Holland as soon as the twelve-year truce lapsed. That threat was below the horizon, though the Pilgrim leaders showed their awareness of it.

Over the years, the congregation had made themselves liked or at least they had made themselves trusted in Leyden:

> Though many of them were poor yet, there was none so poor but if they were known to be of that congregation, the Dutch (either bakers or others) would trust them in any reasonable matter when they had no money. Because they had found by experience how careful they were to keep their word, and saw them so hardworking and diligent in their callings; yet they would strive to get their custom and to employ them above others in their work.

The diligence of Master Brewster, however, made him much disliked by no less a person than King James I of England. About the end of 1616 Brewster set up as a publisher of books and pamphlets. His partner was Thomas Brewer, a well-to-do gentleman of Kent who was studying at the University of Leyden and who attended the Scottish Calvinist church. He, we may suppose, supplied most of the finance. He had arrived in Leyden some years after the Pilgrims and had bought a large house, the Groenehuis—Green House—very close to the Pilgrims' "Green Gate" in the Klooksteeg. The Green House had become something of a gathering place for English and other students at the university. The publishing office and print shop was set up in No. 15 Pieterskerkkoorsteeg—15 St. Peter's Church, Choir Lane (or alley if we must give that semi-slum sound proper to a tightly packed sixteenth-century city), handy to Brewster's house; in fact, Brewster's was a back entrance or the other way about, and the imprint of the press gave the address Choir Alley in Latin—Vicus Choralis (which is the name that street—or alley—now bears in honor of what is referred to as The Pilgrims Press). Brewer brought over a qualified or master printer named John Reynolds, and his asistant was twenty-two-year-old Edward Winslow, a name of much honor in the later annals of the Pilgrims.

The type was probably set up in Choir Alley and run off by one of the Dutch jobbing printers, so that incriminating evidence could be hidden quickly in Vicus Choralis and a "Who? Me?" expression assumed, for Brewster at any rate was not so much interested in the fine art of printing as in the coarser art of spreading propaganda or the Light, or, as King James had it, sedition. Only the first three books published bore the imprint of the press, and they were quite uncontroversial. Those that followed (we do not know exactly how many, fifteen, say, at the most) were less likely to be welcomed by English authority, and one, the *Perth Assembly*, raised such a rare old fuss that it put an end to Messrs. Brewster and Brewer, Publishers. *Perth Assembly*, written by David Calderwood was an attack on James I for his attempt to wish bishops on the Scottish Kirk at a General Assembly of that Church in 1618. In the manner of his times, Calderwood blasted James with a number of virulent nouns and full-flavored adjectives.

Most of the copies were smuggled across to England and Scotland, where they were much enjoyed by many, but not by the authorities, who brought a copy to James. He got into a splendid rage and insisted on action. An innocent Edinburgh printer was arrested, but before anything drastic could happen to him a report was received from the English ambassador at The Hague. He had seen, he said, a copy of a scurrilous pamphlet that he wished to bring to the notice of His Majesty. It had been printed, he thought, by a certain "William Brewster, a Brownist, who hath been for some years an inhabitant and printer at Leyden." As would be seen, it was a pernicious libel on His Majesty and entitled the *Perth Assembly*.

The hunt was up for Brewster, and for one reason or another the States General was inclined to join in, but Brewster had disappeared; some said three months back, the ambassador said three weeks back. In fact, Brewster had been in London on delicate negotiation with the Virginia Company when he took alarm at the discovery of the *Perth Assembly* pamphlet, although he was not immediately suspected of having printed it. Then ensued one of those farcical pursuits in which the villain bobs up in several different places at the same time, false clues are swiftly followed, the wrong man is arrested, and such devoted servants of His Majesty as the ambassador are made to look fools by bungling underlings but have to take the rap. He got a nasty rap from James, who also told him to "move the States General to take some strict order through all their Provinces for the preventing of the like abuses and licentiousness in publishing, printing, and vending such scandalous and libellous pamphlets."

Brewster had gone underground to save his ears and nose, which might have been sliced off in the pillory; or he might have been hanged; not a quick death in those days and very horrible trimmings added if he were to be convicted of treason. Brewster emerges from underground onto the deck of a ship at sea, the consort to the *Mayflower*.

Brewer was arrested, but the university exercised their privilege of keeping him in their own lockup. Finally, he was persuaded by eminent professors to appear in London for examination, the King to pay his expenses. The authorities in London got nowhere with him at all and he was released, but as James, who hated parting with any money at all, would only pay his fare from, and not back to, Leyden, Brewer felt free in his turn to disappear out of harm's way in case someone, somewhere, might dig up some nasty bits of evidence. In the long run, someone did and he was jailed for fourteen years—for another piece of sedition—but that was in 1626.

11   The Drums of War

For some time, the Pilgrims had been getting unsettled, uneasy in their situation, like a flock of birds a few days before the time of their annual migration. Secretary Nathaniel Morton, writing, in 1669, a *New England Memorial*, says: "They foresaw that Holland would be no place for their church and posterity to continue comfortably," and goes on to expound five reasons which it is clear he has taken from William Bradford's manuscript, from which manuscript we may as well quote direct (although not quite verbatim—and Bradford gives only four reasons):

After they had lived in this city some eleven or twelve years, and sundry of them were taken away by death; and many others began to be well stricken in years, the governors with sundry of the sagest members began to apprehend their present dangers and wisely to foresee the future, and think of timely remedy. In the agitation of their thoughts and much discourse of things hereabout, at length they began to incline to this conclusion, of removal to some other place. Not out of any newfangledness or other such giddy humour . . . but for sundry weighty and solid reasons some of the chief of which I will here briefly touch.
First—they saw and found by experience the hardness of the place and country to be such as few would come to them, and fewer

that would bide it out and continue with them. For many that came to them could not endure the great labour and hard fare with other inconveniences . . . yea some preferred and chose the prisons in England rather than this liberty in Holland.

Secondly—They saw that though the people generally bore all these difficulties very cheerfully and with a resolute courage being in the best of their years yet old age began to steal on many of them (and their great and continual labours hastened it before their time) so as it was not only thought probable but was apparent that within a few years more they would be in danger of scattering, or sinking under their burdens, or both.

Thirdly—As necessity was a taskmaster to them so they were forced to be the same not only to their servants, but (in a sort) to their dearest children. For many of their children . . . were so oppressed with their heavy labours, that though their minds were free and willing, yet their bodies bowed under the weight of the same and became decrepit in their early youth. But that which was the more lamentable, and of all sorrows most heavy to be borne was that many of their children by . . . the great licentiousness of youth in that country, and the manifold temptations of the place were drawn away by evil examples into extravagant and dangerous courses, getting the reins off their neck and departing from their parents. Some became soldiers, others took upon them far voyages by sea, and some worse courses, tending to dissoluteness and the danger of their souls to the great grief of their parents and dishonour of God. So that they saw their posterity would be in danger to degenerate and be corrupted.

Lastly—(and which was not the least) a great hope and inward zeal they had of laying some good foundation . . . for the propagating and advancing the kingdom of Christ[1] in those remote parts of the world.

Morton adds: "Their posterity would in a few generations become Dutch and so lose their interest in the English nation they being desirous rather to enlarge His Majesty's Dominions and to live under their natural Prince."

The first and second of the reasons simply say that life was tough in Leyden and the third that it was also hard going for the children, who were being seduced to an ungodly way of life. But life was tough everywhere in industrial cities; maybe they missed the natural rhythm of honest husbandry; no foreman wants you to speed up hand milking; oxen cannot be forced to a gallop in plowing; in hand reaping you have only to keep in line; there is an easy tempo in binding sheaves or using a flail. But somehow these reasons ring hollow except for the point that the children are getting less keen to walk the Pilgrim way with God. And lastly the missionary zeal is not the least thin among the reasons. But Morton must have got his reason from the Pilgrims themselves and it sounds absolutely genuine patriotism—a desire to remain English. Then, at the very end of the chapter, a solid and powerful argument appears for getting away from Holland:

> They lived here but as men in exile, and in a poor condition; and as great miseries might befall them in this place for the twelve years of truce were now out; and there was nothing but beating of drums and preparing for war, the events of which are always uncertain. The Spaniard might prove as cruel as the savages of America, and the famine and pestilence as sore here as there.

The drums the Pilgrims heard were beating in far-off Bohemia, where the series of four consecutive wars between Catholics and Protestants known as the Thirty Years' War had already begun, in 1618. Holland well knew what such a war might mean to her, and the air of Leyden must have been full of rumors. When peace came, thirty years later, Germany had been devastated, Spain was ruined, but the Dutch, though swept into the war, emerged wealthier than ever. Sweden was at her peak of military glory and France the most powerful state in Europe. The cost in lives was over eight million. England had pursued a safe but inglorious course, and at the end of the Thirty Years' War was in the hands of Oliver Cromwell. So the drums the Pilgrims heard were a warning they did well to heed, a warning to move to America, out of earshot. But where, exactly? Like a family today scanning the brochures to choose a place to spend their holidays, the Pilgrims could read a large number of pamphlets: Sir Walter Raleigh's *Discoverie of the large rich and beautiful Empire of Guiana* (1596), Whitaker's *Good News from Virginia* (1613), and of course the very large but more difficult selection in Purchas's *Pilgrims* and Hakluyt's *Voyages of the English Nation* —and so:

After their humble prayers unto God for His direction and assistance, they consulted what particular place to pitch on and prepare
for. Some (and none of the meanest) were earnest for Guiana or
some of those fertile places in those hot climates; others were for
some parts of Virginia where the English had already made entrance.

Those for Guiana had really fallen for the advertising:

The countrie was rich, fruitful and blessed with a perpetual spring,
where nature brought forth all things in abundance without any
great labour or art of man. So as it must needs make the inhabitants
rich, seeing less provision of clothing and other things would serve
than in colder and less fruitful countries must be had.

It does not sound like a Pilgrim talking. Fortunately, someone
had read Purchas ("many of our men fell sick, some of agues,
some of fluxes whereby they would often fall down which grew
chiefly out of the excessive heat of the sun, and of the extreme
damp of the earth") and the echo comes in Bradford:

Such hot countries are subject to grievous diseases, and many
noisome impediments which other more temperate places are freer
from.

And another pertinent objection:

Again if they should there live and do well the jealous Spaniard
would never suffer them long but would overthrow them as he did
the French in Florida.[2]

Virginia seemed to be the best bet, but an objection much
more in the Pilgrim tone was offered:

that if they lived among the English which were there planted already, or so near them as to be under their government they should
be in as great danger to be troubled and persecuted for the cause of
religion as if they lived in England and it might be worse.

This objection was carefully and hopefully noted when they
decided for Virginia:

to live as a distinct body by themselves under the general government of Virginia and by their friends to sue to His Majesty that he
would be pleased to grant them freedom of religion.

It is worth noting here that the Pilgrims, judging by Bradford's
account of the discussion or conference, did not even consider
settling in New England. A settlement made in 1608 not much
farther north than Plymouth was abandoned as "over cold and in
respect of that not habitable by our nation." The settlement was
on the Kennebec River, Maine, but the report could have taken
New England off the agenda as being the same kind of inhospi-
table place. In which case the Pilgrims had not yet seen or not
believed the reports on New England published by Captain John
Smith in 1616. He had sailed into and named Plymouth Harbor,
explored the coast and named New England, made a surprisingly
accurate map, and printed an enthusiastic recommendation of
New England as a "fit place for habitation."

However, Guiana is out, New England is not considered (on
the record), and they hope to get to the northern part of Virginia. There are just the little matters of (a) a patent (that is, a
written permission to settle on the lands for which the First Virginia Company of London has a grant or charter from the king
and can, as it were, sublet), (b) the king's permission, and (c)
finance.

Two were chosen and sent into England who found the Virginia
Company very desirous to have them go and willing to grant them a
patent.

The company was only too glad to have the Pilgrims as
settlers, because it was in a poor financial state and until it could
get a plantation made, or a fishing and trading station manned, it
was not in business. If it had settlers who had signed up for
America it could attract capital from speculators.

The "two who were chosen" were two deacons of the church,
Robert Cushman and John Carver. Cushman was a Canterbury
man and a wool comber in a fair way of business, and may have
been one of those who came over to the Pilgrims from the
congregation of Francis Johnson. He had bought himself a

largish house in Nuns Alley—the Nonnensteeg—near the university, and had just married a second wife. He played a major part in the protracted negotiations and stayed in England to see them through. In any language, it can be said that he was to have one hell of a time from both sides.

John Carver, now over fifty years of age, came from Doncaster, less than ten miles up the Great North Road from Scrooby, but he had not been a member of the Scrooby congregation; he must have made his own way to Holland and Leyden, and does not appear in the Pilgrim records (such as they are) before 1616. After that he is a prominent figure among them and reputed one of the richest. He had married one of the White girls of Sturton-le-Steeple, a sister to Robinson's wife Bridget.

Next in a long line of priorities was the job of getting the consent of the king.

It proved a harder piece of work than they took it for; for though many means were used to bring it about, yet it could not be effected; for there were many of good worth laboured with the King to obtain it (amongst whom was one of his Chief Secretaries) but it proved all in vain.

The chief secretary was Sir Robert Nanton, but he was procured (Winslow's word) by the useful and friendly Sir Edwin Sandys to put a private motion to His Majesty, and for once we get a little authentic dialogue:

NANTON: (He asks His Majesty) to give way to such people, who could not so comfortably live under the government of another State, to enjoy their liberty of Conscience under his gracious protection in America, where they would endeavour the advancement of His Majesty's Dominions and the enlargement of the Gospel by all due means.

JAMES: This is a good and honest motion. What profit might arise in the part they intend?

NANTON: Fishing.

JAMES: So God have my soul 'tis an honest trade. 'Twas the Apostles' own calling.

Then James told him the applicants should refer to the bishops. But the applicants were tipped off "not to entangle themselves with the bishops" but "to take what they had of the King's approbation"—which Bradford translates as

Yet thus far they prevailed, in sounding His Majesty's mind, that he would connive at them and not molest them provided they carried themselves peaceably. But to allow or tolerate them by his public authority, under his seal, they found it would not be.

And later on Bradford adds an opinion from "some of the chiefest" among the Pilgrims that if there was no security in what they had understood as the king's meaning there was none either in a written permission: "Though they had a seal as broad as the house floor it would not serve the turn, for there would be means enough found to recall or reverse it." It was not the king they distrusted so much as the bishops. But there were others against them, including the great Lord Bacon. He was not in favor of Brownists and suchlike being allowed to set up their churches in the new plantations, "else it will take a schism and a rent in Christ's coat which must be seamless." This kind of opposition moved the Pilgrims to set out a very fine line in smooth talk in a list of seven articles of their beliefs shown to the Virginia Company by Sir Edwin Sandys and to anyone else who questioned their absolute devotion to the king and their devout admiration for the king's Established Church. On the showing of these seven articles there was not a hair of difference between them and the Church of England—on these seven points anyway. They did the trick with the company. Sir Edwin Sandys reported that the articles had given the Company "that good degree of satisfaction which has carried them on to set forward your desire." But the Privy Council was not taken in and raised some pertinent questions which very much disturbed some at Leyden so that quite a few withdrew their support.

Meanwhile a letter came from Cushman dated May 8, 1619. He and Brewster had been sent to conclude arrangements with the Company, a line in the letter says: "Mr. B. is not well at this time; whether he will come back to you or go into the north yet I

know not." And that of course meant that Mr. Brewster had gone
into hiding over the Perth Assembly affair. Another piece of news
in the same letter must have spread some alarm and despond-
ency among those at Leyden. It told of the end of Francis Johnson's "ancient brethren" who had gone first to Emden in Friesland and then had drifted back to Amsterdam. Under Ruling
Elder Blackwell they had set sail for Virginia in the autumn of
1618. Since Cushman's is the only record of any sort about this
voyage, here are his words: "Going towards winter they still had
norwest winds, which carried them to the southward beyond
their course. And the master of the ship and some six of the mariners dying, it seems they could not find the bay until after long
seeking and beating about. Mr. Blackwell is dead, and Mr.
Maggner the Captain, yea there are dead 130 persons . . . it is
said there was in all 180 persons in the ship, so as they were
packed together like herrings. They had among them the flux, so
as it is here rather wondered at that so many are alive than that
so many are dead. . . . I see none here discouraged much but
rather desire to learn to beware by other men's harms, and to
amend that wherein they have failed."

It was a miserable end, but whoever was mourned by the
Pilgrims it was not Blackwell, "who," says Bradford, "declined
from the truth with Mr. Johnson and went with him when they
parted asunder in that woeful manner which brought so great
dishonor to God, scandal to the truth and outward ruin to themselves in the world." After detailing some treacheries and ro-
gueries on the part of Blackwell (and there is a good deal of
other evidence to the same effect), "I hope, notwithstanding,
through the mercies of the Lord their souls are now at rest with
Him in the heavens," which acquits Bradford of out-and-out bigotry at least.

Dismissing all these letters as "thus much by the way," he gets
down to brass tacks:

But at last they had a patent granted them. By the advice of some
friends this patent was not taken in the name of any of their own
but in the name of Mr. John Wincob who intended to go with them.

We do not know the terms of the patent, and above all we do not know for what tract of land it was issued, because the document was never directly referred to after it was sent to Leyden, but from some sentences in Bradford's book it can be inferred that the land was around the mouth of Hudson's river. It was certainly not for any land north of 41° latitude—for which the London company had no grant.

They began to choose who should go and who should stay, but "it was also promised to those that went first, by the body of the rest, that if the Lord gave them life and means and opportunity, they would come to them as soon as they could."

(Winslow gives fuller details about the principles of selection. It may be noted that of, say, three hundred in Leyden less than half eventually reached New England, and those that remained were so thoroughly absorbed in the Dutch population that in 1859 not more than three names of families could be traced bearing any resemblance to those known to have been of the Robinson church. [Note on page 98 of 1912 edition of Bradford])

They chose Brewster to be a leader to the New World without knowing just where he was in the Old at the moment, but in the certain faith that he would appear at Southampton. Pastor Robinson was to mind the Leyden flock pending further emigration if affairs went well. At this time they had an offer from the New Netherland Company, who had already founded a trading station at Manhattan, to settle them in New Amsterdam (now New York), to provide free shipping under Dutch naval escort, and give them cattle when they arrived. Bradford calls it "a fair offer." It was more than that, it was a generous offer, although it shows the anxiety of the Dutch to have useful settlers around their trading post. But then along came Mr. Weston, who persuaded them "not to meddle with the Dutch or too much to depend on the Virginia Company." In short, leave it all to Weston, he'll fix everything, shipping, money—the lot. Meanwhile they were to draw up a contract that he would take to friends of his who were anxious to adventure some capital.

Thomas Weston was an ironmonger and a citizen of London. He was also a member of one or another company of merchant venturers and had dabbled in a number of trading enterprises and investments in the Newfoundland fisheries. He had also been warned off from illegal trading in cloth in other people's territory in Holland. There were a number of his kind around, bold, enterprising, taking a hand in any large affair that would make money; a most useful man, but not a safe and steady man. He may have known Edward Pickering, a merchant and one of the Leyden congregation, who became a shareholder, as did Brewer (still loose in England). Most of the seventy Weston got to subscribe were of London, and some put in five hundred pounds (in money of the time) though most invested much smaller sums. Captain John Smith, in his *Generall Historie*, says: "Some were Gentlemen, some merchants, some handycrafts men. These dwell most about London, they are not a corporation but knit together by a voluntary combination without constraint or penalty, aiming to do good and plant religion."

Weston then heard that the Second (Plymouth) Virginia Company was seeking to establish clear rights to the northern part of the Virginian grant, and to call it New England. Both Weston and some at Leyden thought they should go there because of the excellent fishing. This was rash of them; the Pilgrims knew something of half a dozen trades connected with cloth, silk, and so on, and something, not a lot, about farming, but nothing whatsoever about deep-sea or even inshore fishing.

Bradford sets out the state of the party just when matters were coming to a head; it was getting on time to go, if they were to go:

> But as in all business the acting part is the most difficult, especially where the work of many agents must concur; for some of those that should have gone who were in England fell off and would not go; other merchants and friends that had offered to adventure money withdrew, and pretended many excuses. Some disliking they went not to Guiana, others again would adventure nothing except they went to Virginia. Some again (and those that were most relied on) fell into utter dislike with Virginia and would do nothing if they went thither.

Confusion enough one would say but made worse by a communication from Cushman and Carver, their agents in London.

The contract drawn up in Leyden, which Weston had seemed to approve, had been amended by the company and the amendments agreed to by Weston, Carver, and Cushman without any consultation with Leyden. The new contract had ten articles, and as these were to be the background to the first seven years, they are important enough to give in full, or nearly so:

1. The adventurers and planters do agree that every person (that goeth) aged 16 years and upward be rated at £10 and £10 to be accounted a single share.
2. Each settler furnishing himself out with £10 either in money or other provisions shall be accounted to have £20 in stock and so in the division of assets have a double share.
3. The partnership between the adventurers and the settlers shall last seven years, during which time all profits remain in the common stock.
4. After landing, some will be employed in fishing at sea and the rest building houses and farming the land.
5. After seven years capital and profits including houses, lands, goods and chattels to be divided equally between adventurers and settlers, after which each side shall be clear of the other.
6. Any late comer or investor shall receive his proportionate share.
7. Wife, children or servants over 16 have a single share, a double share if "furnished out." Children between 10 and 16 a half share.
8. Children now under ten no share other than 50 acres of unmanured land.
9. Executors to have the proportionate share of any who die.
10. All settlers to have food and clothing out of the common stock.

Leyden accepted these ten articles. What annoyed them was that two articles had been deleted from the original agreement. One was that at the end of the seven years, the houses, their gardens, and the improved land should not go into the kitty but remain the property of the settlers; the second, "that they should have two days a week for their own private employment for the more comfort of themselves and their families."

A furious correspondence began, John Robinson writing "To their loving friends John Carver and Robert Cushman" in terms that did not conceal an unloving and acid dislike of Cushman and all his works, and Cushman alternating between patient explanation and an exasperated ramming home of the realities of his and their position. His language is too vigorous to let go by précis. He is here replying to Robinson point by point. We take him up at No. 3: "This will hinder the building of fair houses. *Answer*. Our purpose is to build for the present such houses as, if need be, we may with little grief set on fire, and run away with the light. Our riches shall not be in pomp but in strength. 4. The Government may prevent excess in building—*Answer*. But if it be resolved on to build mean houses the Government's labour is spared. 5. All men are not of one condition. *Answer*. If by condition you mean wealth, you are mistaken; if you mean by condition qualities, then I say that he that is not content his neighbour shall have as good a house, fare, means, etc., is not of a good quality. And so on to 9. Great profit is like to be made by trucking [trading or barter] and fishing. *Answer*. As it is better for them so for us. 10. Our hazard is greater than theirs. *Answer*. True, but do they put us upon it? do they urge or egg us? hath not the motion and resolution been always in ourselves? If we will not go they are content to keep their money." And he now lets fly: "If the congregation think me to be the Jonas let them cast me off before we go; I shall be content to stay with good will, having but the clothes on my back, only let us have quietness and no more of these clamours."

Some of the Amsterdam congregation who were to join them backed down and their money was refunded, leaving the venture short of both money and people. The merchant adventurers took a grip on the situation and recruited in London for settlers without bothering much about the religious convictions of the recruits, and this group had an agent of their own appointed, Christopher Martin, an extreme Puritan, irritable and arrogant. The three agents went shopping for the voyage each without much regard for what the other two were doing, or as Cushman says, "There is fallen already amongst us a flat schism and we are readier to go to dispute than to set forward a voyage." Martin, in Kent, "set down his resolution how much he would have of everything without respect to any counsel or exception. Surely he that is in a society and yet regards not counsel may better be a King."

Quite suddenly in Bradford's account, things begin to move. "At length after much travail and these debates all things were got ready and provided. A small ship was bought"—but he does not name either of the ships. Morton expands Bradford: "A small ship was bought and fitted out in Holland, about sixty tons, called the *Speedwell,* so as to transport some of them over, so also to stay in the country and attend upon fishing and such other affairs as might benefit the colony. Another ship was hired in London of burden about 180 tons called the *Mayflower"* and then Bradford's famous "loath to depart":

And the time being come that they must depart, they were accompanied with most of their brethren out of the city unto a town, sundry miles off, called Delftshaven where the ship lay ready to receive them. So they left the goodly and pleasant city which had been their resting place near twelve years; but they knew they were pilgrims[3] and looked not much on those things but lifted their eyes to the heavens, their dearest country, and quieted their spirits.

12 The *Mayflower*

"Doleful was the sight of that sad and mournful parting"; the shadow of Blackwell's voyage must have hung over Delftshaven Quay and chilled many a heart. Some complete families were going, but others were divided, the wife staying behind with the children or the wife taking some children and leaving others. Bradford took his wife, Dorothy, but left his son at Leyden. Mary Brewster, hoping her husband would join her in England, took her two youngest and left the older children. Isaac Allerton took his pregnant wife and their three small children, a complete family. Almost half the party, of fewer than fifty, were children. There was no apparent pattern; perhaps each did as seemed best to him.

The *Speedwell*, Captain Reynolds, set sail on July 22, 1620, dropped down and out of the broad estuary of the River Maas past the Hook of Holland into the North Sea heading west-southwest for the Straits of Dover and along the English coast to Southampton. A "prosperous wind" had taken them there in an easy four days, the last piece of good luck for some time. *Mayflower* and the London contingent had arrived a week before. In 1620 Southampton was in something of a decline. The Italians, whose argosies had once used the port, had lost most of

their Eastern trade; the very last Venetian great ship to Southampton had sunk off the Needles in 1587. What Far and Near
East trade there was now went to London. Perhaps the Pilgrims
went ashore in Southampton to have a long letter from Pastor
Robinson read to them. It was full of good advice and warm feeling. He had already told them that they "should use all means to
avoid and shake off the name of Brownists, being a mere nickname and brand to make religion odious."

The first to board them when they anchored was a quartet of
trouble: Carver, Cushman, Martin, and Weston. Carver said he
had been getting in stores there at Southampton and knew not
well what the others had done in London. Cushman said seven
hundred pounds had been spent there "upon what I know not."
Martin refused to give any account of what he had spent, and
denounced Cushman for betraying them to the adventurers,
whom he called bloodsuckers. Weston presented the new contract to be properly signed by the leaders, which they refused to
do and said "that he knew right well that these were not according to the first agreement, neither could they yield to them
without the consent of the rest that were behind. At which he
was much offended and told them they must then look to stand
on their own legs."

This was awkward, for they needed one hundred pounds to
clear port, most of it due for repairs to the *Speedwell*. Weston
meant what he said and would not "disburse a penny." As the
best way to raise money they sold "three or four score firkins of
butter" (that is, 1½ to 2 tons, or 3360 to 4480 pounds), butter
being readily salable.

They thought it wise to write to the adventurers, saying that
they had hoped to see them all at Southampton to discuss the
contract, to which Weston should never have agreed. But to
show they were reasonable people they would modify the article
about including houses and plots of land in the final division
after seven years, and what was more if the adventurers had not
made large profits after seven years they would "continue together longer with you." They ended: "We are in such a strait at
present as we are forced to sell away £60 worth of our provision
to clear the Haven, scarce having any butter, no oil, not a sole to

mend a shoe, nor every man a sword to his side, wanting many muskets, much armour etc."

The passengers were parceled out between the two ships, and a governor with assistants appointed to each "to order the people." Martin was governor of the *Mayflower,* by which we may judge that most of the Leyden people were aboard the *Speedwell.*

On August 5, the *Speedwell* being thought seaworthy, they set sail for the New World. Six days later, they put into Dartmouth, and from there Robert Cushman writes one of his vivid letters. He had obviously been horribly seasick. "Our pinnace [the *Speedwell*] will not cease leaking, else I think we had been halfway at Virginia, our voyage hither hath been as full of crosses, as ourselves have been of crookedness. We put in here to trim her; if we had stayed at sea three or four hours more she would have sank right down. She is as leaky and open as a sieve, and there was a board a man might have pulled off with his finger where the water came in as at a mole hole." He then complains about the arrogant Martin, and wallows in pessimism about the whole enterprise: "Friend, if we ever make a plantation God works a miracle, especially considering how scant we shall be of victuals. Poor William Ring and myself do strive who shall be meat first for the fishes," and ends: "Pass by my weak manner, for my head is weak and my body feeble."

They remained nine or ten days at Dartmouth while the *Speedwell* was gone over by shipwrights. The Pilgrims must have gone ashore, and they could have gotten good advice about fishing, about the right hooks to use for cod, for instance, but judging by later events it seems that they did not bother. Dartmouth was a center for the ships going out to the Newfoundland Banks in spring of each year, returning in the early autumn, and the town was rich on the great hauls of fine cod. The fleet would still have been away when the *Speedwell* was being overhauled.

So with good hopes from hence they put to sea again conceiving they should go comfortably on, not looking for any more lets [delays] of this kind; but it fell out otherwise for after they were gone to sea again above one hundred leagues without the lands end the master of the small ship complained his ship was so leaky as he must bear up or sink at sea.

They decided to put back into Plymouth, but they could not have sailed one hundred leagues, which is three hundred miles, past Land's End from Dartmouth and back to Plymouth in the time. When Bradford wrote this he could have had no chart to hand. He has two explanations for the bad performance of the *Speedwell*. At Plymouth she was found to be overmasted, tight enough in harbor but under full sail liable to start her timbers and let in the sea. Later she was sold, put back in her old trim, and so gave good service for many years. The other explanation slots into the Pilgrim pattern of being exploited by rogues. "By the cunning and deceit of the master and his company, who were hired to stay a whole year in the country [Virginia] and now fearing want of victuals, they plotted this stratagem to free themselves," and at first sight this does not sound true if, in fact, the *Speedwell* was taking in more water than the pumps could cope with (and the Leyden people were aboard to see for themselves) but, he adds, "as afterwards was known and by some of them confessed." Bradford or Brewster must have gotten this information from two of the *Mayflower* crew, long after, in Plimouth. The question hangs in the air: it is not impossible that the crew members were either guessing or lying.

The Pilgrims were in Plymouth for fourteen days. Twenty were to return to London in the *Speedwell,* leaving one hundred and two to be packed into the *Mayflower.* Anyway, some had had enough or, as Bradford puts it, "either out of some discontent or fear they conceived of the ill success of the voyage seeing so many crosses befall and the year time so far spent." Cushman was one, and Bradford's comments on his defection are rather mean, picking him out as a man whose courage had failed him, though afterward he says he became "a special instrument for their good."

Whatever there was known about the distant seas for which the Pilgrims were bound was known in Plymouth. Most of the expeditions of the English probing into the New World had gone out from there. It was the home port of a fishing fleet of fifty or more vessels sailing each year to the Banks of Newfoundland, and other ships trading down the North American coast (Maine was the name they used) for furs. Plymouth was also the lair of the English pirates, as the Spaniard quite accurately called them, who were not only the licensed privateers of the Channel, but also those bold and famous seamen who would venture any-where they could float on the chance of relieving the Spaniard (with whom they were at peace) of gold and silver or anything else worth looting from town or ship in America or sailing from it. Plymouth had founded the English branch of the ancient trade in slaves. There were plenty of men in Plymouth (it was the fishing season, but they could not all have been away) who could have told the Pilgrims how, one morning in 1580, a ship lost for three years had suddenly appeared in Plymouth Harbor laden with a fabulous treasure gotten by Master Drake in a voyage around the world. They would have told of the Armada, of raids on the Spanish mainland and raids on the Spanish main, of adventures stranger than those printed by Hakluyt, but one imagines the Pilgrims no more interested in these matters than they were in the flowering of great art in the Holland they had just left. They must have seen the exotic furs, the costly tobacco, and the healthful sassafras brought from temporary trading posts on the coast of Maine. Indians had been visitors to Plymouth and they might at least have been curious about them.

They went ashore, where vast amounts of information were available, and they met Captain John Smith, that relentless propagandist for New England, and they got his map and his book *A Description of New England* (at least, when Brewster died there was a copy in his library), but very little seems to have sunk in. We don't know, we can only judge by the records they left—there is very little there of Plymouth's hard-garnered knowledge. Captain Smith wanted to go with them to lead and advise them. They declined, no doubt with great courtesy, and he wrote that their "humourous ignorance caused them for more than a year to endure a wonderful deal of misery with infinite patience . . . thinking to find things better than I advised them." One wonders whether some of the un-Separated London contin-gent dipped in the roaring taverns, famous in Elizabethan times (according to Heywood, the playwright), or had the Puritan blight descended on these "boozing kens"? On one plane at least, the Pilgrims met the life of Plymouth, for Puritanism was strong not only in the town but in the country around, and *Mourt's Relation* (Winslow and Bradford probably wrote it) opens with a tribute to the people of Plymouth, fellow walkers with God, we may be sure:

Wednesday the sixth of September, the wind coming east-north-west, a fine small gale, we loosed from Plymouth, having been kindly entertained and courteously used by divers friends there dwelling.

All Bradford or anyone else gives in description of the *Mayflower* is that she was "of burthen about a score," taken to be about 180 tons by the standard of 1582. We are not likely to get any nearer to her appearance and measurements than the replica *Mayflower II*, now moored at Plymouth, Massachusetts. This was designed by William A. Baker, the American naval architect, and he worked very closely to the working drawings and ships' profiles of one of the master shipwrights of Elizabethan times contained in a notebook now in Magdalene College, Cambridge. The replica was built at Brixham, where there were still people who could use an adze, and was sailed to Plymouth, Massachusetts, by Captain Villiers in 1957. She had a crew of thirty-three and took fifty-three days, sailing down to the Canaries on the northeast trades, there picking up the southeast trades to make a passage of 5,420 nautical miles. We don't know the route the *Mayflower I* took, but her voyage lasted sixty-six days.

Taking *Mayflower II* as being as near as we can get to *Mayflower I*, Captain Jones's ship was 104 feet long over all and 78 feet 8 inches at the water line. Her beam was 21½ feet, and she had a draft of 13 feet. In modern terms she would be 220 tons net and 365 tons displacement. Walking over *Mayflower II*, she seems surprisingly roomy, with a great cabin 25×15 feet at its broadest and a main deck 75×20 feet, though maybe *Mayflower I* did not seem roomy to the 102 passengers and the crew of twenty-five. The space works out at about 6×3 feet for each passenger, but a few people slept in the longboat and others in the shallop. Wherever they were, they must have been in fair discomfort when a storm tossed them around and the waves seeped through the leaky decks.

The history of the *Mayflower* has been thoroughly researched, but the gaps in port registers leave many questions unanswered, and moreover there were several *Mayflowers*, three of them in Plymouth in the year 1620. It seems best to take a line through the proved facts but linking in the possible and sometimes the doubtful; many a scholar of the Pilgrims will want to alter a detail here and there, to be contradicted by other scholars, of whom there is an abundant supply. So—the *Mayflower* was chartered for the Armada action in 1588, when one of her owners was John Vassal, who in 1591 moved from Ratcliffe, London, to Leigh-on-Sea. The Vassal family had a shipbuilding yard at Leigh-on-Sea and a house at Cocksey Hurst, Eastwood, near Leigh. (Essex historians are inclined to claim that *Mayflower* was built in the Leigh-on-Sea shipyards, and they are supported by Professor Horrocks of University College, Southampton.) In 1606 she was carrying cloth to Middelburg. In 1607 she had a cargo of wine from Gascony. In 1609 Christopher Jones first appears as master and also as quarter-owner. In 1611 Jones moved to Rotherhithe to live, and there in St. Mary's churchyard he is buried. He was born in Maldon, Essex, and was married in Harwich. To return to his ship: We can follow the *Mayflower* fairly accurately from the time Jones took over, carrying cloth mostly to the west-coast ports of France, bringing back wine and cognac, so that she would have been what seamen call a sweet ship. Early in spring 1620 she was moored at Leigh-on-Sea, and it is there that she embarked the Essex contingent, who had been assembled at Billericay. Captain Jones had already picked up the London party at Rotherhithe after he had discharged his cargo of wine. London was his port of registration.

Of those Captain Jones had brought to Southampton, forty were now at sea on the *Mayflower*, 17 men, 9 women, 14 children, and with them forty-one from Leyden, 17 men, 10 women, 14 children.[4] This almost exact balance may have a reason behind

it; if so, nobody has given the reason. There were, as well, 18 servants and 5 hired men, which makes a total of 104, but following
Bradford's list, two sailors are deleted as not of the company.
These were Ely (or Ellis) and Trevore, who later returned to
England. Two others of the hired hands were mariners, one to
take charge of the shallop (an open boat with oars and sail,
nearly longboat size, cut down and stowed away on the main
deck), the other to go back for the next party from Leyden. The
fifth hired man was John Alden, cooper of Harwich, "a hopfull
yong man," to become more famous as a figure in fiction than for
his sterling worth in the colony. The Scrooby originals were
down to Bradford and Ruling Elder William Brewster with his
wife Mary. Mary had brought two sons and Bradford his wife,
Dorothy.

There was a one-man army aboard in the person of Captain
Myles Standish, of whom we know nothing for certain until he
steps ashore in America. We can infer that he was short ("Captain Shrimp"), had reddish hair and a ruddy complexion, and
that he was an experienced soldier and leader of men. The
Plymouth folk version of his history takes him to Holland at the
age of twenty to fight for the Dutch against the Spanish in the
small force sent by Queen Elizabeth. That force came back in
1609, and he seems to have met Robinson before then at Amsterdam or Leyden and much impressed the pastor. We would like
to know where he spent the next eleven years: In the service of
the Dutch? He might have been a non-practicing Catholic, since
he was the only leading Pilgrim who was not a member of the
Plymouth congregation. In his will he claimed that he was the
rightful heir of the large Standish estates, but no proof of this has
ever been uncovered, and he can only have been a remote kinsman to the Standishes of Standish Hall. Duxbury, Chorley, Lancashire, is claimed as his birthplace.

Stephen Hopkins of London but late of Wootton-under-Edge,
in the Cotswolds, had brought the largest family, a wife and
three children together with one to be born at sea and to be
named Oceanus. Historians of Essex claim that of those aboard
the *Mayflower* twenty-one had their home town or village in
Essex, but this statement raises the hackles of other authorities.

It may be true. Southeastern England, and Essex in particular, was full of Puritans and extreme Calvinists, and we can trace many little Separatist congregations through the records of arrests and imprisonments. Calvinist immigrants from France and the Low Countries were mostly clothworkers, and they found both work and coreligionists in Essex and other southeastern counties. For a large proportion of the workingmen in this part of England, to march against authority was to walk with God. This intransigent attitude can be traced throughout their history and can be seen, in a mild form, among the *Mayflower* party when they first got to America. Just how many of the Southampton contingent were straight Church of England we do not know, probably very few of them, but even if the claims of Essex are thinned out, quite a number were from southeastern England. American scholars quite often ignored the differences that still exist in the temperaments of the people as between one county and another; an Essex countryman, for instance, will oppose you directly if he does not agree with you, whereas a Sussex man will not, although he will never cease working to get his own way. (Marxist and other theorists deny this in one breath and explain it in another, usually in economic or socioeconomic terms.)

Of the eighteen servants aboard, eleven were young men, indentured for we do not know how many years—seven was usual. The word indenture came from the document or agreement between master and servant indented or notched on the edges. The servant bound himself (or herself) to work for his master and no other (unless he was transferred to another by the master) for the stipulated period, and the master bound himself to feed, clothe, and house him, and of course the master covered every other expense, for usually the servant got no wages, or very little. With children the master often contracted to teach them reading or some craft, for the indentures with the servants were an extension of the ordinary apprentice's indentures. These men were bond servants but not bondslaves, as some have called them, and they were indentured for their labor and not for personal service, as were maidservants. There was only one maidservant, and we do not know her name. She came with Carver and may not have been indentured. Just what the terms were for the children we do not know, but we have to remember that children were then treated as little adults. Indentured children were often orphans from the poorhouse; indeed, there were four of them surnamed More from London. Weston had roped them in and put a boy to Carver, a girl to Winslow, and two boys to Brewster.

Indentured service became common in the colonies, and even before the Pilgrims' time Sir George Peckham, speaking of Humphrey Gilbert's expedition, had noted: "There are great numbers which live in much penury and want, as they could be contented to hazard their lives, and to serve for one year for meat, drink and apparel only, without wages, in hope thereby to amend their estates."

The crew included four mates and a master gunner. The first officer, who was to be very useful to the Pilgrims, was John Clarke. He had been to the New World before. There was also a ship's doctor, Giles Heale, though the Pilgrims had brought their own, apparently unqualified physician Deacon Samuel Fuller.

Bradford wastes very few words on the voyage: "According to the usual manner many were affected with sea sickness," he says, but he details three incidents. In the first the hand of God appears.

There was a proud and very profane young man, one of the seamen of a lusty able body which made him the more haughty; he would always be despising the poor people and cursing them daily in their sickness with grievous execrations, and did not refrain from telling them that he hoped to cast half of them overboard before their journeys end and to make merry with what they had. But it pleased God before they came half-way over, to smite this young man with a grievous disease of which he died in a desperate manner, and so was himself the first that was thrown overboard. Thus his curses lighted on his own head, and it was an astonishment to all his fellows, for they noted it to be the just hand of God upon him.

Until, presumably, halfway over (Bradford says "half-seas over") they had good weather and a fair wind, but then they ran into the autumn gales. The heavily laden ship took them badly, and in one storm, which must have been fierce, one of the main deck beams cracked. The mariners "feared the sufficiency of the ship" and there were mutterings about turning back. But Captain Jones knew his ship, and knew she was firm and strong below the water line, "and for the buckling o' the main beam there was a great iron screw the passengers brought out of Holland which would raise the beam into his place." With a post under it the job was done. Surely if the hand of God felled the mocking mariner His providence is to be seen in the presence of this great iron screw, not a normal piece of passenger's baggage. Was it, as has been surmised, part of a printing press, a souvenir of Vicus Choralis? Were Winslow and Brewster aiming to set up shop in northern Virginia to print Bibles in the Indian tongues one day, or could they not bear to part with the gear? But it may have been one of those cumbrous but powerful lifting jacks used in building.

Incident number three also has elements of the marvelous:

> In sundry of these storms the winds were so fierce, and the seas so high, as they could not bear a knot of sail, but were forced to hull [lay to under shortened sail and drift with the wind] for divers days together. And in one of them as they lay at hull in a mighty storm, a lusty young man called John Howland, coming upon some occasion above the gratings was with a roll of the ship thrown into the sea, but it pleased God that he caught hold of the topsail halliards which hung overboard and ran out at length. Yet he held his hold, though sundry fathoms under water.

They hauled him in and fished him out with a boat hook.

On November 6 a youth, William Butten, servant to Samuel Fuller, died, but that was in no way remarkable. The remarkable thing was that his was the only death among the Pilgrims, especially when one considers that they were awash for a good part of the voyage, "the ship shrewdly shaken and her upper works made very leaky." It is odd, though, that Bradford should call Butten a youth, if he was the William Butten who was baptized in Austerfield Church on 12 February 1598. He died as "they drew near the coast, which is called Cape Cod, the which being made and certainly known to be it they were not a little joyful." The North Atlantic is as dangerous as any ocean in the world and they could not have chosen a worse time to cross it.

Their joy was a little premature, for the seas on the Atlantic side of Cape Cod are treacherous in the extreme, and if we are to believe that their destination was around Hudson's river they still had well over 250 miles to sail. But in Bradford's account they have just sighted land, have confirmed their position, and are joyful.

> After some deliberation amongst themselves and with the master of the ship, they tacked about and resolved to stand for the southward (the wind and weather being fine) to find some place about Hudson's river for their habitation. But after they had sailed that course about half the day they fell among dangerous shoals and roaring breakers, and they were so far entangled therewith as they conceived themselves in great danger, and the wind shrinking upon them withal they resolved to bear up again for the Cape and thought themselves happy to get out of those dangers before night overtook them, and the next day they got into the Cape Harbour where they rode in safety.

Here Bradford adds a note about Captain Gosnold's expedition of 1602 and "that point which first showed the dangerous shoals unto them they called Point Care and Tuckers Terror." This all sounds very clear and sensible, but in 1669 Nathaniel Morton, in his *New England's Memorial,* started a hare running about the "fraudulency and contrivance" of Captain Jones, "for their intention was to Hudson's river, but some of the Dutch having notice of their intentions and having thoughts about the same time of erecting a plantation there likewise, they fraudulently hired the said Jones, by delays, while they were in England, and now under pretence of the danger of the shoals . . . to disappoint them in their going thither." And in the margin of his book he adds that, of the plot, "I have had late and certain intelligence." Morton was secretary to the Colony, so that we may take it he wrote in good faith; in any case it was a little late in the day to establish an alibi for the Pilgrims. There is no mention anywhere in the writings of anyone else to support this idea of a plot except some other vague accusations against the Dutch on a paper that has disappeared. And Morton is horribly wrong about the danger of the shoals being a "pretence." Rear Admiral Samuel Eliot Morison, the leading authority on Pilgrim history and on

American naval history, says, in his introduction to a version of William Bradford in modern English: "No seaman who has weathered Cape Cod needs any better explanation than a head wind on unbuoyed Pollock Rip."[5]

But there is another school of thought which says that in 1620 there was a spit of land projecting from the Eastham shore named Île Nauset by Captain John Smith, and it was the surf breaking on the north side of this land or shoal that Gosnold named Tuckers Terror, and which made the *Mayflower* turn back. Île Nauset, which was also Point Care, has since been washed away. Those who agree with Admiral Morison place the turning point off Monomoy. If true, Bradford was wrong in identifying Monomoy with Tuckers Terror. The long, thin spit of Monomoy Beach hangs from the funny bone of the bent arm of Cape Cod. And from Monomoy Point, the tip of what it is only good manners to call a peninsula, the shoals are thickly scattered eastward into the Atlantic for around six or seven nautical miles. A veritable chain of bell buoys and horns now stretches across them. Behind the easternmost part runs Pollock Rip, into which the *Mayflower* was headed. Warned by the boiling surf, Captain Jones seems to have gone about on the starboard tack sailing ENE for the open Atlantic. He then sailed north up the arm of the Cape, following roughly the twenty-fathom curve right around the hand, curving in after a certain amount of tacking about to anchor behind the hook of land depending from the fist.

There they began "to look out a place for habitation." It has been flatly stated by some authorities that the Pilgrims intended to come to this part of New England from the very beginning of the voyage. In that case, why were they sailing south? Who were they supposed to be deceiving? Not the adventurers, who, when they heard of it, accepted the situation quite blandly. It is much more likely that they were making the best of things following the setback at Pollock Rip. They had no right north of the forty-first parallel, no patent, but there they were; there was no English governor, no English Church; there was a chunk of the New World around them; Captain Jones wanted to get away; very well, "look out a place for habitation." It was 11 November 1620.

13   Cape Cod

Being thus passed the vast ocean, they had not no friends to welcome them, no inns to entertain or refresh their weather-beaten
bodies, no houses or much less towns to repair to, to seek for suc-
cour. . . . And for the season it was winter, and they that know the
winters of that country know them to be sharp and violent and subject to cruel and fierce storms dangerous to travel to known places
and more so to search an unknown coast. Besides what could they
see but a hideous and desolate wilderness full of wild beasts and
wild men.

They had arrived so late in the year that after the first "joyful"
relief had faded any place at all in those latitudes would have
looked forbidding, and what is now Provincetown stands on a
very curious and, at first sight, not an attractive piece of land.
The whole of Cape Cod is geologically very curious. The bent
arm of land runs about twenty-five miles eastward from the
mainland of Massachusetts, then about thirty miles north and
northwest, curling around at the tip to point south with, as it
were, a little hook fetching a half circle to point north. Nowhere
is it more than ten miles wide, and only a mile or two separated
the Pilgrims from the Atlantic. The Cape is a relic of the last
great glacial epoch, which ended about ten thousand years ago,

so that Cape Cod is, as geological time goes, very young. The Ice Age began about one million years ago. Ice sheets spread down over the mainland of America, dragging with them sand, gravel, clay, and boulders. At their furthermost edge the ice sheets ended in immensely thick glaciers, which melted and deposited their load of debris to form Martha's Vineyard and Nantucket. That ice retreated, and another line of glaciers made a stand for some thousands of years at the northern edge of what is now Cape Cod. Streams of melted ice emerged from the glaciers as the climate warmed up and carried soil and rocks to form thick deposits on the old coastal plain, which was largely clay. As the ice finally retreated it left immense blocks of dense ice behind, covered with debris, and when this ice slowly melted the soil cover collapsed into the hole and formed the often-circular large ponds scattered over the Cape, and the glaciers left behind immense, as well as large and small, rocks that they had carried from such far-off places as Maine. The process was, of course, much more complex than this simple outline. As the ice melted and retreated from all over the Northern Hemisphere the level of the sea rose and entered Cape Cod bay, isolating a wide ridge of deposits to form Cape Cod—in a very ragged and tattered form. Then the waves of the Atlantic got to work, eroding, washing up sand, and carrying and filling in the long smooth curve of the forearm. Shore-drifting sand was carried by the southwest wind and Atlantic currents around the northern tip to form wrist and hand, and eventually the currents swung a thin, curved hook in to complete the great and safe harbor for the *Mayflower*.

The land was not quite so bleak as Bradford paints it. There was mile after mile of virgin forest down to the water's edge; as *Mourt's Relation* has it, "It is compassed about to the very sea with oaks, pines, juniper, sassafras and other sweet woods," and "The ground or earth sand hills much like the Downs in Holland but much better and all wooded; the crust of the earth a spit's depth excellent black earth." There were plenty of walnut, ash, and birch trees, and in the frequent swamps gigantic cedars bordered with fine red maples on the higher ground. Not until the eighteenth or nineteenth century were these magnificent forests squandered to leave mostly stunted pines and scrub oak and a full-sized job for the reforestation efforts of this century.

Cape Cod has had many other names, and it is just possible that the first was Vinland the Good. Some of the heroic Icelandic sagas tell of Bjorne Herulfson, who discovered it, and of the two sons of Eric the Red and another Viking, Thorfinn Karlsefne the Icelander, who made voyages there around A.D. 1003–15. They belonged to that bloody-minded period when the Scandinavian world seemed to explode. The Vikings reached Constantinople and beyond, up into the rivers of Russia. They pushed into Europe anywhere a boat could reach. They were most certainly settled in Greenland when the whole Northern Hemisphere was warmer than it is now, and they could have been blown down or sailed down the coast of North America. The sagas speak of them wintering on Vinland and of the "wonderstrand" they saw, and some scholars have identified Vinland with Cape Cod or with Martha's Vineyard. Both had abundant wild grapes, perhaps more luxuriant then; and the "wonderstrand" they saw was the long bright sands of Monomoy. Also, there is a very suspicious-looking map showing Cape Cod as Vinland. Well, it isn't wise to deny the sagas, but neither is it wise to wish too much into them; theirs is a splendid, mad, harsh world, and in it Vinland is real enough, even if America isn't.

The history of the discovery of Cape Cod is a blank for five hundred years after the Vikings, blank as far as any record goes; there is not even another legend. Then, in 1498, John Cabot sailed past on his way to the Carolinas; a Portuguese nobleman was cast away at nearby Narragansett; Giovanni da Verrazano spent a fortnight in Narragansett Bay in 1524; in 1525 a Spaniard cruised around New England for two months and had a map made with the whole area named after himself, Tierra de Esteban Gómez. But none of these said they had actually put a foot on Cape Cod. Then there is another blank of over seventy-five years. If we dismiss the Vikings, no European has yet landed on the Cape. If stray English, French, Dutch, Breton, or any other fishermen went ashore or even skirted Cape Cod, they left no record; not even a folk tale survives. In 1602 Captain Gosnold came on the *Concord* and anchored off the tip, the hand, on the

Atlantic side and found such large shoals of codfish around him
that after hauling in all he could cope with he gave the whole
land the name which has resisted all efforts to change it. He sent
a party ashore for firewood, and then sailed off south, where he
nearly ran aground on the shoals off Eastham, which he named
Tucker's Terror, and named the point of the Île Nauset, Point
Care. Continuing south he managed to round Monomoy Point,
and after a short stay ashore on one of the islands in Buzzards
Bay he turned back home with a cargo of what he came for, sassafras ("of sovereign virtue for the French pox"). Bristol merchants, much encouraged by Gosnold's valuable cargo, and
backed by Hakluyt, sent out Martin Pring on the *Speedwell* in
company with the *Discoverer*, but he avoided Cape Cod and
settled for a little while in a stockade he built in Plimouth which
he called Whitson Bay. Here he collected sassafras, and his men
and the Indians vastly entertained each other until the Indians
thought a little warfare would afford better sport. However, two
enormous trained mastiffs frightened the wits out of them and
they then "in a friendly manner turned all to a jest or sport."
Pring's men would not play and soon after left to carry back
news of treacherous Indians, which for a time rather put adventurers against the idea of sending settlers to that part of America.
The next visitors were under the command of the great Samuel
de Champlain, geographer, cartographer, and founder of Canada
for the French. Over a period of about three years he steadily
explored and meticulously mapped New England. Naturally he
called it New France. His base was the French colony in Nova
Scotia. His was the first thorough survey of Cape Cod. His maps
were delightful and accurate pictures and his voluminous writings a pleasure to read. He had a disastrous encounter with four
hundred Indian braves at Eastham, Cape Cod, and lost five men.
The French took their revenge a few days later by methodically
picking off half a dozen Indians. The French never returned to
New England—or New France. In 1613 Adrian Block from the
Dutch trading post at Manhattan laid claim to all the Cape and
called it Nieu Nederlant. Then followed three other visitors to
New England (to be), each of whom had a part in, or an
influence on, the Pilgrim story. First, Captain John Smith, who

came in 1614, mapped and named New England, Plymouth, and Massachusetts, and during a three months' stay got so filled with enthusiasm for the whole place that he spent the last eighteen years of his life trying to persuade the English to settle there. He himself never came back, though he wanted to lead the Pilgrim adventure, and he wanted to be the founder and governor of New England. He had already served as governor in Virginia. Cape Cod he called Cape James, but it didn't stick.

The next to arrive was Captain Thomas Hunt, who filled up with codfish but saw a profile sideline going begging. He landed at Plimouth, captured twenty Indians, and sold them in Málaga slave market for twenty pounds apiece. This was scowled at by every English authority and merchant venturer who heard of it, not out of jealousy or out of any disapproval of slave trading but because word would soon get around among the Indians and create dangerous conditions for any plantation. No adventurer would commission Hunt for further voyages to the New World. One of the shanghaied Indians, by an almost miraculous series of circumstances, found his way back to Plymouth just before the Pilgrims arrived there. The instrument for the return of the Indian was a Captain Dermer, who got to Cape Cod Bay in 1619.

Every one of these voyages to Cape Cod Bay was a separate adventure story full of highlights, miseries, and remarkable characters, and together they form a background to the situation of the Pilgrims gathered on the *Mayflower* on a cold November day in 1620. For the Pilgrims the situation was normal—trouble brewing:

I shall . . . begin with a combination made by them before they came ashore, being the first foundation of their government in this place; occasioned partly by the discontented and mutinous speeches that some of the strangers amongst them had let fall from them in the ship; that when they came ashore they would use their own liberty, for none had power to command them, the patent they had being for Virginia and not for New England, which belonged to another Government [company] with which the Virginia Company had nothing to do. And partly that such an act by them done might be as firm as any patent, and in some respects more sure.

Bradford names no names, but lively imaginations have been put to work to uncover some of these incipient mutineers. At first sight one of the strangers, Stephen Hopkins, looks a likely candidate, if he was the same Stephen Hopkins who had been at the center of a mutiny on Bermuda in 1609, when a convoy to Virginia had been scattered by a hurricane and the flagship wrecked on Bermuda. The crew was put to work to build pinnaces to take them to Virginia, but insubordination broke out among the men, who saw themselves spending their lives working in Virginia for the adventurers. (Other arguments were not unlike those Bradford had noted among the *Mayflower* "strangers.") Before a full-scale mutiny could be organized, a group of the leaders were court-martialed and executed: all except Stephen Hopkins, who begged off on compassionate grounds although there is some evidence that he was the principal agitator. (The shipwreck and the Bermuda adventure came to Shakespeare's notice a year or two later and he made magic with the tale in *The Tempest.*) But, in 1620, times had altered for Stephen Hopkins. On the *Mayflower* he was a gentleman with two servants, Edward Doty and Edward Leister. These two fought a duel at Plymouth, and they had a pretty poor record afterward so they were likely enough lads to start trouble. And their master, who may not have been involved at all in this muttering on the *Mayflower,* and was quite possibly not the Bermuda Stephen Hopkins, showed by his later history that he was no disciplinarian. It was known that Hopkins had been in the New World before, and if not in Virginia (and Bermuda), where? It may be significant that only four of the indentured servants were invited (or told) to sign the compact, and Doty and Leister were two of them.

Although the Pilgrims had no right in New England, Brewster would have been aware of a resolution or order by the Virginia Company to the effect that the leaders of any plantation could form an association to make orders and ordinances, et cetera, until a form of government had been settled, but the company could not have envisaged "a combination made by them" in such a document as the Mayflower Compact, which after a loyal preamble ran (in modern spelling):

[We] Having undertaken for the glory of God and advancement of the Christian faith and honor of our king and country a voyage to plant the first colony in the northern part of Virginia, do by these presents solemnly and mutually in the presence of God and of one another covenant and combine ourselves together into a civil body politic, for our better ordering and preservation and furtherance of the ends aforesaid; and by virtue hereof to enact, constitute, and frame such just and equal laws, ordinances, acts, constitutions, and offices, from time to time, as shall be thought most meet and convenient for the general good of the colony, unto which we promise all due submission and obedience. In witness whereof we have hereunder subscribed our names.

The names that follow are of every male passenger known to be of age, except two sailors who were not to be permanent settlers. Four of the ten menservants signed. This compact, of course, put an end to the idea that some of the company would "use their own liberty," though muttering continued for a time.

What is extraordinary about this compact, or contract, is that it established government, by consent at a time when England's liberties were still conditioned by the remnants of feudalism. It was not "the cornerstone of American democracy," as some enthusiasts have claimed; equal votes and rights for all was some way away, but it put down a sound foundation for local self-government, and the words of John Quincy Adams, who disinterred the compact in 1802, are perfectly valid. "It was," he said, "the first example in modern times of a social compact or system of government instituted by voluntary agreement conformably to the laws of nature, by men of equal rights and about to establish their community in a new country."

The legal terminology "do by these presents" may be due to Brewster, and there is an echo of Robinson, who told them they should form a "civil body politic." There is also a feeling hovering over the compact of the church covenants familiar to the Separatist Calvinist Pilgrims.

After the signing of the document, they elected John Carver to be their first governor, and this too is significant, for Carver held no Church office. They had separated Church and state. In fu-

ture, no Church officer held a political post and no political
officer, the governor for instance, was an officer of the Church.

Sixteen men now volunteered to go ashore and reconnoiter
while the carpenters got to work assembling and repairing the
shallop,[6] which last was to take longer than they thought. The
shore party used one of the ship's boats and brought back some
juniper firewood and a report that they had seen no Indians, nor
any sign of Indian houses, nor sweet water. The next day was a
Sabbath, and there was a full program of psalms, prayer, medita-
tion and preaching—the New World could wait. No doubt the
crew were putting the ship to rights—or did they go ashore to
stretch their legs, or fish? Monday the thirteenth (this and all
other Pilgrim dates are Old Style, which had become out of
phase with the sun, but the New Style was not introduced into
England until 1752, when Wednesday, September 2, was followed by Thursday, September 14, to a great cry from the populace of "Give us back our eleven days," but as they had only lost
ten that is the number we add to Pilgrim dates—so Monday the
thirteenth is to us Monday the twenty-third. When the Pilgrims
came to adjust their calendar they too got it wrong, adding
eleven days instead of ten) was washing day and the piles of
dirty and salty linen were taken to an oval pond about three
quarters of a mile long. The only record of the pond is a vague
folk memory. There were a great number of other ponds, but
that was the nearest. The water was brackish, being fresh water
forced up by the heavier, salty, ground water on which it floated,
the level rising with the tide, the pond being close to the
foreshore. Further inland, the same conditions apply but the
fresh water displaces more salt water and so is deeper and
sweeter.

Sentries were put out and the children ran wild on the sands.
A gang of carpenters got to work on the shallop, which was
taken ashore, and those not otherwise occupied searched for
shellfish. There were the fair-sized steamer clams and the delicious quahogs (or quahaugs) called in New York hard-shell
clams, but on the Cape called in their three qualities, littlenecks,
cherry stones, and brights. The Pilgrims did not know how to
locate the clams, and later the Indians had to show them, but

there were too many on the Cape beach to be altogether missed and the Pilgrims made a feast with the first fresh food they had tasted for over two months. They also gathered the large, fat mussels and made themselves to "cast and scour," as Mourt puts it; sick as dogs, the sailors would say.

Two days went by but, the shallop not being ready, "a few tendered themselves to go by land and discover those nearest places. It was conceived there might be some danger in the attempt, yet seeing them resolute they were permitted to go, being sixteen of them well armed under the conduct of Captain Standish." And that is the first mention of Captain Standish in the Pilgrim annals. Each man was armed with matchlock musket, sword, and corselet. The muskets were about five feet long, smooth-bore and of a caliber of around .75, and they took a long time to load. A set charge of black powder was poured down the muzzle, tamped and wadded, a lead ball dropped in, and a thick pad rammed home. The firing mechanism was simple but needed exact drill. Fine-grain powder was tipped onto the flash pan, and this was ignited by the glowing end of a slow match pressed down by being part of a hammer rather like an old-fashioned 12-gauge shotgun. It was released by a trigger. The ball would smash a large hole in a man, but the matchlock was useless in damp or windy weather. What frightened the Indians was the flame, the smoke, the noise, and the velocity of the bullet, but as an all-purpose weapon their own bows and arrows were superior.

When they had marched about the space of a mile by the seaside they espied five or six persons with a dog coming towards them, and ran up into the woods and the English followed them partly to see if they could speak to them and partly to discover if there might not be more of them lying in ambush.

This is a puzzle; Bradford cannot mean that Standish was inviting the Indians to ambush him. How did he deploy his men? Did he open them out into two flanks and one main party or what? However, the Indians ran for it and Standish and his armored men plodded after them following their tracks in the sandy dunes. One can imagine that it was tiring work and they camped for the night, setting out sentries. It was a good tactical position for a camp, at the head of an arm of East Harbor (since silted at the entrance to form Pilgrim Lake), with a strip of dunes only a few hundred yards wide before them, the Atlantic on their left, and East Harbor on the right front. Next day they put their noses to the tracks again and got among a tangle of vicious thorns, which "were ready to tear their clothes and armour in pieces, but were most distressed for want of drink." By this time they had lost track of the tracks, "but at length they found water and refreshed themselves, being the first New England water they had drunk of, and was now in their great thirst as pleasant unto them as wine and beer had been aforetimes." The point here is that like most English countrymen water was not their usual choice of drink; indeed, it was thought downright unhealthy. Pilgrim Spring, as the place is now called, is remote and attractive enough, but the spring is a mere trickle.

Four miles from their camp they headed down to the bay shore, and there they found cleared ground and several odd mounds. Digging into one, they found old arrows and a bow and, rightly taking it to be a warrior's grave, they filled it in and restored the mound, saying, according to Mourt, "it would be odious unto them to ransack their sepulchres," and also in old English superstition exceedingly unlucky. They followed the shore to the river they had seen, checked that it might make a harbor, and turned back along the shore the way they had come. Coming into a large meadow again, they saw curious mounds but these were different, not graves, they thought. "They digging [them] up found in them divers fair Indian baskets filled with corn, and some in ears fair and good, of divers colours which seemed to them a very goodly sight (having never seen any such before)." They had picked up an old iron ship's kettle (stolen by Indians from a ship's boat or thrown away by the French perhaps) and they filled this with the maize (or Indian corn) and filled all their pockets. It was a new kind of grain to them, but they recognized its value as seed and vowed to pay the Indians for it somehow. (In fact they did, six months later.) They returned along the thin ridge of dunes to the site of their first camp, cut down to the seashore and along to the *Mayflower*, showing their loot to their brethren, "of which and their return they were marvellously glad."

About this time Mrs. Susannah White gave birth to a son, Peregrine, the first Englishman to be born in New England. He lived until he was eighty-three. It was a nice name, Peregrine, meaning a pilgrim; it also means a trader.

For ten days, the Pilgrims did nothing more about "their place of habitation." Then, the shallop being fit to launch though not thoroughly repaired, a strong party set out for the river and the place where they had found the corn. Captain Jones volunteered to head the expedition. Halfway, the weather "grew strong" and the shallop had to turn back, but some of the Pilgrims insisted on going ashore and waded up onto the beach waist-deep in icy waters. Mourt, who gives a very full account of this foray, says: "Many took the original of their death here, it did blow and snow all that day and night and froze withal."

They were taken up by the shallop next morning, and the party went on to explore the river (Pamet was the name of the local Indian tribe and so the river was later named). It turned out to be not so much a river as a swampy tidal estuary, and, getting tired of "the toil of making their way up and down hills and valleys covered with six inches of snow," they made for Corn Hill (its present name). The ground was frozen hard but they attacked it with sword and dagger (why no spades?), and from one place and another they got ten bushels of corn and a bag of beans:

> And here it to be noticed a special providence of God, and a great mercy to this poor people, that here they got seed to plant them corn the next year or else they might have starved, for they had none, nor any likelihood to get any till the season had been past (as the sequel did manifest) [as events showed]. But the Lord is never wanting unto His in their greatest needs: let His holy name have all the praise.

The Pilgrims have been heavily blamed for robbing the poor Indian of his seed corn, and they well knew it was neither moral nor likely to make them popular, but the Indians themselves were often light-fingered and not always out of necessity. If they fancied any object they took it if they could, although perhaps they did not thank their gods for putting temptation in their way.

The Pilgrims, although they did not know it, were in light contact with the Pamets, a subtribe of the Wampanoag Federation,
itself a subnation of the great Algonquin Nation. The Wampanoags for hundreds of years had hunted the Cape as part of an
immensely wider area. They lived in small villages, not in wig-
wams but in well-constructed permanent huts. They were a mild-
mannered people; a sailor of Gosnold's expedition said they were
"exceedingly courteous, gentle of disposition and well conditioned." But they were, if annoyed, quite prepared to fight it out,
and they had been severely annoyed by the French and by what
they had heard of Master Hunt's slave raid. They had no idea of
what the Pilgrims were up to, but they were, very reasonably,
suspicious. It would seem that the first Indians seen by Standish
and his company were a scouting party taking a look at the
Mayflower, and that their report made the Indians leave the
nearest Pamet villages, which is why the second expedition
found some deserted huts. These they looted, and they also
opened up a few more graves.

When the corn had been stacked away on the *Mayflower* and
the men were back on board, a debate opened "about their place
of habitation." Some were for settling by the Pamet River. There
was good corn there, and the corn they had stolen or borrowed
"would be natural seed for the same." (They were, naturally,
looking for ground near the sea with fresh water handy.) There
was good fishing, and, the strongest argument, "they would not
go on coasting and discovery without danger of losing both men
and boat and cold and wet lodging had so tainted their people as
scarce any of them were free from vehement coughs."

Against this, others said the Pamet was not a river; fresh water
would have to come from the nearby pond, and so on. Then Robert Coppin (also written Coffin), who had been in New England
before, spoke of a "navigable river and good harbour almost
right over against Cape Cod," in other words straight across the
bay. They decided to send out their shallop "with ten of their
principal men and some seamen upon further discovery intend-
ing to circulate that deep bay of Cape Cod. The weather was
very cold and it froze so hard as the spray lighting on their coats
they were as if they had been glassed [glazed]."

The average temperature at this time of the year (December 6) on Cape Cod[7] is around the freezing point, and in recent years —6, that is, 38 degrees of frost, has been recorded, so that it is not surprising that two of the men in the shallop fainted with the cold. They sailed on down past Corn Hill to what is now Wellfleet Bay, where they saw some Indians clustered around a black object on the beach. They put ashore a mile or so away from the Indians, who danced about for a while and then ran off into the woods. First of all, the Pilgrims built a good fire and around it a rough stockade or barricade, then put out sentinels and "betook them to rest." They were not disturbed by the Indians.

The next morning, they split up. One party marched along the shore, the other coasted in the shallop. The shore party found the black object to be a grampus, or blackfish, about fifteen feet long:

So they ranged up and down all that day but found no people nor any place they liked. When the sun grew low they hastened out of the woods to meet with their shallop. . . .

They made a barricade and settled around their fire:

But about midnight they heard a hideous and great cry, and their sentinel called, "Arm, arm," so they bestirred themselves and stood to their arms.

One of the mariners said that the noise was the howling of wolves; he had heard them in Newfoundland; so back to rest they went until five in the morning. Some began to prepare breakfast, some, against the advice of Standish and others, took their muskets down to put in the boat, but as the tide was not yet in they laid their arms on the creek side wrapped in coats and came back for breakfast:

All on the sudden, they heard a great and strange cry which they knew to be the same voices they heard in the night, though they varied their notes, and one of their company came running in and cried, "Men! Indians! Indians!" and withal their arrows came flying amongst them.

Standish and another man had their guns with them. These were flintlocks or snaphances, much more quickly got ready, and the fire from these two gave the matchlocks time to prime and light slow matches. Standish gave the proper order to hold fire until they had a clear target. The Indians tried to cut off the men dashing down to the creek for their guns, "but some running out with coats of mail on and cutlasses in their hands, they soon got their arms and let fly amongst them and quickly stopped their violence. Yet there was a lusty man and no less valiant stood behind a tree within half a musket shot, and let his arrows fly. He stood three shot of a musket until one (it was Standish) taking full aim at him and made the bark or splinters of the tree fly about his ears, after which he gave an extraordinary shrike and away they went all of them." To show they were not afraid of Indians, they followed them some way, loosing off a round or two. None of the Pilgrims was hurt, although "sundry of their coats which hung up in the barricado were shot through and through."

This brush with the Nauset Indians (more of a warrior tribe than the Pamets), they called First Encounter, and now there is a tablet and comfort station to mark the spot. The nearest tree is well out of bowshot and is much too slender to protect the body of a lusty Indian even if there happened to be one still surviving on the Cape. The creek is down to a trickle over the sands. But it is a charming little bay, at its best when summer has gone and the sand bars at low tide are thick with wildfowl.

Mourt gives the names of the ten Pilgrims in the shallop party: Standish, Carver the governor, Bradford, Winslow; John and Edward Tilley, the first a silkworker, the second a clothworker; John Howland, "a plain good-hearted Christian" servant to Carver, and two of the mariners hired by the Pilgrims. Of the London contingent, or "strangers": Warren, a merchant; the experienced Hopkins, and his quarrelsome servant, Edward Doty. From the *Mayflower* crew came two who had been in the New World before, Clarke the first mate and Coppin the pilot. The master gunner and perhaps three or four more completed the party. A pleasant game can be had trying to guess which of them were too cocky to take orders from Standish about the guns. Doty for one?

"Afterwards they gave God solemn thanks and praise for their deliverance," in which all would have joined, for it is a mistake to suppose that the sailors were any less pious than the Pilgrims, although they may have been less assiduous in their devotions.

Had the Nausets exterminated the party, they would only have delayed slightly the inevitable process of their own extermination. The two civilizations were incompatible.

The weather looked like doing the Nausets' job for them; as the shallop explored the southern shores of Cape Cod Bay and, seeing no "place likely for harbour," turned north along the mainland shore to find "good harbour," foul weather set in.

After some hours sailing it began to snow and rain, and about the middle of the afternoon, the wind increased and the sea became very rough, and they broke their rudder and it was as much as two men could do to steer her with a couple of oars. But their pilot bade them be of good cheer for he saw the harbour, but the storm increasing and night drawing on they bore what sail they could to get in. But therewith they broke their mast in three pieces and their sail fell overboard in a very grown sea, so as they had like to be cast away; yet by God's mercy they recovered themselves and having the flood with them struck in the harbour. But when it came to, the pilot was deceived in the place and said the Lord be merciful unto them for his eyes never saw that place before, and he and the master mate would have run her ashore in a cove full of breakers before the wind. But a lusty seaman who steered bade those who rowed if they were men "about with her" or else they were all cast away; the which they did with speed. So he bade them be of good cheer and row lustily for there was a fair sound before them and he doubted not that they should find one place or another where they might ride in safety. And though it was very dark and rained sore yet in the end they got under the lee of a small island, and remained there all night in safety.

We can imagine the scene, held for a split second at its most dramatic, as in one of those fearful steel engravings of a boat leaving a ship breaking up on a lee shore, the snow blurring the foaming breakers, the icy spray whipping over the boat, and a flash of lightning picking out the erect figure of the unknown lusty sailor who has taken command and is leaning on the oar

which is turning them hard to port as he bellows encouragement
to the men at the oars. There would be a huddled group of
women but there are none in our picture.

There are several opinions of the course of the shallop, of
which three may be enough. 1. It was blowing a winter south-
easter. They passed Manomet Point without seeing it in the mist
and rain. They rowed west-northwest from the Point and just
cleared the eastern end of Brown's Island into the strong flood
tide. The gale carrying them across the channel, they saw two
high points, the Gurnet and Saquish Head, connected by a low
sandy beach forming Saquish Cove, which was the "cove full
of breakers." The pilot mistook the two high points for two islands and, not at first seeing the low beach, thought the entrance lay between the islands—until he saw the breakers ahead
and "his eyes never saw that place before." 2. The pilot mistook
the Gurnet for Saquish Head and Saquish Head for Goose Point.
Steering between them, he suddenly saw the breakers in Saquish
Cove. The wind blew from the northeast and not from southeast, and the shallop, following the shoreline, worked through
the boat channel between Brown's Bank and Long Beach and
suddenly faced the breakers in Warrens Cove.[8]

They thought it wise to spend the rest of the night in the boat
because of possible Indian attacks, but the wet and cold beat the
wisdom out of them and they went ashore, first one group and
then the others, lit a fire and watched the night out:

> The next day was a fair sunshining day, and they found themselves
> to be on an island secure from the Indians, where they might dry
> their stuff, fix their pieces and rest themselves.

It was also the Sabbath and therefore no day for further explo-
ration. They stayed put on the island, and called it Clarke's
Island after the friendly chief mate. (Why not the lusty sailor?—
then we would have known his name.) On Monday, December
11 (21st on our reckoning), "they sounded the harbour and
found it fit for shipping, and marched into the land and found
divers cornfields and little running brooks, a place (as they supposed) fit for habitation, at least it was the best they could find

and the season and their present necessity made them glad to accept of it. So they returned to their ship (the *Mayflower*) again with this news to the rest of their people which did much comfort their hearts." Bradford's narrative continues with the ship leaving for Plymouth. Only in his pocket notebook, where he kept bare factual records, does he make a note under Deaths: "Dorothy May wife to Mr. William Bradford." She was twenty-three years old, and Bradford must have been told when he returned to the *Mayflower* that she had fallen overboard and been drowned. Nowhere does he ever mention her again. His silence has suggested to most commentators that Dorothy May had committed suicide, then and until our own times considered one of the gravest crimes in the eyes of God and man. The verdict should be "not proven," though conditions and prospects on the *Mayflower* were desperate enough to drive any sensitive woman into temporary insanity.

On 15th December they weighed anchor to go to the place they had discovered.

14 "If We Ever Make a Plantation God Works a Miracle" (Cushman)

Beating against a head wind, it was Saturday, December 16, before the *Mayflower* covered the thirty or less miles across the bay to anchor in the channel behind the tip of Plymouth Beach. The Sabbath was devoted to prayer. On Monday, a well-armed party went ashore to check on the country. Again they noted that the land had been cleared of trees for some way back from the shore and on each side of a fine sweet-water brook. There were clear signs that there had been large cornfields on this cleared land, but they could not understand the equally obvious signs that no corn had been planted for at least a year. The soil seemed good, and outside the mysteriously abandoned fields there was a fine display of berried bushes and fine timber. There were good deposits of workable clay and gravel. An expedition to the north of the harbor found a tidal river, which they named for the *Mayflower* skipper Jones River, and here some suggested that a settlement should be made, but the forest would have to be cleared back and the roots dug or burned out. Moreover, the forest would give cover to attacking Indians. Neither was Jones River handy to what they hoped would be profitable fishing grounds. Clarke's Island was also considered as being safest from Indians, but that too was rejected. The captain, in spite of the Pil-

grims' efforts to secure immortality for the name of Jones, showed
some irritation at all this fossicking around and dithering. He
wanted to conserve his victuals, especially his beer, and he
wanted the Pilgrims to get off his ship as soon as possible. He had
had, one may think, quite enough of their company.

Rather suddenly, the Pilgrims decided to set their plantation[9]
upon the ground on the north side of the brook, where the land
rose fairly steeply to a hill that commanded the harbor and the
country around; it was ideal for defense, the hill would take a
nice platform for the cannon they had brought. The shallop put
twenty men ashore to cut wood, and there they were marooned
for a couple of days while a storm tossed the anchored *Mayflower*
around and Mary Allerton, the tailor's wife, gave birth to a still-
born child.

Christmas Day brought a full working party ashore, for the
Pilgrims did not observe pagan feasts. "We went ashore, some to
fell timber, some to rive[10] [split the timber], some to saw and
some to carry so no man rested all day." But Captain Jones and
the crew thought this Christmas night quite bleak enough without unseasonable austerity, broke out a barrel of Christmas cheer
or beer and very decently invited the Pilgrims to share.

During the succeeding days, New Plymouth (they spelled it
Plimoth) was planned, and building began on a common house
twenty feet square. A short street was laid out on the higher, or
north, bank of the brook (it has never had any name other than
simply Town Brook), running up to the foot of the hill on which
Standish was leveling off ground for his gun platform. Lots were
marked off on both sides of the street, the south-side lots backing
onto the brook. These lots were narrow, $\frac{1}{2} \times 3$ poles ($8 \times 49\frac{1}{2}$
feet). Each person was allocated one lot, and the single men
being persuaded to attach themselves to a family of their own
choice, the number of proposed houses was kept to nineteen,
space was saved, and the surrounding stockade kept to a reasonable length. For these lots, lots were drawn; only Standish, with
a plot next to the fort (to be), and the governor, given a large
corner site, were left out of the draw. Some of the plots were siz-
able, where there were, say, six in a family and six lots were
allocated. The intention was to complete the common house to-

gether, then each family could get to work building their own houses "thinking by that course men would make more haste than building in common."

They were still eating the dried and salted food they had brought with them on the ship; no hunting or fishing parties had yet gone out; they were working in the open in cold and rain, and soon the effects of exposure accelerated the symptoms of scurvy. Bradford collapsed as he worked. Six had died before the end of December; before the end of January, eight more died, including Christopher Martin and Rose, the wife of Captain Standish. The common house held rows of sick men. The fact that no Indians had been seen merely added to the general unease. One day, two dogs snuffling around Peter Browne and John Goodman as they gathered reeds for thatching, took off after a deer, the men following the dogs into the woods in hope of fresh meat. When this casual hunting party did not return the next day, a search party fanned through the woods until dark but found no trace of them. The Indians, they feared, had got them. An Indian would have followed the signs of their passage, but the Pilgrims had no such refined woodcraft. The two men found their way back that night after having spent the previous night pacing about in the frost and snow in fear of wolves they heard howling. They were chilled and starving, and Goodman's shoes had to be cut from his frostbitten feet. He died not very long after.

On January 14, a spark caught the thatch of the common house, which held not only many rows of sick including Carver and Bradford, but several barrels of gunpowder, some of them open. The sick tottered up, moved the barrels outside, and saved the timber structure but lost a good deal of clothing, and there is no doubt that the chills some caught hastened their deaths.

Not until March 21 were enough small houses built for the last of the Pilgrims to leave the *Mayflower* and come ashore to "the firm and stable earth their proper element," and this long delay, occasioned mainly by bad weather, sickness, and death, further lowered their resistance, as Bradford somberly recalls:

In two or three months half of their company died, especially in January and February being the depth of winter, and wanting houses and other comforts, being affected with the scurvy and other diseases which this long voyage and lack of accommodation had brought upon them, so as there died some two or three a day in the aforesaid time; that of 100 and odd persons scarce fifty remained. And of these in the time of most distress there were but six or seven sound persons who to their great commendation be it spoken spared no pains night nor day but with abundance of toil and hazard of their own health, fetched them wood, made them fires, dressed them meat, made their beds, washed their loathsome clothes, clothed and unclothed them; in a word did all the homely and necessary offices for them which dainty and queasy stomachs cannot endure to hear named, and all this willingly and cheerfully without any grudging in the least.

Two of these seven he says were William Brewster and Miles Standish "and yet the Lord so upheld these persons as in this general calamity they were not at all infected either with sickness or any other disability." A man with less faith in the Lord might have said He was being a shade too choosy. Plimouth in the winter of 1620–21 bears a horrible resemblance to a pestilence-stricken labor camp in Siberia. Deaths from all causes were in December six, January eight, February seventeen, March thirteen, and six more later in the year. (As a comparison, 5,649 emigrants left England for Virginia during the period 1606–25; in 1,625 only 1095 had survived.)

Four whole families were wiped out. Only five out of eighteen wives survived; the servants and single men were reduced from twenty-nine to nineteen. No girl children died and only three of the thirteen sons. Either the children had the best food and the most care, or the hard, unremitting toil of the men and women was more than many of them should have undertaken in their weakened state. It is said that the winter of 1620–21 was rather milder than average, but that means temperatures a little above and a little below freezing, and some of the Pilgrims would have died from pneumonia and tuberculosis.

The *Mayflower* crew, who do not seem to have given much assistance to the Pilgrims ashore, nevertheless lost nearly half their number "because their bodies were corrupted with sea diet," but contagious tuberculosis caught from the Pilgrims must have contributed.

The dead were buried at night in the ground later known as Coles Hill and every precaution taken to conceal the graves, for they did not want the Indians to know how their numbers were diminishing. They felt that the nearby forest was full of watchful eyes. They knew Indians were about; how many, they could not guess. Captain Jones had seen two on Clarke's Island. One of the Pilgrims out to snare duck saw from his hide in the reeds a file of warriors headed for the plantation. He crept away and gave the alarm, and those working on the edge of the woods downed tools and ran for their muskets to cover a withdrawal to the fort of the common house. No Indian came near them, but the shock made them set about organizing their defenses on a less haphazard basis. On going back for the tools they had left in the clearing, they found them gone, obviously stolen by the Indians. A meeting was called next day, and as all appointments had to be discussed and put to the vote, Carver put forward Miles Standish to be their captain-general. A majority of votes made it so. (Another Pilgrim puzzle: whom did the minority support?) Standish held the post for almost forty years, but his immediate job was to set out guard duties in decent military order. Immediately Standish took up his command, that is within minutes, two Indians appeared on a hill across the brook and made "Come here" signs, to which Standish made "No, you come here" signs. Stalemate: until Standish and Hopkins slowly advanced on the Indians, putting a musket on the ground as a sign of peace. But something about them, probably the looks of little Standish, unnerved the warriors, who took off down the hill into the woods, whence enough noise came to suggest a largish body of Indians.

Captain Standish saw that it was high time to call up the artillery. A long minion, a gun of 3-inch bore, was brought from the ship, and a larger gun which had already been brought ashore but left lying on the foreshore were hauled up the hill to the gun platform. These and a couple of smaller cannon would make an intimidating noise although they might not do much damage to a skirmishing line of braves. Nothing more was seen or heard of the Indians for some weeks, but three questions concerning them must have given rise to endless discussion. Why had all the land around the harbor been abandoned by the Indians? How many Indians were lurking in the woods? Would they come in force to claim their fields and throw out invaders?

The next contact with the Indians could not have been more surprising. A tall, black-haired Indian carrying bow and arrows came out of the woods, walked boldly across the clearing to the street, and while the Pilgrims gaped or reached for their muskets he came striding up to a group of the men and, in English, said, "Welcome." (One toys with the idea that someone said, "Er— how d'ye do?" or "I didn't quite catch your name" or even "Hi!") He spoke broken but understandable English, said his name was Samoset, was a stranger in these parts himself, had learned his English from the crews of fishing vessels in his native place, which turned out to be Monhegan Island, up on the coast of Maine, and had they any beer? No. They were sorry about this but wondered if he would care for a noggin of brandy or gin with a biscuit "and butter, cheese and pudding" with a slice of duck, "all of which he liked well." As he was practically naked save for a little paint and a morsel of leather apron, they added a long, red horseman's coat more for their own comfort than his. Samoset was "free in speech"; indeed he was a loquacious talker of considerable stamina, and the Pilgrims were a keen audience for some hours, but as night fell and Samoset showed no signs of either drying up or getting out, they suggested that he might like to be put up on the *Mayflower* for the night. Jones's turn, they seemed to think, but a head wind and low water kept the shallop from leaving the little harbor by the brook, and Samoset was lodged in Stephen Hopkins' house under unobtrusive guard. The Pilgrims had by now the answer to some of their worrying questions. The cornfields had been abandoned because the tribe who owned them were all dead, exterminated by plague which had broken out some three years back (the Indians had no resistance to many of the white man's diseases: tuberculosis, smallpox, measles, and others). This plague may have been some form of typhus brought in by rats from one of the European ships. There was one survivor known to Samoset, who, by the way, spoke English better than he (Somoset) did. The Indian name for Plymouth was Patuxet (Little Bay), and the Patuxet Indians, like all the Indians in southeastern New England, including their belligerent friends of First Encounter, the Nausets, came under the general dominion of chief Massasoit, whose own tribe was the Wampanoag. Samoset knew all about the attack at First Encounter, which he said arose out of the Nausets' enmity to all members of Captain Hunt, the slaver's, people. He said that the Nausets had also killed Captain Dermer and three of his men.

The next day, a Saturday, Samoset was given a knife, a bracelet, and a ring on his promise to bring in some of the Wampanoag, with any furs or whatever they had to trade. He was back the next day with five braves bearing deerskins and some beaver furs, which was very awkward, since the Pilgrims could not trade on a Sunday, and neither could they applaud the Indians, who began a wild dance in appreciation of Pilgrim hospitality. The Pilgrims told the Indians to come again another day bringing all the furs they could find and in the meantime—au revoir. The Indians left, but not Samoset, who stuck around until the following Wednesday on a steady diet of butter, cheese, etc. However, the Indians had brought back the stolen tools, an unexpected sign of honesty, which greatly encouraged the Pilgrims. On the Wednesday, as no Indians or furs had shown up, Samoset was sent to find them.

With the Indians now gathering in the neighborhood and the Pilgrims uncertain of their intentions in spite of the recent jolly meeting, Standish set to work organizing and drilling his miniature army. Two Indians appeared on the same little hill opposite the fort and made fighting gestures but melted back into the woods when Standish made toward them.

On March 21, the last of the stores were landed from the ship and stowed in the repaired common house. All the women and children had come ashore. Again two Indians appeared and there was an alarm, but it was Samoset and his English-speaking friend Tisquantum, or Squanto, as he came to be called. They brought news of the first importance. The great Chief Massasoit was nearby and was proposing to visit them in person. Quite soon, he appeared on the little hill, looking very much a chief, imposing and dignified, with an army of sixty ferocious-looking braves around him. After a certain amount of diplomatic who-goes-to-whom young Edward Winslow went to the hill as ambas-

sador, his first appointment to a post he was to continue to fill
most effectively in the years to come. To Massasoit he brought a
pair of knives, a jewel, biscuits, butter, and of course a jar of the
real stuff, or "withall a Pot of strong water." These went down
well enough, but the king, prince, or chief wanted to bargain for
Winslow's armor and sword. As a good diplomat should, Winslow fended him off with a fine, long oration, Squanto interpret-
ing, to the effect that King James was keen to have Massasoit as
an ally. Whatever Squanto made of the speech, it was arranged
that Winslow should stay with the braves and Massasoit with a
bodyguard of twenty should visit the plantation. Standish put on
as good a show as he could, with armor, flags, and military bits
and pieces, a trumpet sounding the equivalent of a royal salute
and the guard presenting arms.

Massasoit was a most impressive man, and a tribute paid to
him later by Winslow is worth quoting: "He was no liar, he was
not bloody and cruel like other Indians; in anger and passion he
was soon reclaimed; easy to be reconciled towards such as had
offended him, ruled by reason in such measure as he would not
scorn the advice of mean men; and that he governed his men better with few strokes than others did with many."

His regalia on this occasion was a massive chain of bone beads
with a long knife hanging down in front and a deerskin tobacco
pouch behind. He was led to one of the houses, where a colored
rug and cushions were set out. With a flourish of trumpets, Governor Carver entered. Massasoit greeted him and a larger pot of
brandy (or Hollands perhaps) was handed to the chief, who had
a go at downing it in one, which "made him sweat all the time
after."

This conference, meeting, or pow-wow turned out to be the
most important event in the life of Plymouth Plantation since the
landing, and the basis for their future security. Then and there, a
peace treaty was signed, which in spite of some tiffs and some
dangerous disagreements was to last for the remaining forty
years of Massasoit's life and was renewed until 1675 by his sons.
The treaty was also a pact of mutual assistance. If the Indians
were unjustly attacked, Plimouth would come to their assistance,

and Massasoit to theirs in like case. There was an agreement to send on to the other any who should break the peace.

Massasoit left, but various braves kept dropping in on the Pilgrims until eventually they had to send to Massasoit to call them off. One Indian they did not want to send away was Squanto. Bradford is speaking of Massasoit's departure after the treaty:

> After these things he returned to his place called Sowains [now Bur-rington, Rhode Island, though Warren also claims the honor] some forty miles from this place, but Squanto continued with them and was their interpreter and was a special instrument sent of God for their good beyond their expectation.

And he gives some detail: "He directed them how to set their corn, where to take fish and procure other commodities, and was also their pilot to bring them to unknown places for their profit and never left them till he died."

It could be said that Squanto was host rather than guest. As the only survivor of the Patuxet tribe, he owned the land on which the plantation stood. Individual Indians did not own land; land was held by the tribe in common.

One of the chief difficulties the early settlers in America had was in communicating with the Indians with any exactness, and it is doubtful whether the treaty with Massasoit would have been signed had not Squanto been present as interpreter. The Al-mighty spent a long time and used many agents in the training of Squanto as a special instrument for the good of the Pilgrims, the first agent being George Waymouth.

Captain George Waymouth, exploring on behalf of the English Plymouth Company in 1605, had taken Squanto to England. We don't know what Squanto did there apart from learning English, but in 1614 he returned to New England as interpreter to Cap-tain John Smith. Smith sailed for home leaving one of his ships under Captain John Hunt to load up with fish and whatever furs he could get. Hunt put in at Patuxet (or Plymouth), lured twenty Indians including Squanto on board, and took them to Spain. There in the Málaga slave market he sold them for twenty pounds apiece. Some were taken off to North Africa; a few were taken by an order of friars so that they might be instructed in the Christian faith and make themselves generally useful; Squanto was one of these doubtful converts. Then comes a gap, since no publisher ever got hold of Squanto, and if he, Squanto, told the whole story no one printed it. But somehow he found his way back to London, where he lived on Cornhill with John Slany, a London merchant. Slany lent him as guide/interpreter to someone on a voyage to Newfoundland, though that someone must have intended trading voyages into Massachusetts. Squanto next appears to be at the disposal of Governor John Mason of Newfoundland, who gave, lent or posted him to Captain John Dermer when the captain set out to explore New England in 1619. Dermer dropped Squanto off in Patuxet, and his record says: "I arrived at my savage's native country (finding all dead)." The next year, Dermer himself died of Indian arrow wounds gotten in a battle on Martha's Vineyard, and in that year the Pilgrims arrived in Patuxet—alias Whitson Bay, Port du Cap St. Louis, Cranes Bay, Accomack, Thievish Harbour, or New Plimoth, but from thenceforward, for us, Plymouth. After 1621 the plantation as a whole was called New Plymouth and the little village or town Plymouth, which does not prevent Bradford, as late as 1630, calling it Plimmoth.

In late March Captain Jones prepared to take his ship home. He had stayed far longer than either he or the adventurers could have expected, partly because "of the necessity and danger" in which the Pilgrims stood and partly because of his own men; "many of the ablest of them [were] dead and of the rest many lay sick and weak and the master dare not put to sea till he saw his men begin to recover and the heart of the winter over." The *Mayflower* set sail on 5 April with no cargo at all for the adventurers, for the Pilgrims had not yet cut enough timber or sawn enough clapboard for their own use; they had not gotten the proper nets and hooks for cod, and probably not enough beaver furs for a single bale. Captain Jones arrived in London on May 6, 1621, and after a refit took up his old trade with the French ports —but not for long. He died, perhaps from the aftereffects of his stay in Plymouth, and was buried in Rotherhithe on 5 March 1622. The *Mayflower,* it is thought, never made another voyage after that date, and in 1624 she was rotting at her moorings in Rotherhithe. Claims have been made that some of the *Mayflower*'s timbers were used in building a barn in Buckinghamshire and a chapel in Oxfordshire. Both buildings still stand, but such claims should not be pushed to the proof; they are better left to the eye of faith, like pieces of the True Cross and Plymouth Rock.

The Pilgrims now had New England and its Indians all to themselves, and their plans for each were fairly simple. The land must supply food, shelter, and timber, and the Indians must supply beaver furs. Squanto had already put the good word around the neighborhood that the Pilgrims were willing to trade or truck for any number of beaver pelts.

With the spring of the year, there must have been a general feeling of optimism, for not one Pilgrim sought a passage home on the *Mayflower,* though this is not to discount the tenacity, even downright pigheadedness, of their kind of Englishman. The word courage has also been used.

Not long after the *Mayflower* left, Governor Carver came in from the fields complaining of a headache, took to his bed, sank into a coma, and in a day or two he died. He was fifty-four, the same age as Elder Brewster. Carver had been much respected, even by the disgruntled section of the "strangers," for his patience and tolerance. His wife survived him by only five or six weeks, "being only a weak woman," says Bradford ambiguously; he may have been referring to her health or the fact that she died of a broken heart. She had been born Catherine White of Sturton-le-Steeple.

William Bradford was elected as the new governor, but as he had not recovered his health, Isaac Allerton became his assistant. Bradford was to be re-elected governor every year for more than thirty years. The leadership of the little colony now rested firmly on the younger group. Elder Brewster was perfectly happy to be the elder statesman and to care for what he saw as the heart of the whole enterprise—the Separated Church of Christ. Bradford was thirty-one, a cool organizer and competent administrator; Allerton, thirty-four, ex-tailor and a sharp business man (too sharp, as it turned out later); Standish, thirty-six, fiery-tempered but an excellent commando-type soldier as well as a good staff man, and Winslow, twenty-five, a smooth, enterprising, and tactful negotiator. Hopkins too always seemed to be to the fore in any enterprise that seemed dangerous. He was aged about thirty-five years. None of these five, of course, were officers of the church. The Pilgrims were lucky in the quality of their leading men and clearly trusted them, while still able to vote against any of their decisions in open meeting.

In April they began to plant their Indian corn and such seed as they had brought with them. For the corn, Squanto was agricultural adviser. The time of planting was "when the leaves of the white oak were as large as a mouse's ear." Twenty acres of ground were dug with mattock and hoe and little hillocks made three to four feet apart. No doubt they also used what existing hillocks there were. In each hillock three herrings (they called them alewives, and strictly the alewife is of the shad genus) were set spokewise a few inches down, covered, and a few seeds planted over them, to be thinned to the strongest plant when they grew. Squanto showed them how to set fish traps for the herring which were now swarming up the brook. Later, ten thousand and more would be trapped in a weir on a single tide. There were over ninety-six thousand hillocks to prepare and forty tons of fish manure to trap and carry to the fields in baskets, and it was a crop that needed watching day and night to keep the crows from the seed and the wolves from digging up the fish. As the maize grew, each hillock had to be earthed up and the ground well hoed. This crop, when it was harvested, "saved them from starvation," and that seems an extraordinary statement to make. They were in a land full of game and wildfowl; deer, duck of every variety by the hundred thousand, wild turkey and partridges; clams and oysters thick on the seashore; fat eels in the streams; lobster and cod with a wealth of other fish in the sea and above all the striped bass of which William Wood in his *New England's Prospect* (1634) says: "Though men are often wearied with other fish yet they are never with bass. They swarm around the mouths of streams and are easily taken." Yet the Pilgrims were often on the verge of starvation. Even though the fish nets they brought were useless, as were the overlarge fish hooks, Squanto must have shown them the Indian techniques. It may be that most of the Pilgrims were truly English in despising food to which they were unaccustomed, and game, berries, and shellfish were not eaten by them unless they were ravenously hungry. Some of those half poisoned by the mussels at Cape Cod may have distrusted all shellfish. They preferred salt fish to fresh, and bread, mutton, beef, or pork to anything else, although they would make do with dried peas, beans, and oatmeal. They were happy enough on a diet of bread, butter, and cheese; a great deal of bread and a little of the others would do, but none of these foods could they get except from diminishing stores. Their tastes were to change eventually and they took to Indian corn well enough after the first harvest although it too was to them (and the rest of Europe) an unfamiliar cereal.

In May, Edward Winslow, six weeks a widower, married Mrs. Susanna White, widow of William White, who had died in the winter. The marriage, the first in Plymouth, was "according to the laudable custom of the Low Countries," and Bradford as magistrate officiated. The Separatists never recognized marriage as a sacrament, "being but a civil thing."

Friendly Indians were now becoming a nuisance, drifting in at any time of the day or night, sometimes with their wives and families, ready to receive anything going in the way of hospitality. Sometimes these visits were fortuitous in that it was the lobster season; the Pilgrims were settled hard by some of the best lobster grounds and the Indians made a habit of following their food around; the presence of the Pilgrims with their strange and delicious foods and strong waters was a bonus. Since the Pilgrims could not refuse some measure of hospitality, it was decided to send a deputation to Massasoit asking him to call the guests off before they ate the Pilgrims down to danger level. Winslow and Hopkins were the ambassadors selected, and they set out on their forty-mile journey in early summer, with Squanto as guide and interpreter. Winslow wrote a dryly amusing account of the journey, which was printed in *Mourt's Relation*. Everywhere, they were well received and entertained on the outward leg. The Indians were much impressed by the muskets, particularly by the smoke and noise, though they were not keen to handle them. Winslow, who had probably never used a musket before coming to America, seems to have been something of a marksman, and at one village excited great admiration by shooting a crow at eighty yards' range. With roasted crab and shad and other fish they did very well until, after some delay, they met Massasoit, who had apparently run out of food. They had first to listen to a deal of tedious oratory from the chief before they got down to business. Massasoit promised to make sure that "his men would no longer pester them" but that he would tell them all that they would be welcome if they brought their beaver skins to Plymouth to trade for what the Pilgrims had to offer. He added that he considered himself King James's man. The Pilgrims for their part presented Massasoit with a red horseman's coat trimmed with lace in which he paraded up and down in great delight. He was also given a copper chain for any messenger of his to wear as a sign that he was the chief's own messenger. They also told Massasoit that if the Indians from whom they had "borrowed" the corn would fix a price for it they would pay them. There was no sign of any food, but Massasoit insisted that his guests should sleep that night on the royal bed, "it being only planks laid a foot from the ground, and a thin mat upon them. Two more of his chief men, for want of room, pressed by and upon us, so that we were worse weary of our lodging than of our journey."

The next day, they put the muskets through their paces and about one o'clock dinner was served, "being two fishes like bream but three times as big and better meat. These being boiled there were at least forty looked for share in them, the most ate of them." They took their leave early one morning, "we very much feeling we should not be able to recover home for want of strength." They got nothing but snacks of fish on the way back and sent a runner ahead to the last stage to ask for a meal to be made ready. "But, God be praised we came safe home that night though wet, weary, and surbuted [footsore]." Bradford, though not Mourt, comments on Massasoit's home place: "The soil good and the people not many; being dead and abundantly wasted in the late great mortality which fell in all these parts about three years before the coming of the English, wherein thousands of them died they not being able to bury one another their skulls and bones were found in many places lying still above ground."

Another Indian, Hobomok, a member of Massasoit's council, came to live at Plymouth and never left them until he died. He was a link with the chief and seemed to have acted as an intelligence agent for him. He became Standish's man as Squanto was Bradford's, and a good deal of jealousy grew up between the two Indians. The Pilgrims encouraged this jealous rivalry, playing one against the other to "make them both more diligent," but it was a dangerous game and it nearly cost Squanto his life later.

One day, the two of them had gone to Nemasket (now Middleborough), an Indian camp some fifteen miles to the west. A few days later, Hobomok came back saying that Squanto had been murdered by the Nemasket chief, Corbitant, who had also attempted to stab him, Hobomok. As Bradford says, Corbitant "was never any good friend to the English to this day." As he drew his knife on Hobomok, he had shouted that "if Squanto is killed the English have lost their tongue."

There was a rumor, too, that the powerful Narragansett tribe had, with Corbitant's help, captured Massasoit, and "if they should suffer their friends and their messengers thus to be wronged they should have none would cleave to them." A council was summoned, and here we can note for the first time but not the last that the Pilgrims were more faithful to Christian tradition than to Christian precept; instead of turning the other cheek, they lashed out. "It was resolved to send the Captain and fourteen men well armed and go and fall on them in the night." They set out for Nemasket and surrounded Corbitant's house during the night, and at a signal fired several muskets in the air, sending a wave of terror through the village. Men, women, and children were ordered not to stir, but several braves broke for the woods and three were wounded. Corbitant, it seems, had not even waited for the English. Then Squanto appeared out of the hubbub accompanied by trembling Indians, "who brought with them the best provisions they had" as a peace offering. Squanto had been threatened with death but had not yet been harmed.

All were told that although Corbitant had got away this time "yet there is no place shall secure him and his from us if he continues his threatening." The three wounded men were taken to Plymouth and their wounds dressed, and no doubt they were also given some entertainment before they were sent home.

The result of this affair was very satisfactory for the Pilgrims. The sachems, or chiefs, of nine tribes came in to offer themselves and their tribes as allies. The Pilgrims accepted, on condition that they all signed themselves as loyal subjects of King James. Even Corbitant offered submission through the good offices of Massasoit, "but was shy to come near them until a long while after."

Before this demonstration in force, an expedition had set out in the shallop to pick up a boy, John Billington, who had got lost and had wandered down to Cape Cod, where he had been passed from tribe to tribe and was now, Massasoit reported, near Corn Hill. The Billington family, father John and two sons John and Francis, were natural delinquents from London, "one of the profanest families amongst them and I know not by what friends shuffled into their company," says Bradford. At first landing on Cape Cod Francis had nearly blown them all sky high by making fireworks near the powder barrels, but at Plymouth one of his escapades had a useful end. He climbed to the top of a high tree and discovered a large lake to the west, which was called and is still called Billington Sea. Billington senior, no doubt a troublemaker on board the *Mayflower,* at Plymouth had been tied neck and heels "for his contempt of Captain Standish's lawful command." From then on, for some years, he went his own crooked way until eventually he was hanged for murder. The Pilgrims recovered the wandering Billington and a fascinating story Mourt makes of the expedition, although he got the date wrong. The Nausets, who had attacked them at First Encounter, made their peace while the Pilgrims were there, and the Pilgrims "gave full satisfaction to those whose corn they had found."

In September the shallop was sent on another expedition, up into what is now Boston Harbor. They met the local chief, who said he and his people had to keep on the move because of neighboring enemies. Make yourself King James's man as many have done, said the Pilgrims' Army of Ten and we will be "safeguard from your enemies, which he did." They sailed across the bay with their new ally looking for his enemies and of course trade. They could find no men at first, only a fair number of frightened women all wearing magnificent beaver-skin wraps. Squanto suggested that they should be stripped of their furs because they were unfriendly people. No, said the Pilgrims, unfriendly words break no bones, but if they offered unfriendly deeds "then we would deal far worse than he desired." One trembling brave came to them, but when he found they were only seeking trade he promised them some skins. They returned to the shallop, "almost all the women accompanying us to truck, who sold the coats from their backs and tied boughs about them (but with great shamefacedness, for indeed they are more modest than some of our English women are)."

The islands around the entrance to the bay they named the Brewsters, the long sandy spit to the South Point, Allerton, and a headland, Squantum, which names are still on the map.

They began now to gather in the small harvest they had and to fit up their houses and dwellings against winter being all well recovered in health and strength and had all things in good plenty.

Thus Bradford, but the great American feast of Thanksgiving[11] would not have been established on that slender mention of a harvest festival. Mourt gives the details that launched millions of turkeys and seas or bogs of cranberry sauce—in due course.

Our harvest being gotten in, our governor sent four men on fowling so we might after a special manner rejoice together after we had gathered the fruit of our labours. They four in one day killed as much fowl as, with a little help beside, served the company almost a week.

The Indians, whether invited or scenting the feast from afar, came in, ninety strong, headed by Massasoit. As their contribution they went out and killed five deer. We don't know the date of this feast but it would have been after the lobster season, which with the main fishing season finished around the end of August. There were, though, plenty of cod and eels about. The wildfowl come to the bay from September to March and, judging by the number killed by the four men, it would be at least September end and probably October. John Pory, who came on a visit to Plymouth in 1623 on his way back to England from Virginia, after listing the fish to be caught from Plymouth ranges over other gifts of nature: "Touching their fruit I will not speak of their meaner sort as of raspberries, gooseberries, strawberries, delicate plums and others. But they have commonly through the country five several sorts of grapes being fairer and larger than any I ever saw in the South Colony [Virginia]." He also mentions the turkeys as large and fat. And with all this protein they could now have their carbohydrates in corn bread, with vitamin C in watercress, leeks, and other salads topped up with stewed fruit and washed down with wine both white and red "very sweet and strong." Of the seed the Pilgrims had brought with them, barley and peas gave a poor crop. We have no report of the small garden seeds.

There was no doubt that a good time was had by all, in a festival with a thoroughly pagan background. Each year, they were to hold their harvest thanksgiving even if they had very little to be thankful for, and it became a tradition throughout New England, centering in the later years on turkey, which the Pilgrims certainly had in 1621, and cranberries, which they had not, although they had acres of cranberries in easy reach. In 1863 President Lincoln made the last Thursday in November a national Thanksgiving Day. In November 1621 the high mood of thanksgiving at Plymouth fell sharply away. Taking stock of their harvest, they found the yield very much less than their estimate, and rations of meal were at once cut in half. And in November came the ill-named ship *Fortune.* She was a small ship of fifty-five tons, "unexpected or looked for," with thirty-five passengers aboard, most of whom were "strangers," but Robert Cushman (their agent with the adventurers) had come to leave his son Thomas, aged fourteen, with them, and Jonathan Brewster son of the elder, Thomas Morton from Harworth near Scrooby, young Philippe de la Noye (whose descendants come down to our own time as Delano), and several others were from Leyden. The strangers aboard had made quite a fuss when they got to Cape Cod "and there saw nothing but a naked and barren place. They began to think what should become of them if the people here were dead or cut off by Indians." The captain said if that were so he had just enough ships victuals to take them on to Virginia, for Weston had sent this shipload out without provisions or any supplies at all for the colony; "there was not so much as bisquit bread, or any other victuals for them, neither had they any bedding, nor pot nor pan to dress any meat in, nor over many clothes." What Weston had sent was a letter complaining that the *Mayflower* had been returned with no cargo, "a quarter of the time you spent in discoursing, arguing and consulting," he said, might have produced something. He had not, he said, told the adventurers that the Pilgrims refused to sign the agreement; he was afraid that, had they known, they would not have advanced another halfpenny; another thing—"give us an account how our monies were laid out." Cushman persuaded them to sign the agreement they so much disliked; he pointed out that without the adventurers' support there could be no more immigrants from Leyden. He also gave a long sermon to the whole colony, much of it directed at those strangers who wanted the common lands divided up and every man to work for himself. Cushman may not have convinced these free enterprisers, but they had no immediate answer to his persuasive Christian communism. Their time was to come. One good thing came with the *Fortune;* the adventurers had got a charter for the plantation from the New England Company, and their occupation of Plymouth was for the first time legal. The Pilgrims could not have felt guilty about the empty holds of the *Mayflower,* but they put all they could into the *Fortune,* loading her "with good clapboard (oak staves, not the modern clapboard) as full as she could stow, and two hogsheads of beaver and otter skins." The freight was estimated to be worth near five hundred pounds. Since this was about half their debt to the adventurers, they expected not only supplies of trade goods and provisions to come to them in return but a more agreeable communication from Weston, to whom Bradford had sent an indignant letter. Cushman returned to England on the *Fortune* bearing the detested agreement signed by the leaders at Plymouth.

The *Fortune* got as far as the Channel when she was brought to under the guns of a French privateer, taken to a small port in France, stripped of everything of value, her passengers and crew robbed down to their shoes, and finally ship, crew, and passengers were allowed to go on to London.

The French ignored a packet of manuscripts in Cushman's

possession entitled *A Relation or Journal of the Beginnings and Proceedings of the English Plantation settled at Plymouth, New England.* Cushman saw it through the press adding an essay on *The Lawfulness of Plantations.* The author was shown as G. Mourt and nobody knows who G. Mourt was, but *Mourt's Relation* must be the work of Bradford and Winslow.

At Plymouth, feeling they had done well by the adventurers, the Pilgrims set about assimilating the newcomers, particularly the seventeen men, two women, and four children who were strangers and who were distributed among the seven houses already built. Although no one says so, some of the single men must have slept in the common house and messed either together or with the families to which they were attached.

Glowing accounts of the wealth of fish, flesh, fowl, and fruit in Plymouth had been given in the propaganda of Captain John Smith, and those accounts had been backed up by letters sent in the *Mayflower.* Even the adventurers might be excused for sending no supplies of food to such an apparent paradise. A clear case of oversell. The newcomers must have been shocked by the reality of Plymouth; it was winter, there were plenty of wildfowl about, but the fish had not yet come in, there was only water and a little wine to drink, no milk, butter, or cheese, since there were no domestic beasts; and the remnants of the supplies the *Mayflower* had brought plus what the exuberant thanksgiving had left of the harvest would scarcely last until next harvest even on half rations. Hope, of which the Pilgrims in these early years had to keep a large supply, told them that in return for the rich cargo of the *Fortune* the adventurers would send ample provisions, and that before very many months had passed.

Word soon spread among the Indians that the *Fortune* had brought mouths but no food, and the Narragansett Indians, no friends of Massasoit, nor of his allies the Pilgrims, nor of Europeans in general, obviously thought the time ripe for a demonstration, and if that went well to consider an attack. One of their warriors stalked into Plymouth and presented a bundle of arrows wrapped in a snakeskin. This, Squanto declared to be a challenge. Whether the Pilgrims were by now versed in the ancient and sinister language of symbols or whether Squanto gave them the idea we do not know, but they filled the snakeskin with powder and bullets and sent it back to the Narragansett Chief Canonicus, and "it was no small terror to the savage king; insomuch as he would not once touch the powder and shot or suffer it to stay in his home and country . . . and having been posted from place to place for a long time, at length came whole back again." But neither Standish nor the other leaders thought that this kind of black magic would hold off several thousand Narragansett warriors for long, so all hands were put to completing the eight-foot (eleven in some accounts) -high palisade around the town. Almost a mile in circumference, it ran down from the common house between the brook and the houses on that side of the street along the high bank by Coles Hill burial ground and back up the far side to the common house. There were flanking towers and three heavy gates, one at the shore end of the street and one at each end of the cross street. These were shut every night and sentries posted. "This was accomplished very cheerfully by the beginning of March [1622] in which every family had a pretty garden plot secured," which means that each garden was fenced one from the other. At this point in his journal, Bradford remembers an incident "rather of mirth than of weight." On Christmas Day most of the strangers said it was against their conscience to work on that day. So Bradford took the rest out to work, "but when they came home at noon from their work, he found them in the street at play, openly; some pitching the bar, and some at stool-ball and suchlike sports. So he went to them and took away their implements and told them that was against his own conscience that they should play and others work. If they made the keeping of it matter of devotion, let them keep their houses but there should be no gaming or revelling in the streets. Since which time nothing hath been attempted that way; at least openly."

At the end of March, keeping a long-promised rendezvous, they prepared to take the shallop up to those Massachusetts Indians whose women had so blithely stripped off their beaver coats. Hobomok, Massasoit's Indian resident, warned them that there was treachery afoot among the Massachusetts backed by the Narragansetts, and he hinted that Squanto was party to the plot because he had seen him whispering in the woods to strange Indians, but the Pilgrims ignored this, knowing the jealousy between the two of them, and set off, taking the two Indians with them. They had not long left when a friend of Squanto's burst into Plymouth with a bloody face saying that the Narragansetts with Corbitant, and Massasoit for good measure, were coming to attack the plantation. A gun was fired to recall the shallop, the defenses were manned all that night, but no Indians came anywhere near. Hobomok was protesting that Massasoit would never conspire against them unless, he added, he [Hobomok] had been told. His wife slipped out to find Massasoit, whom she found quite peacefully at home, and on hearing her news became furiously angry at the suggestion that he might be breaking faith. Very acutely, he said that the whole business was a fabrication of Squanto's. Bradford says the Pilgrims

> began to see that Squanto sought his own ends and played his own game by putting the Indians in fear, and drawing gifts from them to enrich himself; making them believe he could stir up war against whom he would. Yea he made them believe they kept the plague buried in the ground, and could send it amongst whom they would which did much terrify the Indians.

A very useful piece of propaganda, one would say, but Squanto had now overreached himself and it "had like to cost him his life." Several braves arrived bearing Massasoit's demand for Squanto's head. Bradford was in a quandary. The Pilgrims could not afford to lose Massasoit's friendship; moreover, they were bound by treaty to surrender "any that did hurt to them that they may punish him." On the other hand, Squanto had done them much service and this present piece of dangerous nonsense arose only out of Squanto's vanity and rivalry with Hobomok. But there was also the question of jealousy between Squanto and Massasoit, and the latter wanted, literally, the former's head, for which Massasoit had instructed his braves to offer many beaver skins. Bradford replied, rather huffily one feels, that the English do not sell men's lives at a price, but that "when men deserved justly to die to give them their reward." So, coming down on the side of justice and the treaty, he sent for Squanto, who said he would abide by the governor's decision.

> But at the instant when our Governor was ready to deliver him into the hands of his executioners a boat was seen at sea to cross before our town and fall behind a headland not far off. Whereupon having heard many rumours of the French the Governor told the Indians he would first know what boat that was ere he would deliver Squanto to them, but being mad with rage and impatient at delay, they departed in great heat.

Massasoit never lost his keen desire for Squanto's head, but he was fended off one way and another, and Squanto kept as close as he could to the Pilgrims until the day he died a natural death. His plot, which so misfired, was an involved one aimed at securing even more power, or honor as Winslow puts it, among the Indians than he already had.

The boat that put in such a dramatic appearance turned out to be a shallop from the *Sparrow,* a fishing vessel sent out by Weston as a private venture by himself and another of the adventurers to "get up what we are formerly out"; in other words to repay themselves for what they had spent in the Pilgrim adventure. The *Sparrow* brought no provisions or any other supplies for Plymouth but landed seven passengers whom Weston desired them to entertain and "supply with such necessaries as you can spare and they want." The men were to fish, not for Plymouth but for Weston & Partner and were to set up a salt pan on one of the islands in the bay. Weston also wrote that he and his partner would be sending over some more people on their own account; for the Pilgrims not to house and feed them would be "extreme barbarism." How many were to be expected, who they were, or what they proposed to do for a living Weston did not say, but in another letter he told them that the company of adventurers showed signs of disintegrating.

What, exactly, Weston was up to, neither Bradford nor the few others he dared show the letters to could fathom. One thing was very clear: "All this was but cold comfort to fill their hungry bellies." The seven unwelcome guests were housed and fed "as good as any of [our] own," went out fishing so that they were no help in planting the spring corn, and in due course sailed to Virginia, where they sold both ship and fish. But the *Sparrow* was the bearer of another letter from a Captain John Huddleston, fishing in Maine waters, "a stranger of whose name they had here heard before." His letter began: "Friends, countrymen and neighbours. I salute you and wish you all health and happiness in the Lord" and went on to tell them of a terrible disaster in Virginia, where nearly four hundred (actually 347) of the colonists had been killed by Indians, and added: "Happy is he whom other men's harms do make beware." The starving Pilgrims reacted by sending Winslow up the Maine coast to thank the captain for his courtesy, and by the way had he any spare provisions? He had and gave them all he could spare, but would not accept payment and sent them with a letter to all the other English boats, who, between them, loaded the shallop to the gunwales, though "it arose but to a quarter of a pound a day to each person," which was doled out daily; otherwise "they would have eaten it up and then starved."

Spurred on perhaps by the Virginia massacre, "they built a fort with strong timber both strong and comely." On the flat roof, which commanded all the countryside and the bay, they mounted their cannon, and for many years this fort with its slit windows served as meetinghouse, jail, and court of justice.

About the middle of summer, two more ships sailed into the bay—the *Charity* and the *Swan*—and the Pilgrims thought that here at last they might again taste butter and cheese, bread, and maybe beer. What they got was an elucidation of Weston's mysterious letter by another letter, which said that for one thing he was no longer one of the adventurers, "so I am quit of you and you of me for the matter" and for another, would they please look after the sixty or so men on the two ships until such time as the men were ready to make a settlement for which he had a patent for himself. The patent turned out to be for land at the lower end of Boston Bay. Weston also advised them to do as he had done and cut loose from the adventurers, and as matters turned out this would have been greatly to their advantage, but unfortunately they did not share Weston's moral flexibility and

thought it "neither lawful nor profitable." Other letters had come
by the ships, including one from Cushman, and the general tenor
of their contents was: beware of Weston and his men; they are
not your kind of people.

They soon found this to be true. "They were an unruly company and had no good government over them." Weston's men
stayed the best part of the summer, and although the Pilgrims
shared what little food was available, some of the men took every
opportunity to steal the growing ears of corn. Eventually they
sailed for Massachusetts, "yet they left all their sick folk here till
they were settled and housed." These were sent on as they
recovered, for being all men, it was thought that their help
would be needed in the new settlement—to be called Wessagusset, but now the city of Weymouth, twenty-five miles north of
Plymouth.

"Now the welcome time of harvest in which all had their
hungry bellies full." This can only mean that bellies were filled
once, at a thanksgiving, and then back to the tight belts, for it
was a poor harvest; they had not yet got the hang of growing Indian corn, and the unripe corn had been picked both by Weston's
men and some of the strangers among the Pilgrims, "and though
they were well whipt for a few ears of corn yet hunger made
others to venture." The obvious thing to do, if they were not to
suffer another and maybe worse famine in 1623 was to buy corn
from the Indians—but they had no trade goods, no knives to
spare, no beads and no trinkets left, but "Behold now another
providence of God, a ship comes into the harbour." This was the
Discovery, of London, fitted out to trade along the coast of
America, and she had a large store of English beads, "which
were then good trade," and some knives. Bradford makes great
moan about the price he was charged in beaver skins and the
like, but it must be remembered that the *Discovery* could have
got very much higher prices (or more skins) from the Indians.
The skipper of the *Discovery* was another Captain Jones, but not
as pleasant a man as the *Mayflower* Jones. At one time and
another he was accused of piracy in various seas and of robbing
the Indians.

Weston's men at Wessagusset soon heard that Plymouth had

now gotten trade goods, and as they too were short of food they
offered to send their small ship, the *Swan*, on a joint trading expedition. They would pay their share of the capital outlay, they
said, when Mr. Weston arrived with supplies. This foraging
voyage got off to an unlucky start. With Standish in charge, the
Swan and the shallop were driven back by a storm. Setting out
again, Standish fell ill and the ship or boats put back into
Plymouth, sailing out again with Bradford in command and
Squanto to pilot them down the dangerous Atlantic forearm of
Cape Cod through the boiling shoals of Monomoy and around to
the south shore of the Cape. But Squanto's knowledge of the
shoals was not good enough, and "the master durst not venture
any further," so they put in to that harbor of Monomoy, now
Chatham, where Champlain had his bloody affair with the suspicious and truculent Indians. There were no Indians in sight, but
Bradford now knew enough about Indians to send Squanto into
the woods to allay their suspicions and flush them out to trade.
At length they came, Winslow says, "welcoming our Governor
according to their savage manner; refreshing them very well with
store of venison and other victuals which they brought to them in
great abundance." They were still rather suspicious, playing hide
and seek with their huts, moving them from place to place, but
eventually Squanto got them to settle down to trade and Bradford got eight hogsheads of corn and beans.

It was the last service Squanto did for them; suddenly he took
ill, and within a few days died, asking that Bradford pray for
him "that he might go to the Englishman's God in heaven." Bradford says that his English friends had suffered a great loss, and
we may be sure he was sincere in lamenting the loss of a friend.
The Pilgrims were always grateful to those who helped them
(and spiteful to those who didn't). The lament may have been
even more sincere for the loss of a valuable and almost ir-
replaceable asset. Squanto's one fault was that he tried too hard
to be honored among his own kind, not, we may think, a grievous
fault. But we feel cheated by Bradford; we would like to haul
him out of that Englishman's heaven to which he undoubtedly
went, to ask him at least one question: your friend, the last of the
Patuxets, was one of the early discoverers of Europe: what ad-

ventures had he there? And what were his views on the natives, and—please don't go, Master Bradford, we have a schedule of a thousand and one questions.

They sailed back to the Massachusetts country, but there was some kind of plague among the Indians and all they got were complaints about Weston's men, who, the Pilgrims were alarmed to be told, were upsetting the Indian trade, not only by ill conduct but by giving far too much for the Indians' corn, "as much for a quart of corn as we used to do for a beaver's skin." They went back down to the bottom of Cape Cod Bay, where another eight or ten hogsheads of corn were bought, but a storm nearly wrecked the *Swan,* and the shallop was thrown up on the beach. The corn and beans were made up into a mound, covered, and left in charge of the Indians to be collected somehow later. Weston's men sailed back in the *Swan,* dropping off ten hogsheads of corn in Plymouth, while Bradford's men set out to walk the forty miles to Plymouth. Almost at once, Bradford set off again, covering a good deal of country around the shoulder of the cape, buying corn which squaws toted back to Plymouth, visiting chiefs, and generally making friends and influencing people.

Bradford ends his journal for the year 1622 with an ominous glance at the affairs of Weston's gang of ill-conditioned settlers twenty-five miles up the coast, at Wessagussett. The year ended, as it had done since the twelfth century, on March 24. March 25 was New Year's Day 1623.

16   That Conceit of Plato's

The lurid drama of The End of Wessagussett may conveniently open with a little curtain raiser set in Manomet (Bourne) with Captain Standish center stage. There is a prologue. During February, Standish had taken the shallop to pick up Bradford's purchases at Nauset (Eastham), where he reacted to some petty thieving of beads, etc., with a show of such military might as he had. As the Indians had most carefully guarded the mound of corn left in their care, the chief was surprised at the captain's mistrust of them, as were the Indians at the captain's next call, at Commaquid (Barnstable). These last had brought in the half-frozen Pilgrims from the shallop, warmed them, fed them, and sold them corn. Again some trinkets were missing, and again Standish staged a bad-tempered demonstration. In the first case the stolen trifles were restored and the enterprising thief punished, and in the other the trinkets reappeared. The Pilgrims interpreted these petty acts as a sign of growing hostility. In March, having taken the corn back to Plymouth, Standish came with a party to Manomet (Bourne), where he immediately got suspicious because his reception was not as warm as that accorded to Bradford some time back. There are two versions of what followed, but Winslow's is clear enough and is the original.

It is, though, compiled with hindsight, and to put it mildly, Winslow does not disclose the sources of his information.

> Captain Standish was not long at Canacum the sachem's house but in came two of the Massachusetts [Indians]. The chief of them was called Wituwamat, a notable insulting villain, one who had formerly imbrued his hands in the blood of English and French and had oft boasted of his own valour, especially because as he said they died crying, making sour faces more like children than men.

Winslow, after presenting this stock picture of the savage Indian, details the plot. There was to be an attack on Wessagusset and Plymouth and our savage was at Manomet to persuade the Indians there to join in. "Standish on his guard and watchful escaped any mishap but treasured up his anger against Wituwamat." The curtain raiser ends then with the choleric eye of the little captain fixed on the not so noble savage, and we move to the scene of the forthcoming drama.

Wessagusset was in a bad way. The men had been reckless in using up their food, and to get corn or meat some of them "sold away their clothes, others (so base were they) became servants to the Indians, cut wood for them and fetched them water for a cupful of corn, others fell to plain stealing, both night and day from the Indians. In the end they came to that misery that some starved and died with cold and hunger." The Indians treated these men with great contempt and where they had got some food "they would take it out of their pots and eat it before their faces, yea if in anything they gainsaid them they were ready to hold a knife at their breasts." In an attempt to conciliate the Indians, Weston's men publicly hanged one of their own number for stealing the Indians' corn, but followed up the hanging by a sharp attack on the Indian audience. After this, the English withdrew into their palisades, and Sanders, their leader, sent a letter to Plymouth to ask advice as to whether they should attack the Indians and force them to sell corn.

There is an interlude at Sowams, Massasoit's home, where the chief is dangerously ill "and like to die." Winslow, Hobomok, and John Hampden, "a gentleman of London" (of whom we know

nothing except that he was not the great John Hampden, M.P.),
set out to visit him, Bradford having "fitted them with some cor-
dials to administer."[12] Winslow published a very long and de-
tailed account of this mission. On the way south, they heard that
Massasoit was dead, which occasioned the loving tribute to Massasoit, already quoted, that Winslow attributes to Hobomok but
which is quite clearly Winslow's. They pressed on to make
friends with his successor, but found Massasoit in the midst of a
howling, dancing crowd, sinking fast and sightless. When they
told him Winslow had come, he said: "Oh Winsnow [Indian trouble with l and r] I shall never see thee again." Winslow slipped
some conserves into the Chief's swollen mouth with the point of
a knife, learned that he had been constipated for five days and
had not slept for two, carried on from there with a little fruit
juice, some broth and so on, immensely helped by Massasoit in-
sisting on drinking an unskimmed broth thick with fat and being
violently sick. After a good deal of nose bleeding he was cleaned
up by Winslow and slept eight hours. In a day or two he was up
and about. "Now I see the English are my friends and love me
and I will never forget their kindness." Winslow and Hobomok,
accompanied by Corbitant, left, after being well feasted, and
spent the night at Corbitant's home. Part of the entertainment
there was a long discussion on religion, though Winslow the diplomat was content to expound rather than convert, and is civil
enough not to give us the full text. The next day, on the trail to
Plymouth, Hobomok told him that Massasoit had disclosed full
details of the plot to attack Wessagusset and Plymouth, naming
seven tribes who were to join with the Massachusetts.

Bradford says: "This did much trouble them and they took it
in serious deliberation, and found upon examination other evidence to give light hereunto, too long here to relate." An authority on the Pilgrim story and on almost everything connected with
it, George F. Willison, sees the conspiracy story of Winslow's as a
fabrication put out by the Pilgrim propagandists to justify the action Standish took at Wessagussett, and it does seem odd that
Winslow could wander up through the tribes if those tribes had
entered into a conspiracy against Plymouth, and even odder that
he should loiter after he had had Hobomok's warning. If the con-

spiracy story was merely a Winslow public-relations exercise it was well carried out, and we may be sure that Winslow could have explained away any inconsistencies.

The curtain now goes up on the main action. At the yearly court day, March 23, it was decided (and this is Winslow's account) "that Captain Standish should take so many men as he thought sufficient to make his party good against all the Indians in the Massachusetts bay, and to take them in such traps as they lay for others, therefore he should pretend trade, but first go to the English and acquaint them with the plot."

Standish took an army of eight in the shallop and went first to the *Swan*, anchored in the harbor. There was not a soul on board, not even a dog. Standish fired off a few muskets and some of Weston's men appeared on the beach. Why was not the ship guarded? asked Standish, to which they replied that they had no fear of the Indians; they lived among them without a sword or a gun between them. Standish left these contemptible men, as he must have thought them, and looked for the deputy governor of Wessagusset, to whom "he made known the Indians' purpose." An Indian came in with furs with whom Standish traded "as smoothly as possibly he could," but the captain at his smoothest was enough to scare the daylights out of the Indian, who reported back that he saw by the captain's eyes "that he was angry in his heart." This brought out a powerful warrior called Pecksuot and several more, who put a severe strain on the captain's smoothness: "they would whet and sharpen the points of their knives before his face and use many other insulting gestures and speeches." Pecksuot said to him: "You may be a great Captain but you are a little man, I am not a great Chief yet I am a man of great strength and courage." Wituwamat, on whom the Captain had fixed his eye at Manomet, was there bragging about what his knife could do. Standish bided his time, and the next day he lured these two with two others, one of them a youngster, into a room and "gave the word to his men," and the door being fast shut, "began himself with Pecksuot." He snatched Pecksuot's knife from his neck and killed him with it. "Wituwamat and the other man the rest killed and took the youth whom the Captain caused to be hanged." It seems that the Indians put up a terrific fight. "It is incredible how many wounds these pnieses [warriors] received before they died, not making any fearful noise, but catching at their weapons and striving to the last."

Standish then gave orders that every Indian warrior in the town should be killed, but only two could be found. He marched his army out of the town gate, scattering a band of Indians, who retired from tree to tree directing their arrows on Standish and Hobomok. Hobomok got annoyed at this, and being himself a noted warrior, stripped off and went after the Massachusetts "so fast our people were not able to hold way with him." The Massachusetts retreated into a swamp, hurling insults at Standish, who was too good a soldier to venture into the thickly wooded bogs but stood there shouting to their leader to "come out and fight like a man." So the drama ended in true Jacobean style, with the stage strewn with bodies and our hero breathing defiance.

Back in the town, Standish asked Weston's men what their plans now were. Plymouth would harbor them if they wished. They chose to retreat to the *Swan* and sail away to Maine, there to seek passage home on the English fishing fleet. "Thus," says Bradford, "this plantation is broken up in a year; and this is the end of those who being all able men, had boasted of their strength and what they would bring to pass."

The captain brought the head of Wituwamat back to Plymouth and stuck it on a spike at the fort, where it remained for many years. There was nothing unusual in this. Heads decorated Temple Bar, London, and many other places during the seventeenth and even the eighteenth centuries.

A shock wave ran through all the Indian settlements in New England, the Indians leaving their houses and "running to and fro like men distracted, living in swamps and other desert places." Mysteriously, at Manomet, Nauset, and Cummaquid, those three places where the suspicions of the captain were so aroused, the three chiefs became ill and died, as did many others. Usually these recurring waves of illness and death were attributed to some form of typhus or some other white man's disease,[13] which never left the Indian settlements or settlement areas, but there also seems to have been a loss of energy and a kind of despair so that without any catastrophe like the deadly plague of 1616 the Wampanoag Indians of New England dwindled year by year until by the time of the American Revolution there were only hundreds of Indians where once there had been thousands, and before long these hundreds diminished to a miserable handful. There are still a few Wampanoag Indians in New England today, thoroughly integrated, not at all miserable, but very resentful whenever they remember their lost heritage.

Standish had been greeted with joy on his return with his grisly souvenir, but when their pastor at Leyden heard of the affair he sent them a stern rebuke and bid them "consider of the disposition of your Captain, whom I love . . . but, there may be wanting that tenderness of the life of man which is meet." It is not, he wrote, pleasing in God's eye "to be a terror to poor barbarous people."

Plymouth, though still watchful, now considered itself more secure from Indian threats (whether they were ever seriously threatened is a moot point), and with Weston's men gone they had no immediate rivals in the beaver trade, but they were still teetering on the edge of starvation. At first light each day the sentry on the gun platform of the fort would cast a hopeful eye toward the distant tip of Cape Cod looking for the sails of a supply ship, but "they knew not when they might expect any." They kept their shallop busy fishing; as one crew returned another crew put out to sea, taking mostly bass. If the shallop had a poor catch or was out at sea too long, they spread along the seashore at low tide digging clams. Also, in the summer they managed to bag a few deer. In the winter they had wild fowl to shoot and the woods yielded groundnuts.

Up to this time, spring 1623, the fields had been worked in common, and the yield of the harvest put in the common store, but now they decided that their experience had sufficiently proved

the vanity of that conceit of Plato's[14] and other ancients that the taking away of property and bringing in community into a commonwealth would make them happy and flourishing. For the young men that were most able and fit for labour and service did repine that they should spend their time and strength to work for other men's wives and children without any recompense. The strong, or man of parts had no more in division of victuals and clothes than he that was weak and not able to do a quarter the other could. The aged and graver men to be ranked and equalised in labours and victuals, clothes, etc., with the meaner and younger sort thought it some indignity and disrespect unto them. And for men's wives to be commanded to do service for other men as dressing their meat, washing their clothes, etc., they deemed it a kind of slavery neither could many husbands well brook it.

And, says Bradford, it would have been worse had they not been "godly and sober men."

Each family was now assigned land in acres proportionate to its numbers, all boys being assigned to a family. After paying a tax in kind to maintain the fishermen of the plantation, the officers and so on, what the family allotment yielded, the family kept. The change in spirit was immediate, "for it made all hands very industrious, so as much more corn was planted than otherwise would have been. The women now went willingly into the field, and took their little ones with them to set corn, which before would allege weakness and inability, whom to have compelled would have been [formerly] thought great tyranny and oppression."

Although at seed time they did not know or expect it, this year, 1623, was to be a pivotal year, and it was also to be a year of many visitors. The first visitor had come and gone—the irrepressible Weston. "Mr. Weston came over with some of the fishermen [to Maine] under another name and [in] the disguise of a blacksmith, where he heard of the ruin and dissolution of his colony." Out fishing, presumably, his ship had been wrecked, he had just managed to get ashore, where the Indians stripped him to his shirt, and after wandering to the nearest fishing station he borrowed some clothes and found his way to Plymouth. In spite of all the tricks he had played on them, the Pilgrims still felt under some obligation to him, and when he asked for some beaver pelts to set him up in business again (to be repaid of course when his ship came home), Bradford replied that he could not give them to him openly; "it were enough to cause a mutiny amongst the people," but secretly he could have one hundred skins. "But he requited them ill for he proved afterwards a bitter enemy to them upon all occasions," and of course he never paid for the skins.

The next visitor was Captain Thomas West, in the *Plantation,* who presented himself as admiral of New England with powers to stop all fishing along the coast except under license "for a round sum of money" from the council of New England. His appointment as admiral came from Sir Ferdinando Gorges, a very busy colonial developer who had obtained a grant of all the land between the Merrimack (just north of Cape Ann) and the Kennebec rivers. The fishermen using the Maine waters had no intention of taking out a license and told the admiral so, and there was nothing much the admiral could do about these "stubborn fellows." Moreover, they got their owners to complain to Parliament and fishing was made free. However, it was a good try on Sir Ferdinando's part. Captain West noted the starving condition of the Pilgrims and he said he just happened to have two hogsheads of peas to spare. How much? Nine pounds apiece. Robbery! said the Pilgrims. Very well, not a penny less than eight pounds. No, said the Pilgrims, we have "been so long without" and will stay that way rather than pay that price. No sale.

The next visitor was the *Anne,* followed by the *Little James* ten days later, battered and delayed by heavy storms. All together, these ships brought eighty-seven settlers. Twenty-nine were from Leyden, though sadly for the Church their beloved Pastor Robinson was not among them; indeed there seems to have been something of a conspiracy or at least a reluctance on the part of the adventurers to send him over. There were some moving reunions: the two Brewster daughters, Patience and Fear, with the venerable Elder Brewster; his wife and five daughters with Richard Warren, a *Mayflower* Pilgrim; his wife and three children with Francis Cooke, also of the *Mayflower,* and there were two mail-order, or pen-pal, brides: Mrs. Alice Southworth *née* Carpenter from Wrington near Bath, whose first husband had been Edward Southworth from the Scrooby area; and Barbara whose surname we do not know but who was by family tradition the younger sister of Rose, the first wife of Captain Standish. Alice was to marry William Bradford on August 14. Barbara married Myles Standish very soon after landing, and if she was his deceased wife's sister then the Pilgrims ignored the Table of Kindred and Affinity, which is likely since they scorned the rest of the Book of Common Prayer as well. Alice had been brought over by George Morton, the last of the old Scrooby congregation to get to Plymouth. Morton's wife was a sister of Alice.

All together, the strength of the settlement was increased by ninety-three: 28 men, 27 women, 35 children, and 3 servants: thirty-two were Church members, and there was one woman eighty years of age. All counted, Plymouth now had a population of 180, distributed among thirty-two houses. Bradford did not like the look of some of the newcomers: "some were so bad as they were fain to be at charge to send them home again next year." As for most of the newcomers, they did not like the look of the Pilgrims of Plymouth. "These passengers when they saw their low and poor condition ashore, were much daunted and dismayed; some wished themselves in England again, others fell a-weeping, fancying their own misery in what they saw now in others; others pitying the distress they saw their friends had long been in; in a word all were full of sadness." (If they had been reading *Mourt's Relation* (Winslow?) in England they were probably in a state of shock.) Only some of their old friends rejoiced to see them. "And truly it was no marvel they should be thus affected, for they [the Pilgrims] were in a very low condition, many were ragged in apparel, and some little better than half naked. The best dish they could present their friends with was a lobster or a piece of fish without bread or anything else but a cup of fair spring water."

Among the newcomers was a group of ten led by John Oldham who were "on their particular," that is they were to be independent of the Pilgrim settlement except that they came under the general rule of the governor. They were to be allotted lands on which they were to pay a rent of a bushel of corn, and they were liable for military service. They had no rights in the joint stock or capital and could not engage in trade with the Indians. This arrangement was an experiment by the adventurers that was not repeated. Cushman, in a letter, apologized for the general standard of the newcomers: "it grieveth me to see so weak a company sent you, but had I not been here it had been weaker." The fact was that the adventurers had more volunteers offering themselves in London than they had money with which to send them, and any offering to finance themselves were accepted without much question. In those early days of colonization, there were many theories about the best methods of selection. The keen mind of Francis Bacon saw that "the best sort are gardeners, plowmen, labourers, carpenters, surgeons, apothecaries and the like, not the scum of the people and wicked condemned men who will ever live like rogues and not face to work but be lazy and do mischief to the discredit of the Plantation." The adventurers in general avoided the last without seeming to be able to lay their hands on the first category. At least they did not follow the advice of Sir Humphrey Gilbert, who thought the colonies "would relieve England of those needy people who were daily consumed by the gallows." Australia and not America got the benefit of Sir Humphrey's patriotic principles, and anyway the Pilgrims would have shipped them back.

The *Mayflower* and *Fortune* settlers, or the Old Comers, soon got at cross purposes with the Newcomers. It would be a year before the new allotments of land could yield corn, and the Old Comers feared that their next harvest and their present, meager stock would be eaten up. They proposed to Bradford that the Newcomers should live on the supplies the ships had brought and the Old Comers would make do with what they had and what the coming harvest would bring. The Newcomers were delighted to agree.

That summer was hot and dry. No rain fell from the third week in May until the middle of July, and by then the crops were brown and sere and they feared that the whole harvest would be lost. "Upon which they set apart a solemn day of humiliation to seek the Lord by humble and fervent prayer in this great distress and He was pleased to give them a gracious and speedy answer both to their own and the Indians' admiration." When they began their prayer in the morning there was not a cloud to be seen anywhere in the sky, but before they broke up in the late afternoon it began to rain "with sweet and gentle showers. It came without either wind or thunder or any violence and lasted all that night in such abundance as that the earth was thoroughly soaked." From then on showers alternated with warm sunshine until there was "a fruitful and liberal harvest."

The harvest festival of 1623 was, it seems, combined with the wedding feast of William Bradford and Alice Southworth. We owe to Emmanuel Eltham a description of the junketings. Eltham was one of the adventurers, a man keen on profit, but an enthusiast for colonization and an admirer of the Pilgrims, despite the fact that they had not yet yielded much profit to the New Plymouth Company. He had come out as "Captain" of the *Little James;* the actual sailing and working of the vessel came under the "master," although sometimes the same individual was both master and captain. In a letter addressed to his brother he gives a description of Plymouth, an account that Winslow might have envied, of the fantastic wealth of fish in the seas around Cape Cod Bay, a description in equally enthusiastic terms of the timber and furs and of many other natural resources exploitable for profit, and then gets down to "the greater cheer we had at the Governor's marriage. We had about twelve pasty venisons, besides others, pieces of roasted venison and other such good cheer that I could wish you some of our share. For here we have the best grapes that ever you saw, and the biggest, and divers sorts of plums and nuts." Massasoit had been invited, and "he brought three or four bucks and a turkey." With him came the principal of his five wives, four other chiefs, and about one hundred and twenty warriors. "And we had very good pastime in seeing them dance with such a noise that you would wonder." It would be nice to think that, full of good cheer, the Pilgrims shook a leg, but nobody says so.

Eltham also gives the first accurate news we have of domestic beasts and fowl at Plymouth: "six goats, about fifty hogs and pigs, also divers hens." He considered New England a very good place for a plantation—"a better country was never seen nor heard of for here are a multitude of God's blessings," but he was not very impressed with the Pilgrims as planters: "How is it pos-

sible that those men who never saw fishing in their lives should
raise profit by fishing?" And there were too many women and
children. But the Pilgrims were always half-hearted about
fishing, especially after the disastrous fishing voyage and wreck
of their pinnace, the *Little James*. Bradford himself said that
fishing is "a fatal thing to this plantation," though a few months
later he talks wistfully of "the great profit raised by fishing."
However, most of their energies went in getting furs and raising
corn.

There was no halving of rations after this harvest; free enterprise and the sweet and gentle showers had for the first time
made them self-sufficient in basic foods.

The *Anne*, loaded with bales of beaver, oak staves, and cedar
wood, sailed for home on 10 September, with Edward Winslow
as supercargo and Plymouth representative, to put the adventurers more fully into the picture. He took with him the manuscript of *Good News from New England*, to be published the following year, which, while not quite so extravagant in its
descriptions of the new paradise, gave vivid accounts of the
Pilgrims' just dealings with the Indians, including those of Wessagusset.

Hard on the heels of the gay harvest feast, another visitor
came to the neighborhood, to put a damper on any euphoria the
Pilgrims may have had. He was Captain Robert Gorges, son of
Ferdinando, who had arrived in Massachusetts Bay to begin a
plantation and had "pitched upon the place Mr. Weston's people
had forsaken." And further, he had a commission from the council of New England to be governor of the country, which of
course included Plymouth. Bradford would cease to be a governor, although for the time being he would be a member of the
council. Captain Robert came to Plymouth and he and his men
"were kindly entertained for fourteen days." But there was very
unkind entertainment for another visitor, their old friend Weston, who bobbed up unexpectedly in his little boat. Captain
Gorges taxed him with the "ill carriage of his men at Wessagusset." Weston talked his way out of that; he wasn't there and so
on, but he could not talk his way out of another charge that he
had got the backing of Sir Ferdinando to get a license for a

number of heavy cannon to fortify Wessagusset but had in fact taken the guns elsewhere and sold them. Weston tried to ride the high horse with Captain Gorges, who seemed a kindly enough fellow, but the captain lost his temper with him "and vowed he would either curb him or send him home for England." However, Bradford spoke up for him, and Weston set off for Virginia, repaying the Pilgrims with a few malicious cracks. In Virginia, Weston became a member of the House of Burgesses, and later he was a member of the Maryland Assembly, and in neither place is anything known to his discredit. He returned to England in 1642–43 and died in Bristol of the plague.

While his ship refitted at Plymouth, Captain Gorges went back overland to Wessagusset. It seems that the settlers in the new plantation had a disagreeable winter and soon "dispersed themselves, some to England, some to Virginia." As for the captain, he returned to England, "not finding the state of things here to answer his quality and condition"—in other words, New England was no fit place for an English gentleman.

William Bradford, once again governor, with no overlord, decided that for the forthcoming year, 1624, he would take a rest from that office, saying that, if it was an honor, others should have a turn, and if it was a burden, then others should share it. The Pilgrims would not accept his resignation; instead they increased the number of assistant governors to five. If Bradford had offered to resign because he thought that politically the worst was over, and Plymouth was now on a smooth course, he was, for once, too optimistic.

17   On Their Own Feet

At the end of 1623, that is in March, or at the beginning of 1624, Winslow returned to Plymouth in the *Charity* with "a pretty good supply" and the first cattle, three heifers and a bull. He also brought a fine lot of fishing gear, a saltmaker, and a carpenter. The adventurers' plan was that the carpenter would build boats, all hands would fish, the saltmaker would cure the fish, and all concerned would wallow in the great profits. The fishing post was to be on Cape Ann, for which, Cushman said, a patent had been obtained. The carpenter made good boats but the saltmaker knew very little about saltmaking and eventually set fire to the curing sheds at Cape Ann, "and this was the end of that chargeable [expensive] business." The adventurers were extremely ineffective recruiting agents, no doubt because they were usually at loggerheads among themselves not only on economic questions but on religious issues. There was a strong Church of England faction among them, and this faction had persuaded Cushman to accept the Reverend John Lydford to go out to Plymouth and be their pastor. It was probably the same faction that was preventing Pastor John Robinson from joining his flock. Not much is known of Lydford's previous history beyond the fact that he had had a parish in Ireland and that he was a graduate of Magdalen

College, Oxford. There is no contemporary account of Lydford's career in Plymouth other than that in Bradford's journal, and a very unappetizing character it makes of him. "When this man first came ashore he saluted them with that reverence and humility as is seldom to be seen, and indeed made them ashamed he so bowed and cringed unto them." He brought a wife and a swarm of children and in no time at all he was admitted to the Church, confessing that he had been guilty of "disorderly walking," which the Pilgrims understood to mean that he had been a Church of England minister. They were of course joyful at his conversion but it was not long before they saw that he had his own ideas of walking in purity and brotherly love. His brotherly love extended itself more especially to the troublemakers of the town, the "particulars" led by John Oldham, to John Billington, and to other disgruntled settlers. One of these, an Anglican, was worried because his child could not be baptized unless he joined the Separatists, which was against his conscience. Lydford promptly arranged a private service, and baptized the infant with the sign of the cross. This was a rank offense against all the Pilgrims stood for. They had fled to America to avoid such horrors. Bradford and his council took note but no action. In their subtle way they bided their time, and watched their man. The *Charity* was ready to sail, "and it was seen that Lydford was a long time writing and could not forbear to communicate to his intimates such things as made them laugh in their sleeves." The *Charity* cleared the harbor, and some time afterward Bradford put out in the shallop, caught up with the *Charity* over the horizon, and boarded her. William Pierce was the master and a good friend to the Pilgrims and gave every help to Bradford in searching the ship and passengers. There were over twenty letters from Lydford "full of slanders and false accusations" and some of the same kind though more illiterate from Oldham. Some were copied, of others they brought the originals back to Plymouth, put them away, and said nothing. Lydford & Co., when they saw Bradford put back into Plymouth, looked "somewhat blank, but after some weeks when they heard nothing they then were as brisk as ever."

Oldham overdid his briskness by pulling a knife on Standish and refusing to do guard duties in a great burst of foul language.

He was put in irons in the fort, and the Pilgrims, judging the time to be ripe, brought both Oldham and Lydford to trial before the council. The charges against them were read, "but they were stiff and stood resolutely on the denial of most things and required proof." Lydford said that as for the adventurers in England he had no dealings with them. At that point, with a fine sense of dramatic timing Bradford produced the letters and showed them to Lydford, "at which he was struck mute." Not Oldham, though, who threatened them "in very high language" for daring to open his letters, and turning to his supporters called out: "My masters where is your hearts, now show your courage, you have oft complained to me, now is your time, if you will do anything I will stand by you." Bradford says: "Not a man opened his mouth, all were silent." One can suppose that the silence was punctuated by the clinking of the weapons of the two companies of militia that Captain Standish had assembled. The court sentenced them to be expelled from the colony—Oldham at once, though his family were at liberty to stay over the winter; Lydford after six months, and this leniency toward Lydford was "with some eye to his release" if he behaved himself and repented, and repent he did, with a public confession of his sins, and a long professional essay in self-abasement. He knew his audience; they loved that sort of orgy and immediately "they began to conceive good thoughts of him upon his repentance." But after a month or two he made a spectacular backslide with another secret letter to the adventurers, and again Bradford intercepted it. The Lydfords had to go, but before they left Mrs. Lydford came to one of the deacons and told him that her husband was forever meddling with her maids, that he had been forced to leave his parish in Ireland for one adventure with a maid that sounds like a tale from Boccaccio. A young man in his parish thought he loved a young girl but asked Master Lydford's opinion of her "before he suffered his affection to run too far." Master Lydford saw the maid privately several times and finally was able to recommend her highly to her godly swain. They were married but not long after the wedding the young wife's conscience troubled her and she revealed that Master Lydford's check on her suitability had been altogether too thorough or, as

Bradford says, "he satisfied his lust on her." Of course he repented and had to leave Ireland. Lydford was still at Plymouth when Oldham showed up again, in roaring mood, calling them all traitors and rebels. They put him in the jail to cool off and then made him run the gantlet to the boat, every musketeer giving him "a thump on the breech with the butt end of his musket."

Winslow and Captain William Pierce came ashore at this moment, quite unnoticed, because all the Pilgrims were busy with Oldham's send-off. They had brought from England the patent for a fishing post at Cape Ann, that post where the salt-maker burned down the warehouse or salting shed. Lydford, Oldham, and some others took their landing stage over at one point, and Standish had to be restrained from declaring war on them. But that was smoothed over by Pierce and Roger Conant.

Lydford and Oldham had joined the settlement begun by the Reverend John White of Dorchester, who was later to be called the father of the movement to Massachusetts. Cape Ann was his first venture and a failure. Roger Conant was the head of the tiny settlement, and afterward he was to found the town of Salem. Oldham became a successful trader at Salem, made friends with the Pilgrims again, and "seemed to have an honourable respect of them." He was allowed to come and go at Plymouth "at his pleasure." Lydford they would have no more to do with; he preached some years in Salem (then called Naumkeag), until the Puritans came under John Endicott, when he left for Virginia, where he died.

The case against Oldham has few overtones; he was a noisy man of some ability and he did not like the way the Pilgrims ran Plymouth. There was no room for him there anywhere near the top, even if he had been admitted to the Church. The case against Lydford seems perfectly clear; he was an unctuous and treacherous lecher. He may have had a point or two in the long list of charges he made against the Pilgrims, but they had no trouble in refuting such accusations as that the Plymouth Church would have "no others to live here but themselves," and "that if any are not of the Separation they will quickly distaste them." The adventurers put the charge more bluntly: "You are Brownists condemning all other churches and persons but yourselves and those in your way, and you are contentious, cruel and hard-hearted . . . towards such as in all points both civil and religious jump not with you." To which the Pilgrims replied to the effect that some of their best friends were not Separatists. It remained true that they were not ready to extend full religious tolerance, that all the colony, whether Church members or not, had to attend Sunday service, and that they were very careful as to whom they admitted to full membership of their Church. There were furious quarrels over the Pilgrims among the adventurers, who, after the Lydford-Oldham business, fell apart completely. Only a few agreed to carry on the company, and on behalf of these few James Sherley and three others signed a long, loving, and tedious letter (though not as tedious as the letter the breakaway group sent) telling the Pilgrims to behave themselves wisely and "to go on fairly as men whose hope is not in this life," not to disperse any of the goods in the common store for any "private ends" but to add to them by gathering "such commodities as the country yields" and send them over to England to clear their debts, which now amounted to fourteen hundred pounds, "and lastly be you all entreated to walk circumspectly and carry yourselves so uprightly as," et cetera. The letter was penned in Cushman's hand and there is no doubt that he it was who persuaded the few to go on backing the Plymouth plantation. With many expressions of loving-kindness, they had sent over cattle, cloth, shoes, and so on, not for the common stock but to be sold at exorbitant rates for their own private profit.

The *Little James*, that pinnace of ill fortune, which had gone to the bottom once and been raised with the help of the Maine fishermen, was now loaded with dried cod and bales of beaver pelts and sent off to England, towed by the *Charity*. Captain Pierce wanted to put the valuable furs into the big ship, but Winslow insisted that he was under bond to send them into London on the *Little James*. In the English Channel, almost in sight of Plymouth, the tow had to be cut in heavy weather; a swift-sailing Barbary pirate pounced on the *Little James* and took her down into Salé, "where the master and men were made slaves and many of the beaver skins were sold for four pence apiece." Salé was on the Barbary coast of what was until recently French

Morocco (and is the Sallee where American troops landed in November 1942 to take part in the North African campaign of World War II). Tunis, Tripoli, Salé, and Algiers were all pirate nests whose ships preyed on the commerce of Europe almost without check, and the raiders were usually referred to as Turkish pirates or Sallee Rovers, but the ships were manned by enterprising villains of a score of nationalities.

The greatest part of the loss fell, of course, on the adventurers, and Bradford unkindly observes: "Some thought this a Hand of God for their too great exaction of the poor Plantation," but covers up quickly with "but God's judgements are unsearchable." In fact, Thomas Fletcher, who had the greatest interest in the cargo, was ruined by the loss of the *Little James*.

Captain Standish had embarked on the *Charity*, fortunately for the Sallee Rovers, for he would have made an awkward slave, although the Arab dealers had a short way with recalcitrant chattels personal. In London he was to negotiate better prices for the Pilgrims, as well as to try to come to terms with those adventurers who had opted out but still made claims under the old agreement and were fitting out ventures encroaching on the Pilgrims' territory, as in the fishing post they had tried to establish at Cape Ann. But Standish could do little business; the plague had been raging in Denmark and at Leyden and had come to London in April. By the end of 1625 it was to claim thirty-five thousand in London alone, and Standish had a tough time raising a loan to purchase goods and to help with his expenses. He got £150, for which he had to pay interest at the fantastic rate of 50 per cent (a usual and legal rate was 8 per cent).

Back at Plimouth, New England, there had been a very good harvest, so good that they loaded some corn into one of the shallops the new carpenter had made and sent her up to the Kennebec river to trade. She brought back seven hundred pounds' worth of fur, mainly beaver, in exchange for "little else but corn."

In April 1626 they heard that Standish had arrived on the coast of Maine, and they sent a shallop to fetch him home. "Welcome he was but the news he brought was sad." James I was dead and the new king, Charles I, it was feared, would drift to popery. The faithful deacon, Cushman, their friend with the adventurers, was dead of the plague. Saddest news of all and a fearful blow to the Pilgrims, John Robinson was dead. They had never until now given up their dearest hope that one day he would come to live among them and be their pastor. They had never considered any other, though without a pastor they had been deprived of the Sacraments. His letters, full of wise counsel and sympathetic understanding of all their problems, had both chided and guided them. A letter from Roger Whyte of Leyden told of his last days: "He fell sick the 22nd February and departed this life 1st March. He had a continual inward ague but free from infection so that all his friends came freely to him. And if either prayers, tears, or means could have saved his life he had not gone hence." On March 4th he was buried in the Pieterskerk, the great cathedral that loomed over the pleasant Green Gate meetinghouse in Bell Alley so well known to the Old Comers in Plymouth. Bradford gave words to the grief of the Pilgrims: "Though they had esteemed him highly whilst he lived and laboured amongst them, yet more after his death when they came to feel the want of his help and saw, by woeful experience, what a treasure they had lost to the grief of their hearts and wounding of their souls."

John Robinson had been under fifty years of age when he died. Within four years, his Leyden congregation dissolved; some part reached America in October 1630, some joined Ainsworth's old church in Amsterdam. Others died of the plague. At Plymouth, the shock of their pastor's death wearing away a little, "they gathered up their spirits and the Lord so helped them, Whose work they had in hand, as now when they were lowest they began to rise again."

The new carpenter who had arrived at the same time as Lydford had already built them a couple of boats and he now undertook some surgery on one of the shallops, cutting it in two, inserting a mid section of five or six feet and so provided them with a roomy, seagoing trading vessel.

One or two small settlements had been established to the north of them by adventurers anxious for the profits of the fur trade and, greatly to the disgust of the Pilgrims, they were giving the

Indians far too big a price for the furs, up to twice as much, but still the Pilgrims did a good and profitable trade. They also managed to buy about two hundred pounds' worth of trading goods from a plantation at Monhegan which "was to break up," a share in the cargo of a French ship cast away at Sacadahock, and a "parcel of goats." These, they paid for with some of the beaver they had gotten in over the winter. They still had enough furs left to pay off Standish's debt, and these they sent to England with Isaac Allerton, who was to be their sole representative with the adventurers. Not much is known about Allerton's earlier life, and nothing at all that would suggest that he was the best man to conduct complicated business affairs except a certain acquisitiveness. (By 1633 he had one of the best houses in Plymouth and paid a higher rate of tax than any other member of the community, almost double that of Bradford and some other leading Pilgrims.) In London he was authorized to borrow a maximum of one hundred pounds to lay out for goods to be transshipped to Plymouth. He borrowed two hundred pounds at 30 per cent, which rate, Bradford remarks with an air of strained tolerance, was less than the 45 per cent they had paid on last year's imported goods. Whether it was due to Allerton's enterprise or to the despair the adventurers felt of ever making a profit out of Plymouth, Allerton brought back with him a new agreement with the adventurers. Up to this time the adventurers had invested a total of seven thousand pounds in the colony, but they agreed to give up all their rights and to make no further claims on Plymouth in return for a sum of eighteen hundred pounds to be paid in nine annual installments. Says Bradford: "This agreement was very well liked of and approved by all the plantation; though they knew not well how to raise the payment, and discharge their other engagements, and supply the wants of the plantation seeing they were forced for their necessities to take up money or goods at so high interest."

Subject to the mortgage of eighteen hundred pounds, the Pilgrims now owned all Plymouth, its houses and gardens, fields, stores, livestock, boats, et cetera, and the good will of the fur trade. But they were not incorporated, nor were they a co-operative, and the question was, how should the assets be apportioned and should those who were not Saints be included in the share-out? They decided to include everybody (except servants), because "first they considered that they had need of men and strength both for defence and carrying on of business. Secondly, most of them had borne their parts in former miseries and wants with them," and then he adds, perhaps to explain his generosity, "but chiefly they saw not how peace would be preserved without so doing."

Trade would be managed as before to help pay off the mortgage. All single free men had a single share and every father of a family had his own share, one for his wife and one for each child. Each shareholder was called a "Purchaser." Each kept his own house and garden, with some give and take for a better or a poorer plot, the livestock was apportioned out, and the open fields were allocated by lot in thirty-acre parcels. The shares carried an obligation (to be paid in corn) to make up any part of the debt "the profits of the trade would not reach to." Those who had signed the agreement with the adventurers and were personally responsible for repayment of the installments were given a monopoly of the trade; this was only fair. Strictly, the monopoly was in the hands of Bradford, Allerton, and Standish, but they could and did elect others to be "undertakers" with them. They chose William Brewster, Edward Winslow, John Alden, John Howland, and Thomas Prence.

The Pilgrims had already made a successful voyage to the Kennebec River, and they now established a trading post there, on the present site of Augusta, Maine, with John Howland in charge. Bradford says that when Allerton went back to England with the agreement he had orders to procure a patent from the council of New England for the Kennebec post, but no application seems to have been made at that time. They did get a patent later for a strip fifteen miles wide on either bank of the Kennebec, and there they built a strong trading station. Bradford was trying to ward off other traders, particularly groups from the fishing vessels on the coast. He claims that the Pilgrims were the first discoverers of this rich fur-trading area. They also established a post at Aptucxet (now Bourne),[15] on the narrow land of the arm of Cape Cod where Scusset Creek running into Cape Cod

Bay and the Manomet River flowing into Buzzards Bay nearly
turn Cape Cod into an island (which is what the modern Cape
Cod Canal in fact does). Through this post, solidly built of oak
timbers, they could deal with the country south of the Cape,
avoiding the dangerous Atlantic shore and the tedious trail
through Narragansett territory. And not far away as distances go
in those parts were their main competitors, the Dutch settlers of
New Netherland. (In November 1626 the Indians had sold the
island of Manhattan to the Dutch for sixty guilders.)

Is his letter book Bradford notes: "This year we had letters
sent to us from the Dutch plantation, of whom we had heard
much by the natives, but never could hear from them nor meet
with them before themselves wrote to us, and after sought us
out." When the charter for the council of New England was issued,
in 1620, the presence of Dutch traders on Hudson's river was ignored, indeed Captain Dermer had warned them off as interlopers. In 1623 Dutch settlers took possession of Manhattan
Island and planted Indian corn. The purchase of Manhattan was
held by them to give them full title. The letter referred to by
Bradford said in effect, we have heard of you at Plymouth, your
country and ours are old allies—let's do business in beaver or
otter or whatever, for ready money; to which Bradford replied
with good wishes and friendship saying that they were bound to
be thankful to the Dutch nation, et cetera, and "in a short time
we may have profitable trade and commerce together. But for
this year we are fully supplied with all necessaries, both for clothing and other things, but hereafter it is like we shall deal with
you if your rates be reasonable. And therefore when you please
to send to us again we desire to know how you will take beaver,
by the pound, and otters by the skin, and how you will deal per
cent. As likewise what other commodities from us may be acceptable to you." Bradford wrote in Dutch and very much to the
Dutch commercial taste, but he added a warning that they, the
Dutch, should not deal with the Indians in Plymouth territory,
that is around Cape Cod and down to the Narragansett River.
He also sent copies of the correspondence to the New England
Council because the Dutch were still regarded as interlopers.
The Dutch governor did likewise to his government, adding that

troops might have to be sent out to protect the New Netherland settlement.

But trade overrode all other, pettier considerations, and a few months later a Dutch ship, the *Nassau*, dropped anchor near Aptucxet and Isaak de Rasieres came ashore "with a noise of trumpets" but did not much care for the idea of a twenty-mile walk to Plymouth "whereof I fear my feet will fail me." A shallop was sent and the Dutch opper koopman (top trading agent) was welcomed and entertained at Plymouth. He brought with him sugar, linen, and both fine and coarse Holland cloth. "But that which turned most to their profit, in time was an entrance into the trade of Wampumpeag." It means white money and was usually shortened to Wampum,[16] and was currency among some Indian tribes on the coast such as the Narragansetts. It came in two kinds, black and white; the white half the value of the black. The white was made from the stems of periwinkle shell, the black from the purple part of the inside of quahaug shells, and these stems were drilled and polished into little cylinders. Several parallel strings made a "belt." The black was valued at about a penny, but of course this varied with the price of beaver skins in England. It was some time before wampum became currency in Plymouth trading areas; in fact it took two years to get rid of the fifty pounds' worth De Rasieres had unloaded on them. Soon it was much sought after by the Indians of the Wampanoag, the Massachusetts, and other tribes, and they preferred it to any trade goods for their furs. And it very much suited the Pilgrims not to have to carry bushels of corn as money. If the Indians wanted trade goods, they paid wampum or beaver. Pilgrim traders could pay wampum or trade goods or corn if necessary. As the Pilgrims had found another source of wampum and the fishermen traders had no wampum, the Pilgrims for a long time had a corner on the fur trade. Europeans tried to make their own wampum, but it was too expensive to prepare and the Indians could detect the forgeries every time.

Allerton, in 1628, managed to get four of the adventurers to become undertakers, including the London Bridge goldsmith James Sherley, who had already shown himself to be a useful friend. The furs Allerton had brought to England reduced the

plantation's debt by a sixth, and it seemed a good time to
implement the plan to bring to New England the remaining
Leyden congregation. Thirty-five of them came to Salem with
John Endicott's advance party of Puritans and were ferried to
Plymouth by the shallops, and the next year the last organized
group of Leyden people came over in the *Handmaid*. There were
sixty of them, and they seem to have been swept up wholesale
with no attempt to weed out unsuitable persons; they were "of
the weakest and poorest without any of note," indeed so unnote-
worthy were they that no record of any of their names has survived. In later years, one or two individuals came from Leyden,
but the congregation there was now dissolved, and its very
presence was forgotten within a few generations. The expense of
bringing over these two contingents increased the Pilgrims' debt
by five hundred pounds. By 1631 the original eighteen hundred
pounds had swollen to not much less than six thousand pounds.
This included the expense of a new patent, but mostly it was the
price paid by innocence to the wiles of two enterprising businessmen whom the Pilgrims trusted, namely Allerton, one of their
own, and Sherley, their best friend among the adventurers. It is
a tangled tale whose outline may reasonably follow the story of
Thomas Morton.

18 The Revels at Merry Mount and Other Troubles

"About three or four years before this time [say 1625] there came over one Captain Wollaston (a man of pretty parts)" who began a settlement just north of Wessagussett where is now the town of Quincy. He called his plantation Mount Wollaston. This was an encroachment on Pilgrim territory but the Pilgrims let it pass for the time being, suspecting that Sir Ferdinando was involved in it somewhere. One of Wollaston's partners was Thomas Morton, who was a gentleman, a classical scholar of Oxford, something of a versifier himself, and a conventional London rake and hell raiser. Wollaston found New England not suited to a gentleman of his condition and took ship for Virginia with a number of indentured servants, whose indentures he sold to the tobacco planters at a very useful profit, sending back one Rasdell to bring him a further supply from Mount Wollaston. Before Rasdell arrived, Morton gathered the servants around him "and got some strong drink and other junkets and made them a feast." He also made a speech telling them to get rid of a lieutenant set over them, and he, Morton, would free them from their indentures and make them partners with him in the settlement. "This was done" (for the full flavor of subsequent events we need Bradford's language, half scornful, half malicious, but exhibiting that peculiar zest the righteous show in describing the sins of the ungodly): "Morton became Lord of Misrule, and maintained as it were a school of Atheism . . . quaffing and drinking both wine and strong waters in great excess, and as some reported, £10's worth in a morning. They also set up a Maypole, drinking and dancing about it many days together, inviting the Indian women for their consorts, dancing and frisking together (like to many fairies, or furies rather) and worse practices. Morton likewise composed sundry rhymes and verses some tending to lasciviousness and others to the detraction and scandal of some persons, which he affixed to this idle or idol Maypole. They changed also the name of their place and instead of calling it Mount Wollaston they called it Merry Mount as if this jollity would have lasted for ever."

Well now, the pagan revels certainly offended Pilgrim nostrils but there were two other offenses, one of which hit them in the pocket and the other endangered their lives. Morton was raking in large quantities of fur, and he was selling muskets to the Indians and teaching them how to shoot. There was also a fear that he would establish a city of refuge for runaway servants. The Pilgrims wrote to Morton but lost heavily in the exchange of words. Morton was not only a wit but had legal training, "upon which they saw there was no way but to take him by force." Bradford's account of the action is sketchy; he makes it appear that the men of Merry Mount were too drunk to make good the armed resistance they had planned: "They were so steeld with drink as their pieces were too heavy for them; [Morton] himself with a carbine overcharged and almost half filled with powder and shot, had thought to have shot Captain Standish, but he [Standish] stepped up to him and put by his piece and took him." Morton's own account is much different, as for instance when he describes his arrest by Standish, "the first Captain in the land (as he supposed)." He says that Standish rushed him, disarmed him, and threw him to the ground, where the rest of Standish's men fell on him. Morton embroiders the whole affair with some amusing and malicious comments on the Pilgrims and "Captain Shrimp (a quandon drummer)" in particular. He says that the captain threatened him with his pistol, took him to

Plymouth and then marooned him on an island "without gun, powder or shot or dog or so much as a knife to get anything to feed upon or any other clothes to shelter him with, at winter, than a thin suit." After a month he was taken off and sent to England in the charge of John Oldham, but, says Bradford, "nothing was done to him, not so much as a rebuke." No doubt Bradford was stung into his malicious account of Merry Mount by "an infamous and scurrilous book"—for Morton took his revenge in 1637 when he published *New England's Canaan,* a satirical mock history in which the Pilgrims as well as the Puritans are brilliantly ridiculed. Bradford did pretty well too, as far as distortion amounting to libel went. Neither account, one feels, is of much use to a precise historian.

Merry Mount was swept into the Massachusetts grant under Governor John Endicott, but the Pilgrims knew that it was outside their jurisdiction. It was a nuisance to them, and they acted in concert with the rest of the scattered New England settlements, seven of whose leaders subscribed to the cost of the operation.

In 1629 the Pilgrims appointed Ralph Smith to be their pastor, the first pastor they had had in Plymouth. Elder Brewster had labored and taught in the word and doctrine, but Robinson himself would have insisted that they must elect a pastor in his place. Smith was a graduate of Christ's College, Cambridge, who had come over to one of the fishing stations and asked Plymouth to find room for him. They did, and "seeing him to be a grave man and understood he had been a minister," they allowed him to join the Church and then "chose him into the ministry." There does not seem to have been any great enthusiasm for his efforts, but then Robinson was a hard man to follow, and anyway there was always Elder Brewster.

In 1630 the troublesome career of John Billington came to a dramatic end. John Newcomen, a newcomer, made an enemy of Billington, not, one would think, a difficult thing to do. While Billington was out shooting one day, he saw Newcomen, who promptly hid himself behind a tree, "perceiving the intent of this Billington." He was right, for Billington shot at him and hit him in the shoulder. He died soon after, Billington was arrested, tried by a jury of twelve, found guilty "by plain and notorious evidence," and sentenced to death. The Pilgrims were not very sure about their authority, and asked Governor John Winthrop of the Massachusetts Bay Company to advise them. Winthrop, as an attorney, had no doubts at all. The man was guilty: hang him; and Plymouth Colony carried out its first execution, "a matter of great sadness unto them."

A disproportionate number of pages in Bradford's journal are taken up with the enterprises and financial contortions of Isaac Allerton, their agent with the adventurers. Not disproportionate to the amount of damage he did to the Pilgrims, for he increased their debt enormously in continual and unsuccessful attempts to enrich himself, but disproportionate to the pattern of the narrative. The details are tedious and the attention wanders, because Bradford himself cannot make head or tail of what Allerton was up to, and neither can we. Bradford did see that Allerton was shipping goods of his own bundled up with theirs and only he knew which were which, and it usually turned out that the goods that sold well were his and the remainder had been brought over for the Pilgrims. Moreover, any goods lost at sea were, by coincidence, the Pilgrims' loss.

How far Allerton was greedy and how far merely incompetent it is difficult to say. Sometimes he acted in the interests of the colony, and sometimes he carried out an able arrangement for them. Whatever he did cost them money. In 1630 he brought over a new patent for Plymouth, from the council for New England, made out to William Bradford as trustee for the colony. It granted to Plymouth all of New England southeast of a line from the southern shore of Boston Bay to the point of Narragansett Bay and extended the area of the grant on the Kennebec (in the actual patent a river was a river, any lesser stream was a Rivolett or Rundlett). This was splendid news—but in fact the Great Seal was not attached, and it was therefore not a royal charter, which fact at the end of the colony's life proved a dire misfortune. With a royal charter, Plymouth would have been the fourteenth founding state. Instead, she was swallowed by Massachusetts.

When Allerton arrived with his invalid charter, he brought

along as his scribe or secretary Thomas Morton of Merry Mount, which Bradford thought insensitive and made Allerton "pack him away."

Also in 1630, Allerton got a patent for land on the Penobscot River without consulting Plymouth but hoping they would see the sense of becoming partners with him. Since a trading post at Penobscot would damage their trade at Kennebec, they thought it best to play in with Allerton but try to take control if they could. But Allerton and Sherley had put the enterprise in charge of a "profane young man," Edward Ashley, and the best the Pilgrims could do was to stock the post with trade goods and infiltrate a trusted man as his assistant. They chose a "discreet Saint," young Thomas Willet[17] (who later on became the first mayor of New York). Ashley did very well as a trader, but their man on the spot reported that Ashley had been "trading powder and shot with the Indians" and had been indulging in "uncleanness" with the Indian women. The Pilgrims moved in, arrested him, and packed him off to England.

Allerton soon after began chartering ships on the basis of any gains are mine, any losses are yours, and finally they got rid of him as their agent following an incredible series of financial disasters. He left Plymouth in 1633, when his second wife, Fear Brewster, died. After that, he was heard of in many places from Marblehead to Manhattan speculating in goods, ships, and so on, making money, losing it, and leaving a trail of debts, but usually with someone's money in hand. He died when he was seventy-three, insolvent.

The Pilgrims were no more fortunate with Sherley in the long run, in spite of his genuine "love and friendship." A final settlement was reached in 1641, when seven of the Plymouth undertakers took over all the assets and all the liabilities of the colony "made or pretended, whether just or unjust from the world's beginning to the present." To get clear, Bradford, Standish, and Alden had each to sell large parcels of land, while Thomas Prence and Winslow had to part with their houses.

The whole situation in New England had changed long before then, and the roots of the changes were in England in and among the growing desperation of the Puritans under Charles I. Charles had married a French Catholic wife but he appeared to be loyal to the Anglican settlement—too loyal for the consciences of the Puritan ministers and lecturers, who soon found reasons to fear for the progress of their own brand of Protestantism. A declaration was made by the king, which is still printed in the Prayer Book, forbidding any controversy over the articles of faith on pain of punishment by the courts, but the great blow was the promotion of William Laud to the see of Canterbury. Laud had many virtues: he was industrious, unselfish, and a fine administrator, but his ambition was to elevate the Church of England into a branch, a reformed branch, of the Universal Catholic Church, neither Roman nor Calvinist. One of his first moves was to withdraw toleration from the Huguenot refugees. They must conform to the Anglican ritual, he proclaimed, and this ritual, he made clear, must include practices and ceremonies that all Puritans found abominable: bowing to the altar, removal of the Communion table to its old position in the chancel (which implied a recognition of the Real Presence in the Lord's Supper), and other observances closer to the Roman than the Reformation model. Persons who denounced or did not comply with the change were fined, imprisoned, and deprived. The Commons complained to the king that Laud was destroying the Protestant character of the Church of England, but the crown backed Laud, and it is strange to find strict Puritans trying to defend the Church of England rituals which they were devoted to erode from within. Laud's object was to destroy Puritanism, and in this he was attacking a form of worship that nearly all the merchants, tradesmen, small gentry, and a large proportion of the ordinary people had accepted as the true path to salvation. The Puritan saw to his horror that the whore of Babylon was again stalking the land, or in less flamboyant terms, Charles defeated Parliament in 1629, which the Puritans saw as the victory of Arminianism and popery. It was time to revolt or go, and the time for revolt was not yet ripe. Some fled to Holland, for there was no refuge in Germany, where Lutherans and Calvinists were under the heel of the Catholic house of Austria. Even in France the Huguenots were held down by a Catholic cardinal, but others began to consider the New World, where the right worship of God could be established, and the handy organization for such a flight was the council for New England.

The council for New England had received a royal charter for the whole of New England in 1620, but they made no real effort to send out colonists, though they were willing to grant patents to settlers for specific areas. The 1623 patent to the Reverend John White and the Dorchester Adventurers was one such patent. By 1629, only a few of those settlers were still hanging on in Salem. In 1628, the council granted a patent to a group of Puritan merchants, mostly from Boston, Lincolnshire, to settle the area from three miles south of the Charles River to three miles north of the Merrimack, and this area included Salem. Captain John Endicott (another Standish in his way, with the same training) sailed to Salem in the *Abigail* with instructions to take over the territory and hold it against any intruders. Particularly, he was to watch out for our old and ambitious friend Oldham. In March 1629, the New England Company being, unlike the Pilgrims, good businessmen, checked that their patent was valid, and to make sure obtained a royal charter confirming the grant and a new title: The Governor and Company of the Massachusetts Bay in New England. How they worked this tricky business just a week before Charles dissolved his last Parliament nobody knows, but, then, that is how businessmen with a political sense work.

And now enter John Winthrop, born 1588 in Groton Manor, Bury St. Edmunds, Suffolk, who was to impinge on the Pilgrims on a great number of occasions. Winthrop was an attorney and a Puritan who fully believed that the judgment of God would shortly descend on England for its perversion, corruption, Arminianism, filthy Roman practices, and so on and began to think of New England: "Who knows, but that God hath provided this place to be a refuge for many whom He means to save out of the general destruction," which may be considered a more positive approach than that of the Pilgrims in Leyden in 1620. Some of the chief Puritans did not approve of such important men as Winthrop leaving the country: "The church and commonwealth here at home hath more need of your best ability in these dangerous times than any remote plantation." The importance of

Winthrop was to the Puritan cause; he held no great position in the land, he was not even in Parliament, indeed the king had dismissed him from his post as attorney to Parliament in the drafting of bills. But his friends in the Bay Company and certain ministers persuaded him that the New World needed him more than the Old. Whether it was Winthrop's idea or not, the company proposed to move its meeting place, what we would now regard as its registered office, out of range of the king and his agents, to New England itself, where it would be a self-governing commonwealth. After a good ideal of discussion, the general court of the company (read board of management) elected John Winthrop as governor, which put him in charge of the whole operation, from chartering ships to the selection of settlers. There was no lack of applicants both godly, and non-Puritans, and no lack of servants, because there was a severe depression in the cloth trade as a result of the Thirty Years' War. The desirable settler was first of all Puritan, secondly moneyed, thirdly useful, and the useful category, carpenters, surgeons, sawyers, coopers, and so on, had to be adequate in numbers. It was altogether a better-organized expedition than that of the Pilgrims. Four hundred men, women, and children, mostly from London and East Anglia, set sail in the *Arabella* and three other ships and made Salem Harbor on June 12, 1630. Six hundred more settlers were on the way from England, including a contingent from the West Country. From Salem, Winthrop explored Boston Bay, made Salem Harbor on June 12, 1630. Six hundred more settlers around the rich lands of the bay. Soon Winthrop and the Charlestown contingent, or most of them, moved to the peninsula of Boston, where good spring water was to be had at the head of a cove.

In spite of their planning they had a hard, hungry winter, in which two hundred died. Many returned home in the spring. But they learned to live with New England and indeed began to do so in a grander manner than the Pilgrims. In the first spring, Winthrop set his servants to cultivate six hundred acres of very good land and put them to building him a stone house. They never had another winter as bad as the first.

The most striking difference between the Pilgrims' settlement

and the Puritans' is the massive scale of the latter.[18] During the
twelve years from 1630 to 1642, upward of fourteen thousand
settlers came to New England under the auspices of the Massachusetts Bay Company. (The figure has been put at twenty
thousand by Sir George Clark.) The settlers were not all Puritans, but every single one of them had to conform to the will of
God as interpreted by Governor Winthrop, his deputy governor,
and eighteen assistants. "When God gives a special commission,"
said Winthrop, "he looks to have it observed in every Article."
Everyone, Puritan or not, was required to attend church, and it
was the duty of everyone to observe and if necessary to censure
everyone else's morals. There were many Separatists among the
immigrants, indeed the instinct to separate from the Church of
England was widespread among these righteous people, who saw
into what foul errors the Church of England had been led.
Winthrop saw Separatism as wrong thinking in itself and as a
grave political danger. It was wrong because it was too exclusive
and a failure of charity, it was dangerous because if Separatism
became dominant, the bishops might get the king to revoke the
Massachusetts Bay Charter. But bishops they could not and
would not have, and the tendency was to organize into two disciplines, the Presbyterian and the Congregationalist. The Presbyterians favored groups of churches formed into presbyteries, with
the presbyteries forming synods, each in its turn exercising control over the lesser organization. The Congregationalists held
that each church, each congregation, was sufficient to itself. This
was the Pilgrims' form of Calvinism, though the Massachusetts
Puritans did not necessarily borrow it from them. There was a
Congregational church in London. The Presbyterians favored the
admission of all who were not obviously unfit by reason of sinful
conduct (a very wide field); the Congregationalists confined
their membership to God's elect, who had to prove by rigorous
examination that God had chosen them for salvation. The Presbyterians could have been considered as Separatists, but the
Congregationalists were indistinguishable from them.

There were, of course, innumerable minor deviations in doctrine gotten from fresh interpretation of Bible texts, and plenty
of backsliders, but nearly all the Massachusetts settlers were in-

tent on founding a kingdom of God on earth, and woe betide those backsliders if they did not repent. The way to repentance was through endless and exhausting reasoning. There were other techniques to deal with the recalcitrant. This theocracy was also a limited democracy. The Bay Company's charter became a constitution for the government of the colony, but a large number of the settlers were admitted to vote as freemen, without the English forty-shilling property qualification. But they had to be Church members. Winthrop and his assistants could have reserved the government to themselves and friends. The pseudo-democratic system served the same end and looked better and was easy to defend.

The bogy of Separatism rose up before the bay government in the attractive personality of Roger Williams, who arrived in Boston after that terrible first winter. He was young, fresh from Cambridge, and had been a private chaplain in Essex. The Boston Church invited Williams to officiate during the absence of the elected minister, but Williams was a pure Separatist and he wanted the Church members to make a public declaration of their repentance for taking Communion "with the churches of England while they lived there" before he would agree to minister. Winthrop immediately stepped in and engaged Williams in debate on this matter, but he was not prepared to debate Williams' next proposition, that civil magistrates had no authority in religious matters and could not even order people to keep the Sabbath. He left the impure Church of Boston and went to Salem, where he charmed the tough John Endicott. Williams was a Saint and so sweet in manner that he attracted even those who found him disruptive. Salem offered him the post of minister, but Winthrop interfered; the views of Williams were too dangerous, which brought Williams to Plymouth. Here he "laboured at the hoe and the oar and lived on small means." He shared the ministry with Smith "and his teaching well approved." But after a year or two, "he this year fell into some strange opinions and from opinion to practice which caused some controversy between the Church and him, and in the end some discontent on his part, by occasion whereof he left them somewhat abruptly." Brewster was willing to let him go, because he thought Williams was inclining to the Anabaptists, of whom the Pilgrims had seen quite enough in Amsterdam. He also questioned whether they had any right to the land on which they were settled, and he did not think that the king had any right to grant patents. The land belonged to the Indians. He further likened His Majesty to certain beasts in the Book of Revelations. But Williams always kept some affection and respect for the Pilgrims and in after years did them good service in their relations with the Indians. When he left Plymouth he got into continual hot water with the authorities in Massachusetts, although for a time Salem took him on again as minister. Finally the general court proposed to ship him back to England as a fascinating nuisance, but in a letter written thirty-five years later he says: "That ever honoured Governor Mr. Winthrop privately wrote to me to steer my course to Narragansett Bay and Indians, for many high and heavenly and public ends. . . . I took his prudent notion as a hint and vow from God and waiving other thoughts and motions I steered my course from Salem (though in winter snow which I feel yet) unto these parts." But he was on Plymouth territory, and Winslow, who always remained his friend, "lovingly advised" him to move across the water. He went with five faithful disciples across Narragansett Bay, and there the great and feared chief of the Narragansett gave him land and he founded the town of Providence and the first Baptist church in America. He had always held that liberty of conscience admitted no restraint by any authority, and in Providence established complete religious toleration and almost complete civil liberty. Canonicus, the sachem or chief, loved him as a brother, and Roger Williams, without turning native, became a profound admirer of the Indians and a student of their language. There have been far too few Roger Williamses in the history of America, indeed in the history of the world.

The Pilgrims were to have a great deal of trouble with ministers not only at Plymouth but in the new towns that were soon to be founded, for as Massachusetts grew, so Plymouth entered a period of great prosperity. The new towns of the Bay Colony wanted all the surplus food that Plymouth could produce, both corn and meat. Corn went to eight shillings a bushel, calves ten pounds a head, and beef cattle up to twenty-eight pounds. They had not the slightest reluctance in accepting or demanding high prices. Business was very much business with both Puritan and Pilgrim, and there was a proper respect for the laws of supply and demand. Moreover, the Puritans were on the whole wealthier than the Pilgrims, and the Pilgrims were reaping the just reward of their bitter struggle for survival. And a further point was that those Puritans would not have come to New England except "that with their miseries they opened a way to these new lands, and, after these storms with what ease other men came to inhabit in them, in respect of [in contrast to] the calamities these men suffered so as they seem to go to a bride feast where all things are provided for them."

Apart from Massachusetts and Plymouth, the only other English colony on the coast of North America in 1630 was Virginia, five hundred miles south, with the Dutch at Manhattan halfway. Virginia had been a crown colony since 1624, with the first American legislature, created in 1619. Also in 1619, Virginia imported the first Negro slaves, who were bought from a Dutch trader. Both Massachusetts and Virginia were for the time being self-contained, but Plymouth, until she turned to livestock and large-scale corn farming, depended for her income on fur, and to get furs had to reach out among the Indians and establish trading posts. Her post at Penobscot, ably run by Thomas Willet, very much annoyed the French, who claimed that Penobscot was French Canadian territory. One day while Willet was down at Plymouth getting fresh supplies, a small French ship put into the harbor. There were only four servants at the post, and by a simple trick the French secured their muskets and at gun point ransacked the store of everything it contained, to the value in beaver alone of some five hundred pounds.

Another post had been established at Sowans, Rhode Island, Massasoit's home ground. Friendly Indians gave them a warning that the Narragansetts were plotting to attack the post. The garrison was four men with four muskets and very little powder, but Captain Standish was in charge. Knowing that Plymouth was short of gunpowder, he sent to Boston for a supply. He got thirty pounds from Governor Winthrop, but Governor Winthrop was severely censured by his council, to whom the Separatist was not much less of an enemy than the Indian. The attack did not materialize, but the Pilgrims noted and resented the unfriendly attitude of the Puritan council.

From Sowans the Pilgrims had explored the fertile country around the Connecticut River, and they proposed to the Puritans that they should jointly develop the area for furs. The Puritans refused to play, fearing that there would be trouble with the powerful Pequot tribe, whose numbers were anything from thirty-five hundred to forty-five hundred and who were already hostile to the encroaching English. Connecticut, said the Puritans, was of no interest to them.

The Pilgrims, acting alone, set about getting timber to build a station, but on their way upriver they found that the Dutch had jumped the claim and met the Pilgrims with two cannons trained on their boat from a fort. Lieutenant Holmes, assistant to Standish, told the Dutch he had orders to go upstream and upstream he was going; "the Dutch threatened them hard but they shot not," and the trading post of the Pilgrims was established upstream, the land for it being first purchased from the Indians. The Dutch then played "the gallant Duke of York," marching seventy men up to the trading post "but seeing them strengthened" marching them back again. The Pilgrims had in fact stolen the fur trade from the Dutch by planting their post higher up the river. In the spring of 1634 a trader named Hocking tried to do the same to them on the Kennebec River; he "would needs go up the river and intercept the trade that should come down to them." John Howland and John Alden tried to reason with Hocking and when that failed sent two men in a canoe to cut the cables of his ship. Hocking, seeing them handling his cable, snatched up a gun and killed one of the two men, whereat his fellow shot and killed Hocking. Governor Winthrop immediately took up the cause of justice and arrested John Alden when he put in at Boston. Certainly there was a murder charge in the affair, but Winthrop's main concern was that unpunished crimes might give an excuse for the king to send over a governor and so upset all the carefully stacked Puritan applecarts. Plymouth sent Standish to demand Alden's release. It was refused, and now Plymouth got extremely angry at the Boston assumption of jurisdiction over Plymouth. However, when Winthrop proposed that the case should come before a court empaneling judges from both plantations, Plymouth agreed. The court found that Hocking was the guilty party, and he being dead, that was that, but in fact that was not that, because Hocking was an employee of Lord Say and Sele, who began to stir himself in the matter. Winslow was sent to England to explain and smooth all down, and he was also to point out to the Commission for Plantations that the Pilgrims had been most loyal subjects of the king in resisting both French and Dutch intrusions. But then up bobbed Sir Ferdinando Gorges with Master Morton of Merry Mount in tow, and Morton brought forward awkward questions about the Pilgrims' patent and the conduct of their Church, which in turn brought Archbishop Laud on the scene to ask a few questions. Had he as a layman taught in the church at Plymouth as Master Morton alleged? Well, yes, said Winslow; to edify the brethren, and he had as a magistrate performed the marriage ceremony, which was a civil affair and "nowhere in the Word of God was it tied to the ministry." Take him away, said Laud, and for seventeen weeks Winslow lay in jail. He got free at last, and Laud especially became diverted by events that were to lead to his own imprisonment by the Puritans and his execution.

In America the Pilgrims were running into other troubles. The French made another attack on the Penobscot trading post and this time not only looted the place but sent Willet and his men back to Plymouth. The Pilgrims hired a ship to overawe the French with its guns, but the attempt ended in farce, the ship firing off all its powder out of range, and the post remained in French hands. The next bother was at their post in Connecticut. Their old friendly pest John Oldham had moved down there from Puritan territory with a party and had bought some land from the Indians immediately outside their post. The Massachusetts Bay people were asked to tell them to move somewhere else. They got no help whatsoever from the bay Puritans, and rather than use force, "they had had enough of that," they worked out a kind of compromise where John Oldham & Co. paid them some compensation and stayed put. Within two years nearly all the West Country congregation who had founded

Dorchester in Massachusetts moved down through the forest trails driving their cattle before them, to found Windsor, Connecticut. That year, Winthrop appealed to Plymouth to help him in a war against the Pequot Indians in Connecticut, that place they had blandly told the Pilgrims was of no interest to them. Nine men working in the fields had been killed by the Pequot. Captain John Endicott had been sent by the Bay Company to demand the surrender of the murderers and a large compensation, and as the Pequot gave him no satisfaction at all he attacked them, killed a large number, and burned whatever goods and chattels of theirs he could find. He then returned, leaving the settlers to face the Indians' revenge. An Indian war was imminent, but the Pilgrims were, naturally enough, not keen to come to the assistance of the Puritans, who had shown themselves very unwilling to help them at Penobscot and on the Kennebec, but, after a good deal of acrid argument they offered to send fifty men under Lieutenant Holmes. They were not needed. A combined force from the Bay and from Connecticut, together with some of the Narragansett Indians, closed in on the Pequot fort or encampment, "approached the same with great silence and surrounded it with both English and Indians, that they might not break out." A large assault party moved in firing into the huts, and very soon the encampment was ablaze. "Those that escaped the fire were slain with the sword, some hewed to pieces, others run through with rapiers, and very few escaped. It was conceived that thus they destroyed about 400 at this time." Another, and perhaps the last large group of the once proud Pequot, eighty men and two hundred women and children, were trapped in a swamp, and Winthrop's report says not twenty escaped, presumably of the men, for he continues: "The prisoners were divided some to those of the river, some to us. Of those we sent the male children to Bermuda [as slaves] and the women and maid children are disposed about in the towns [slaves or servants]. There have now been slain and taken in all about 700." Bradford's comment: "The victory seemed a sweet sacrifice and they gave the praise thereof to God." The Pequots never recovered; the remnants of their tribe took refuge in other tribes who adopted them. The Pequot war was a trailer for that great American epic "The End of the Red Man."

19   No Holding Them Together

With a history of the Pilgrims there is the problem of setting a
term, of coming to an end, because there is no end; American
history continues, Plymouth exists now, and there are, if we accept all the claims, millions of Pilgrim descendants. We can make
an arbitrary end with the last of the *Mayflower* passengers, Mary
Cushman, *née* Allerton, who died in 1699 aged eighty-three,
though Peregrine White, the first child born in New England and
on the *Mayflower*, lived to the same age. After 1691 there was no
Plymouth Colony: it had been absorbed by Massachusetts, and
long before that the old colony had declined, the population was
small and scattered, and no natural resources had been discovered other than those the Pilgrims knew. But since we have
followed William Bradford so closely it seems natural to stay
with him and make an end in 1657. There were stirring events
after his death, notably the Indian, or King Philip's, War,[19]
which involved every colony from Connecticut to Maine, but the
story is mainly one of new men in new towns, and the center of
interest has shifted to Cape Cod, though a strong, indeed relent-
lessly interfering government is still in Plymouth.

During the 1620s the Pilgrims kept to their base at Plymouth.
Trading posts were established wherever there was profit to be

made, but these needed only a few men to man them, and no settlements were made. By 1632, the high prices corn and cattle
were fetching among the new, Puritan settlers in Massachusetts
created a demand for more land, which meant reaching out
beyond the immediate area of Plymouth, and Bradford acidly
comments on the new prosperity that "it turned to their hurt, and
this accession of strength to their weakness . . . there was no
longer any holding of them together. And no man now thought
he could live, except he had cattle and a great deal of ground to
keep them, all striving to increase their stocks. By which means
they were scattered all over the Bay, quickly, and the town in
which they lived compactly till now, was left very thin and in a
short time almost desolate."

The nearest good land was north across the bay, and there
some of the Old Comers settled, Elder Brewster, Alden, and
Standish among them. Standish may have named the place Duxbury after his (possible) birthplace near Chorley, Lancashire.
The name seems to have been pronounced Ducksborrow, and
even spelt that way; but in part of East Anglia *bury* still sounds
like *burra* in the local tongue. At first the Duxbury people were
expected to worship in Plymouth, but the shallop or boats could
not always put to sea, and in bad weather a ten-mile trudge
across country and back was rough going. So the first break-out
was made, and others followed in rapid succession, each forming
a separate Church, "a body by themselves." Winslow took land
farther north, at what was to be called Marshfield, and named
his manor Careswell, after his old home in Worcestershire. He
lived in Plymouth for the time being and his land was farmed by
his servants. But grants of land much farther afield were being
sought by the Pilgrims, by newcomers, and by refugees or dissidents, or whatever stirred them, from Massachusetts. As Plymouth Colony began systematic land records in 1635, we can
trace the movements of settlers fairly exactly. During the succeeding four years, at least 130 individuals and five groups got
grants of land, and of those groups four were from Massachusetts. Of these four, three settled in Sandwich, Taunton,
and Yarmouth; the fourth went to Scituate, which was in Plym-

outh territory, but had been settled in 1633 by another Church, sister to the Separatists.

William Bradford held all the land in Plymouth Colony as trustee, but he now surrendered his jurisdiction to the freemen of Plymouth, after setting aside three large blocks of virgin land for the purchasers (that is those who had bought out the adventurers in 1627). These tracts of land were to be bought from the Indians before any settlement could be made, but the Purchasers had first choice. Originally, the governor and seven assistants, sitting as the Court of Assistants, had the say as to who should receive grants of land, but the new arrangement transferred control over the undistributed land to the freemen. With one exception, no one received a grant of more than three hundred acres at a time; most grants were much smaller. One of the reserved tracts was at Nauset and ran "from sea to sea"; the second stretched eight miles inland from the shores of Buzzards Bay, and the third eight miles inland from the limits of Narragansett Bay.

Also, in 1636 the government of Plymouth Colony was reorganized. A Book of Laws was drawn up, the first codification of law in the history of the colony, and to the existing general court of the governor and seven assistants were added a secretary, a treasurer, and some minor officers down to but not including an ale taster. Elections were to be held annually, as they always had been, and any man, freeman or not, who had taken the oath of allegiance to the colony and was the head of a family and a settled resident could vote, although only freemen could be elected to office. A freeman was not necessarily a member of the Church. Without being a democracy, Plymouth spread political power among the people much more than did Puritan Massachusetts. Each of the new towns sent two deputies to the general court to make or unmake laws, and on the whole the laws of Plymouth were more liberal than those of England. Only eight offenses attracted the death penalty, against hundreds in England, where a child could be hanged for stealing five shillings. In Plymouth, the only executions ever carried out were for murder and sodomy. No witches were executed in the colony, even when Massachusetts was going through one of those frightful bouts of mass hysteria, hanging and beating up old women and girls, and in a time when most ordinary people believed in the power of witchcraft.

The site for Sandwich, the first cape town, was selected because it was not far from the Aptucxet trading post and wide stretches of salt hay on the marshlands bordering the bay gave excellent fodder for cattle, far more than the settlers could use. The pioneer founders in 1637 were Edmund Freeman and ten others, mostly from Lynn, near Boston. Plymouth granted them land for sixty families, and within a year thirty families had arrived and were wrangling bitterly about who had what land. Down from Plymouth came Standish and Alden and settled matters—we don't know how.

Yarmouth, the next town to be founded, was cut out of the thick forest just in from the center of the lowest point of the bay, and by the time the settlers had gotten rough houses, or "booths," built, the routine disputes broke out. Since the settlers could not agree with their own committee, Standish was sent for and he made a completely new distribution. It worried him not at all that some of the townsmen were still disgruntled.

Barnstable was initially founded in 1639 by the Reverend Joseph Hull, who was more attracted by the salt-hay pastures than the prospect of a new congregation. Since coming to America in 1635, his herd of cattle had always had as much attention as his flock of souls, and when John Lothrop arrived in Barnstable from Scituate with his own congregation, Hull's people drifted to the new, less distracted preacher, and Hull himself removed to Yarmouth. Lothrop had preached at the first Congregational Church ever to be founded: Henry Jacobs' church in London, begun in 1616. When Lothrop left for America, some of the congregation came with him to Scituate and followed him to Barnstable so that the Congregational Church that still flourishes in Barnstable can and does claim a very long, uninterrupted pedigree.

The last of the early towns to be established was Eastham, on the Purchasers' reserved tract at Nauset, but that was not until 1644, when the fortunes of the old colony had sharply declined following the desperate tactics of King Charles I in England.

Just before the Civil War broke out, Charles had checked the emigration of Puritans to Massachusetts by closing the English ports, and at once the market for the Pilgrims' meat and corn collapsed. "All men feared a fall in cattle but it was thought it would be by degrees and not be from the highest pitch to the lowest." A cow selling for twenty pounds fell to five pounds, and a goat from three pounds to eight shillings. The incoming tide of Puritans reversed itself when a number of Puritans returned to England partly to fight the good fight and partly to protect their interests. In 1645, Cromwell and his Puritans won a decisive victory at Naseby, and the more fanatic Puritans were at full liberty to complete the destruction of the interiors of the beautiful churches of England. In the name of their meager concept of God's greatness, they destroyed noble and lovely works created by the human spirit to His glory. True, the New Model Army had set out to maintain the rights of the nation against the king; Cromwell's ambition was not a personal one; he had great and unselfish motives; but the end was a Commonwealth of Saints sustained by the sword and detested by the people of England as a tyranny, no less tyrannical by being exercised in the name of God. There were to be no more cakes and ale, no sports, no theaters, no dancing, no spring, no Christmas, and a bleak, unlovely Sunday devoted to the arid Church of the Puritans, to which even the Presbyterians were hostile. It became increasingly difficult to distinguish sincere Puritans from hypocrites, and self-righteous petty tyrants and their sycophantic spies were everywhere in the land.

In the end, Cromwell himself saw that spiritual purity cannot be imposed by force, and in the further end, the New Model Army itself was at its greatest when it laid down its arms and voluntarily went back to the farms and the counters from which it came and each man won his individual victories by the honesty and integrity of his character.

Over the seas, in Plymouth Colony, at the beginning of the short-lived Puritan triumph the Pilgrims were full of joy. "Full little did I think that the downfall of the Bishops with their courts, canons and ceremonies had been so near when I began these scribbled writings. Do you not now see the fruits of your labours O ye servants of the Lord that have suffered for the truth?"

But they feared that with England engrossed in civil war, one or other predatory European nation might descend on the almost defenseless colonies, and Massachusetts, Plymouth, Connecticut, and New Haven together formed a confederation for mutual defense. Naturally Massachusetts, as the most populous and strongest, became the dominant and rather bossy partner.

In that same year, on 16 April 1643, William Brewster died, a Pilgrim from the "very root" of the Scrooby Separatists, a wise, kindly, unambitious Saint and a scholar whose library showed a much wider range of interests than one would guess at from the thin outline of his life, which is all we have. Aristotle, Bacon, and Machiavelli one could expect alongside a large number of religious books, but what was a book on silkworms doing there or a play on the somewhat juicy life of Messalina. Did he expect to find mulberries in the New World? Was the play an exhibit from the museum of the Ungodly, a solitary item in a chamber of horrors?

Around that time, Morton of the Merry Mount showed up again, "starved out of England." It says a good deal for the charity of the Pilgrims that they allowed him to stay with them over the winter. He repaid them by trying, unsuccessfully, to lure some of the Pilgrims to settle in New Haven, though it is doubtful whether he had any interests there or whether it was just a comforting idea. He left in the spring of 1644 and spent a year in a Boston jail. On his release, he went to Sir Ferdinando's colony in Maine, where he died, "old and crazy" two years later.

By 1644, Plymouth, apart from the diminishing fur trade, was back at mere subsistence fishing and farming, and more and more people left the town, because, Bradford says, "of the straightness and barrenness of the same. . . . The Church began seriously to think whether it were not better jointly to remove to some other place than to be thus weakened and as it were insensibly dissolved." After painful discussion and in the face of a large number who said that if the Church did not move elsewhere they must, it was agreed that a move should be made, and an advance or reconnaissance party was sent to Nauset. Nauset was one of the three tracts reserved to the Purchasers in 1640, fifty miles from Plymouth, where the forearm of the Cape turns north, and as yet there were no settlers there. The advance party found that the tract was not large enough to settle all the Plymouth Pilgrims, and "they began to see their error that they had given away already the best and most commodious places to others." But Nauset had good, fertile soil, and the younger end who wanted to get out of Plymouth insisted on settling there, or "such as were before resolved on removal took advantage of [the] agreement and went on, neither could the rest hinder them, they having made some beginning." The Nauset pioneers had, as a beginning, cleared land and planted corn and beans, and in the spring began building their houses. In two years it was incorporated as a town, and three years later the name was changed to Eastham. (Within two generations, the Pilgrim settlers at Nauset had cut down all the wonderful forest around them, and the fertile soil blew away, exposing arid sand. The generations following did exactly the same almost everywhere on the Cape.)

The wholesale emigration left Plymouth desolate; a large part of the life had been withdrawn from the heart of the Community of Saints. Bradford could not see it as another beginning, only as an end: "And thus was this poor church left, like an ancient mother, grown old and forsaken of her children (though not of their affections) yet in regard of their bodily presence and personal helpfulness. Her ancient members being most of them worn away by death, and these of later time being like children translated into other families, and she like a widow left only to trust in God. Thus she that had made many rich became herself poor."

Bradford ends his journal in 1650, after recording that Edward Winslow had left them and had been absent four years. He never returned, but had a most successful career in England and died in 1655 as Cromwell's chief commissioner on an expedition to the West Indies. He is the only Pilgrim of whom we have a portrait. A year later, 1656, Captain Myles Standish, commander-in-chief and resolute soldier, died and was buried in Duxbury. He ended as a well-to-do retired general in his own manor, with no need of that Standish inheritance he had in his last years claimed as his right. In the narrower sense of the word as then used, only he and Winslow among the Pilgrims were gentlemen.

A little more than six months later, in the spring of 1657, William Bradford died, the most valiant for truth of them all. Surely the trumpets sounded for him on the other side. He had been governor thirty times since 1621, and he, more than anyone, had essayed to be the architect of the Community of Saints that had been the dream of John Robinson. On that score alone he is one of the greatest figures of early America, but he was also the author of one of the masterpieces of American literature, *Of Plimmoth Plantation*. Governor Bradford insisted on his right to govern according to the agreed rules and later to the laws of the colony, though he claimed no right to change or vary those laws. None of his successors inherited his virtues. In his last years, he became alarmed about what he saw as a moral decline; he opposed toleration of other Christian sects, and he sanctioned the relentless persecution of Quakers, but he was only being loyal to that religious code he had embraced as a boy in faraway Austerfield, Babworth, and Scrooby.

The Pilgrims were unlucky in their choice of Plymouth. It had no deep-water harbor, no river highway into the hinterland and interior, and the soil was exhausted. It could never have played an important part in the economic development of New England and America. They were lucky in their leaders: in Robinson, their spiritual father; in Brewster; and in Bradford, who gave strength and harmony to a very ordinary body of decent, hard-working, tenacious, and pious, but not dull English men and women. Perhaps the courage and endurance of the Pilgrims when they stood alone are sufficient justification for the honor now given to their name, but they are also remembered for keeping in being some civilized ideas on which a democracy could be built. By the Mayflower Compact, they formed themselves by voluntary agreement into a "civil body politic," a sufficiently remarkable achievement. They firmly established the rule of law, and in 1636 they drew up what amounted to a bill of rights in a code of law; they instituted civil marriage and land records; they ruled that land should descend to all children of a marriage and not wholly to the eldest son; they separated church and state, and they extended open discussion at their church meetings to their town meetings. All these were seeds that others ripened in their own good time.

Thus out of small beginnings greater things have been produced by His hand that made all things of nothing, and gives being to all things that are; and as one small candle may light a thousand, so the light here kindled hath shone to many, yea in some sort to our whole nation; let the glorious name of Jehovah have all the praise.

Notes

1. Chapter 11: "Advancing the Kingdom of Christ," page 106.

And in a note to *Mourt's Relation* Cushman writes of the Pilgrims' duty to go to the Indians and convert them, but in fact they did very little missionary work; they were too intent on survival and in contact with the Indians they were more intent on winning furs than souls. Later on, certain ministers went among the Indians seeking converts, the most notable being Thomas Mayhew, "King of the Isles," John Cotton the younger (around the 1660s); and of course the best of them, Roger Williams. The Puritans in Massachusetts were more active in missionary work, but neither Plymouth nor the Bay Colony made much impression on the Indians.

The Protestants of New England then left the conversion of the Indians to the efforts of individuals, whereas in New Spain the Spanish crown put almost as much energy into converting the Indians to the true faith as in occupying and developing their lands and their mineral wealth of gold and silver. The rulers of Spain, to quote Professor J. H. Parry, "used their power to send into the mission field men of outstanding ability, experience and zeal; men who—considering the smallness of their numbers and the magnitude of their task—achieved an extraordinary degree of success." These men were nearly all friars of the Dominican and Franciscan orders, with the austere Strict Observants of the Franciscans in the majority. During the sixteenth century the Franciscans had founded about 270 churches in New Spain and by 1536 had converted nearly five million Indians, sometimes baptizing fifteen hundred in a single day. These conversions were made by persuasion and not force in any form, and indeed the friars were often unpopular with the Spanish settlers when they insisted that the Indians should be treated with tolerance and humanity. The friars founded mission schools, where the Indian children could learn Spanish and European crafts and a few missions taught Latin and trained native Catholic priests.

It would seem that part at least of the fantastic success of the friars in gaining the confidence of the Indians was due to the austerity of their own lives. But they also filled a vacuum that they had themselves created by utterly destroying the Indian temples and gods, even the little village altars and deities. They also burned every one of the beautiful Indian manuscripts they could lay their hands on.

In 1571, the Holy Inquisition came to South America and the great age of the missionary friars came to an end. The old missionary pioneer mendicant friars were by then dying off, and the parishes and missions were given to secular priests.

2. Chapter 11: "The French in Florida," page 108.

Florida was one of the key places in a comprehensive plan for the defense of the Spanish West Indies against raiders. Opposite Florida was Havana, the assembly point for the treasure fleet. Laudonnière established a Huguenot settlement in Florida, which the Spanish destroyed and replaced by a strong fort.

In the early-seventeenth century the powerful fleets of the Dutch West India Company, raiding through the Caribbean and always ready to pounce on the treasure convoys, concentrated almost all the naval resources of New Spain in defense.

The colonies of Virginia and Plymouth posed no threat and were ignored; moreover, the Spanish settlers in South America and the islands were nearly all hidalgos and upward, there were no peasants among them and few laborers, and they had no taste for lands with temperatures running below zero in winter. In any case, they already had more land than they could settle.

3. Chapter 11: Origins of the term "Pilgrim," page 117.

Bradford's reference in "they knew they were pilgrims" is to the Epistle of Paul to the Hebrews, Chapter XI, with the marvellous first verse: "Now faith is the substance of things hoped for, the evidence of things not seen." Verse 13 ends "and confessed that they were strangers and pilgrims on the earth," and the succeeding verses have a peculiarly poignant relevance to the Leyden Separatists' condition. The Plymouth Separatists were not called the Pilgrims until the 1790s, when the Reverend Robbins in a sermon on Forefathers' Day quoted the pilgrim reference, reinforced by two (at least) hymns, one of which has the line "Hail Pilgrim Fathers of our Race," and thereafter they were Pilgrims. In 1819 the Pilgrim Society was founded, open to all who wished to honor the Pilgrims. By the 1840s, Pilgrims or Pilgrim Fathers was the usual name for the Saints—which is the name they themselves used for their church members.

4. Chapter 12: Passengers on the *Mayflower*. As listed in the appendix to Bradford's *Of Plimmoth Plantation*. (An asterisk indicates those from whom descent can be traced; those marked with a dagger did not survive the first winter.) Page 124.

The names of those which came over first, in ye year 1620, and were by the blessing of God the first beginers and (in a sort) the foundation of all the Plantations and Colonies in New-England; and their families.

MR JOHN CARVER†; KATHRINE†, his wife; DESIRE MINTER; & 2. man-servants, JOHN HOWLAND°, ROGER WILDER†; WILLIAM LATHAM, a boy; & a maid servant,

& a child yt was put to him, called JASPER MORE†. 8

MR WILLIAM BREWSTER°, MARY°, his wife; with 2. sons, whose names were LOVE° & WRASLING; and a boy was put to him called RICHARD MORE°†; and another of his brothers. The rest of his children were left behind, & came over afterwards 6

Mr EDWARD WINSLOW°; ELIZABETH†, his wife; & 2. men servants, caled GEORG SOWLE° and ELIAS STORY†; also a little girl was put to him, caled ELLEN†, the sister of RICHARD MORE. 5

WILLIAM BRADFORD°, and DOROTHY†, his wife; having but one child, a sone, left behind, who came afterward. 2

Mr ISAAK ALLERTON°, and MARY°†, his wife; with 3. children, BARTHOLOMEW, REMEMBER°, & MARY°; and a servant boy, JOHN HOOKE† 6

Mr SAMUEL FULLER°, and a servant, caled WILLIAM BUTTEN. His wife was behind, & a child, which came afterwards 2

JOHN CRAKSTON†, and his sone, JOHN CRAKSTON. 2

CAPTIN MYLES STANDISH°, and ROSE†, his wife. 2

Mr CHRISTOPHER MARTIN†, and his wife†, and 2. servants, SALAMON PROWER† and JOHN LANGEMORE†. 4

Mr WILLIAM MULLINES°†, and his wife°†, and 2. children, JOSEPH† & PRISCILLA°; and a servant, ROBART CARTER†. 5

Mr WILLIAM WHITE°†, and SUSANA°, his wife, and one sone called RESOLVED°, and one borne a ship-bord, caled PEREGRIENE°; & 2. servants, named WILLIAM HOLBECK† & EDWARD THOMSON†. 6

Mr STEVEN HOPKINS°, and ELIZABETH°, his wife, and 2. children, caled GILES°, and CONSTANTA°, a doughter, both by a former wife; and 2. more by this wife, caled DAMARIS & OCEANUS; the last was borne at sea; and 2. servants, called EDWARD DOTY° and EDWARD LITSTER. 8

Mr RICHARD WARREN°; but his wife and children were lefte behind, and came afterwards. 1

JOHN BILLINTON°, and ELEN°, his wife; and 2. sones, JOHN & FRANCIS° 4

EDWARD TILLIE†, and ANN†, his wife; and 2. children that were their cossens, HENERY SAMSON° and HUMILLITY COPER 4

JOHN TILLIE°†, and his wife°†; and EELIZABETH°, their doughter. 3

FRANCIS COOKE°, and his sone JOHN°. But his wife & other children came afterwards.   2

THOMAS ROGERS°†, and JOSEPH°, his sone. His other children came afterwards.   2

THOMAS TINKER†, and his wife†, and a sone†.   3

JOHN RIGDALE†, and ALICE†, his wife.   2

JAMES CHILTON°†, and his wife°†, and MARY°, their doughter. They had an other doughter, y^t was maried, came afterward.   3

EDWARD FULLER°†, and his wife°†, and SAMUELL°, their sonne.   3

JOHN TURNER†, and 2. sones†. He had a dougter came some years after to Salem, wher she is now living.   3

FRANCIS EATON°, and SARAH°†, his wife, and SAMUELL°, their sone, a young child.   3

MOYSES FLETCHER†, JOHN GOODMAN†, THOMAS WILLIAMS†, DIGERIE PREIST†, EDMOND MARGESON†, PETER BROWNE°, RICHARD BRITTERIGE†, RICHARD CLARKE†, RICHARD GARDENAR, GILBART WINSLOW.   10

JOHN ALDEN° was hired for a cooper, at South-Hampton, wher the ship victuled; and being a hopfull yong man, was much desired, but left to his owne liking to go or stay when he came here; but he stayed, and maryed here.   1

JOHN ALLERTON† and THOMAS ENLISH† were both hired, the later to goe m^r of a shalop here, and ye other was reputed as one of ye company, but was to go back (being a seaman) for the help of others behind. But they both dyed here, before the shipe returned.   2

There were allso other 2. seamen hired to stay a year here in the country, WILLIAM TREVORE, and one ELY. But when their time was out, they both returned.   2

These, bening aboute a hundred sowls, came over in this first ship; and began this worke, which God of his goodness hath hithertoo blesed; let his holy name have ye praise.

5. Chapter 12: Pollock Rip, page 130.

As evidence of how dangerous are the waters of the Atlantic off Cape Cod, from the year 1843 to 1859 about five hundred ships were wrecked off the Cape. In 1903 the U. S. Engineers Office at Newport, Rhode Island, made a map showing 540 more between 1880 and 1903 (quoted from *Cape Cod*, by Henry C. Kittredge). A large proportion of these wrecks were off Monomoy, both to the south of the point and on the shoals near Pollock Rip.

6. Chapter 13: The shallop, page 138.

William A. Baker, who designed *Mayflower II*, also designed the shallop replica, and he settled for a "heavily constructed double-ended boat having one mast with a sprit mainsail and what we normally call a jib. The dimensions as finally worked out are length overall 33 feet 3 inches, breadth 9 feet 2 inches and depth 3 feet 3 inches." He says that sloep in Dutch, slup in Swedish, chaloupe in French, and shallop in English were rather loosely applied at different periods, but that the above is about as near as we are likely to get to the *Mayflower* shallop. (From an article in *The American Neptune*, Vol. XVII, No. 2, 1957, reprinted by Plimoth Plantation Inc.)

7. Chapter 13: Winter on Cape Cod, page 143.

The chart on p. 231 gives the precipitation and range over the years 1882–1960 as noted by the U. S. Weather Bureau at Provincetown. It will be seen that mid-December shows the lowest recorded temperature. It was not quite so cold when the Pilgrims were making their reconnaissance of the bay, for 1620–21 was a relatively mild winter. That is what the experts say, but Bradford makes it clear that temperatures were below 32°.

8. Chapter 13: Plymouth Rock and First Landing, page 146.

The first landing in the New World was made on the beach of what is now Provincetown on November 11 (Old Style—for New, or our, style add ten days). The landing at Plymouth was made on December 11 (O.S.) and the party that "marched into the land" did not include John Alden or any women. By their respective family traditions, both Alden and Mary Chilton are given the honor of being the first to step ashore on Plymouth Rock, but the only evidence that the party used the rock as a landing point came from an ancient ruling elder, and came at second hand from Deacon Spooner. The deacon said that one day in 1741, when he was a boy of six, Ruling Elder Thomas Faunce, then aged ninety-five years, had been brought down to the beach and had told a little group that when he was a boy his father had told him that one of the Pilgrims had told him that the first landing had been made on that rock and the ancient Faunce pointed to a very large boulder. This boulder was one of those deposited during the last ice age and had been transported by the glaciers from somewhere north of Massachusetts. Technically it was a glacial erratic. At one time a wharf was built over the rock, and then, on December 22, 1774, chains were put around the rock and thirty pairs of oxen tried to heave

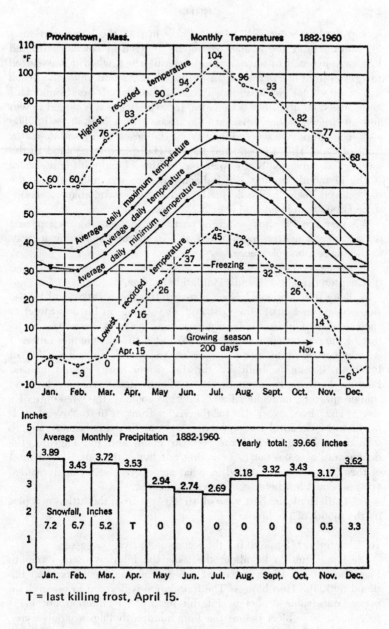

T = last killing frost, April 15.

it onto the higher beach. The rock broke in two, the larger part sinking into the sand, the smaller part being dragged to Town Square and left there exposed to souvenir hunters until 1834, when it was carted to a pit in front of Pilgrim Hall and fenced in. Around 1859, the beach was searched for the abandoned half of the rock. It was found half under the door of an old warehouse, the warehouse was pulled down, and an ornate, rather lopsided, Renaissance arch built over it. The rock seemed to have worked its way up the beach to a position just in front of Coles Hill. In 1880 the Pilgrim Hall piece was joined to the larger piece, and finally, in 1920, on the three hundredth anniversary of the Plymouth landing, the Italianate portico was pulled down, the rock moved below high-tide mark, and a quite unsuitable but handsome Greek temple erected over it.

Whether the Pilgrims' scouting party set foot on the rock or not doesn't greatly matter; myth or not, it is as useful a symbol in its way as the Black Stone of Mecca.

9. Chapter 14: The Plimouth Plantation Replica, page 149.

Walking from Plymouth Rock across to the Town Brook and by the side of the brook up to the grist mill, or walking up Leyden Street to the site of the Old Fort it is very easy to as it were superimpose a picture of the plantation as at, say, 1630, and if the imagination falters it is only necessary to move a mile or two south to the replica of Plimouth Plantation built by the Eel River with Pilgrim houses, Pilgrims in costume, demonstrations of seventeenth-century log and shingle splitting, matchlock firing, Pilgrims cooking, the whole life of a day in 1627 lived every day for the visitor from April to November. It ought to be dreadful but somehow it is not, perhaps because superb scholarship has gone into the reconstruction, and the Pilgrims, the demonstrators, seem not to be acting but living their parts, and most of them are extremely skilled in what anywhere else would be called arts and crafts but here seem necessary chores.

Yet I still think the best view of 1630 is got from the little grass plot by the mouth of the brook.

10. Chapter 14: "Some to fell timber, some to rive," page 149.

We know quite a lot about the tools the Pilgrims used. Plimouth Plantation at Eel River is part of a non-profit-making foundation initiated by Ralph Hornblower. The foundation is devoted to research on every conceivable aspect of Pilgrim history, an ambition not likely to exhaust its subject before the four hundredth Pilgrim anniversary, A.D. 2020. It has the advantages of a most comprehensive reference library both at the plantation and at Pilgrim Hall, and of a staff who respond to any intelligent interest with immediate, courteous—and if provoked, an overwhelming flood of—information. The thirty or more full-time, and up to four times as many part-time and temporary, researchers issue their findings or theses in printed pamphlets, or sometimes typewritten duplicated form, and some of the less recondite information has been used in this book.

Research into the last wills and testaments of the Pilgrims who died before 1640 has revealed fascinating lists of their possessions: furniture, bedding, cooking utensils, tableware, clothing and so on, and tools. Of these the inventories of twenty-three individuals show twenty-six saws, twenty-one augers, twenty axes, sixteen chisels, sixteen planes, fifteen wedges, thirteen hammers, and a range of adzes, files, knives, squares, etc. Some of the saws were cross cut and some whip. Most of the axes were felling axes but some were broad axes for squaring off timber, though in the early days the Pilgrims were sawyers rather than axmen. Since very few of these tools have survived, Plimouth Plantation sent to England to have replicas made from English models or drawings, not for show but for everyday use. The axes, adzes, and sickles were made by a skilled blacksmith, Kenneth Grantham of East Grinstead, Sussex, using the techniques of the sixteenth and seventeenth centuries. Some of these techniques had been used for "time out of mind." An ax, for instance, is made by forging a blank of iron like a double axhead. The two leaves are then folded over a piece of steel on the cutting edge, the three pieces of metal being welded into one axblade. (Steel was scarce and expensive until the late-eighteenth century.) This was also the technique used in forging the ancient swords.

11. Chapter 15: Forefathers' Day and Thanksgiving, page 165.

Before the American Revolution, Forefathers' Day was celebrated around the date of the First Landing in Plymouth. It was dropped for a few years and revived in the 1790s. In 1820, the bicentenary, the Pilgrim Society whipped up rather more and wider interest in the Forefathers. In 1824, Mrs. Hemans wrote her *Pilgrims Ode* and in 1858 Longfellow gave an admiring world *The Courtship of Miles Standish*, both efforts affording splendid publicity to the Pilgrim cause but each owing more to poetic license and imagination than to historical facts. In 1895 Massachusetts established December 21 as a legal holiday to be called Forefathers' Day, and in the following year the very successful Society of Mayflower Descendants was founded. As at 1970, nearly twenty-five thousand descendants had been traced and some sixteen thousand are members of the society. Thanksgiving Day, commemorating that first harvest festival, was a local affair until 1863, when Mrs. Sarah Josepha Hale, a women's magazine editor and authoress of "Mary had a little lamb . . . ," persuaded President Lincoln to make the last Thursday in November a national thanksgiving holiday; rather a late date for a harvest thanksgiving, but by then it was not thanks for the fruits of the earth that were being offered but thanks for God's mercy to the Pilgrims.

12. Chapter 16: Medicine in Plymouth, page 178.

The only doctor among the Pilgrims was Samuel Fuller, the son of a butcher in Norfolk and at one time a silkworker. He may have got his medical knowledge by attending lectures at Leyden University, but he does not seem to have qualified as a doctor there or anywhere else. He appears to have been as able a doctor as most of the qualified men of his time, very few of whom had progressed beyond

> the old Esculapius
> And Deiscorides and eek Rufus
> Old Hippocras, Haly and Galien.

Though he may not have taken the Hippocratic oath he observed it and attended any sick person whether Catholic, Protestant, or pagan, white or Indian. Governor Endicott asked for him to come to Salem when sickness broke out there, and so did Governor Winthrop during the epidemic at Charlestown. Jacobean medicine relied largely on herbs, blending, and powerful purgatives. With the herbs the ancient sympathetic system of "similars" was used; as saffron for jaundice, wormwood for worms, and so on. We know today that many of the herbal extracts were effective but some were superstitious nonsense. The Pilgrims got by on a spare, plain diet, fresh air, and abundant exercise; and for those days they had a high standard of general health and were surprisingly long-lived. Child mortality (that is those the records say "died young") was about 25 per cent. In some parts of the world today it is over 50 per cent. A 21-year-old man could expect to live to sixty-nine (statistically 69.2), a 40-year-old to seventy-six, a 21-year-old woman to only sixty-two years, but after childbearing age the women had a slightly higher life expectancy than the men. In a sample of six hundred deaths in Plymouth, 30.5 per cent of men lived to between seventy and seventy-nine, 22 per cent to eighty-nine, and nearly 6 per cent to over ninety. The two epidemics with high death rates were in the first year and in 1633.

13. Chapter 16: Indians and disease, page 180.

Professor J. H. Parry, in *The Spanish Seaborne Empire*, notes that within a century of the first Spanish settlement of the West Indian Islands the whole native population was extinct. Catholic missionaries blamed ill treatment and overwork of the physically weak primitive Indians, but on the mainland the Indians were strong, healthy, sophisticated, and highly organized, were not much overworked nor ill treated by the Spanish, yet they too suffered a catastrophic decline in numbers. The Indian population of New Spain was estimated at 25 million at the time of the conquest, in about 1520. By 1532 they were down to some 17 million. In areas where the Spanish made no settlements, made no war, nor exacted any forced labor the population also declined sharply. By 1568 the population of New Spain was down to less than 3 million and by 1580 to less than 2 million. At the beginning of the seventeenth century there were fewer than 1¼ million Indians left.

It is usual to blame the white man's diseases for this decline, but Professor Parry adds: "The precise nature of the lethal factors can only be guessed."

14. Chapter 16: That conceit of Plato's, page 181.

In Plato's original conceit parents, wives, children, and property were held in common. He dropped this wholesale communism in favor of only property being held in common, and then like the Pilgrims fell back on private enterprise with a lament that only when the philosopher rules in the city will the ideal state be founded. Neither was the Pilgrims' mutual communism in any degree Marxist. It was nearer that kind of millennialism that Robert Owen tried to establish in New Harmony, Indiana; that experiment also collapsed because the good guys did all the work and the bad guys cashed in, or because human behavior in the mass is extremely patchy in its idealism, and the philosopher has to be a dictator with an efficient police force to establish either millennialism or communism. A community of saints might make it if any who deviated from saintless were eliminated, but that comes to the same thing.

15. Chapter 17: Bourne Trading Post, page 197.

At Aptucxet, or Bourne, the old Pilgrim trading post has been reconstructed and filled with a great assortment of early-colonial relics, all genuine it seems, with the single exception of a very, very doubtful stone engraved with Icelandic rune-staves much too like ogham. But the post is in a delightful situation (the original site), and one can stand and stare down the trail through the forest to the river hoping for Dutchmen with Indian bearers to arrive with trade goods. Nothing seems to have altered for three hundred-odd years.

16. Chapter 17: Wampum, page 199.

Another set of values for wampum is 3 black or 6 white=one penny; one fathom=five shillings. Eventually the Dutch established factories for wampum making and turned it out in such quantities that the market collapsed. The whites stocked up on Dutch wampum but the Indians remained suspicious. Harvard University accepted wampum for tuition but accumulated such a large stock that in 1641 a trading company was required to relieve them of it but not more than £25 at a time. Musket balls were also made legal tender at four a penny "but no man to take more than twelve at a time."

17. Chapter 18: Thomas Willet (page 205) was the son of an English clergyman who came over from Leyden when he was twenty-four. He was posted to the expedition of four ships of the line sent by Charles II to dispossess the Dutch on Hudson River, perhaps because he spoke Dutch, and also because he had lived at New Amsterdam for some years. The British took New Amsterdam, renamed it New York, and Thomas Willet became its first Lord Mayor.

18. Chapter 18: Ships to Massachusetts, page 209.

As a contrast to the meager supplies sent to the Pilgrims, in 1628 the Massachusetts Bay Company sent out to Salem five ships, the *Talbot*, the *George*, the *Four Sisters*, the *Lions Whelp*, and the *Mayflower* (not the Pilgrim *Mayflower*). The *Talbot* had on board:

Salted beef	22 hogsheads
Bread (hard)	12,000
Peas	40 bushels
Oatmeal	20 barrels
Salt fish	450 pounds
Butter	10 firkins
Cheese	1200 pounds
Beer	40 tuns (8,640 gallons)
Brandy	20 gallons
Malaga	20 gallons
Olive Oil	20 gallons

and much else, including pepper, cloves, mace, and cinnamon. Household utensils for each family were listed as "1 Iron Pot, 1 Kettle, 1 Frying Pan, 1 gridiron, 2 Skillets, 1 spit, with wooden platters, dishes, spoons," etc.

19. Chapter 19: King Philip's War (Indian lands), page 216.

Although outside the scope of this book, the Great Indian War is a necessary postscript, for it saw the end of good Indian relations, the virtual end of Massasoit's tribe, the Wampanoags, and very nearly the end of Plymouth Colony. As the settlers took over more and more Indian lands, a conflict was inevitable. The Pilgrims, according to their lights, were just and even fair. No one could acquire land from the Indians except by purchase and only with the consent of the Plymouth court. Indians never owned land as individuals; the whole tribe held certain territory in common, and the chief, or sachem, agreed with his council to sell portions of it for so many hatchets, hoes, knives, yards of cotton cloth, coats, brass kettles, or whatever the Indians coveted, but in Plymouth Colony anyway, no liquor and no firearms, though the Indians did get hold of both one way or another, and no boats or horses. (William Nickerson—a famous name in Cape Cod—bought a thousand acres of land at Chatham in 1656 in exchange for a boat. The Plymouth court fined him so heavily that there was not enough money in the whole colony to pay the fine.) Maybe good land was worth a pound an acre to the colonist, and he paid about one shilling an acre in goods; to that extent the Indian was cheated, but the point is moot and the Indian seldom thought that he had had the worst of the bargain. Only gradually did he realize that he was losing much more than the use of his hunting grounds, and he did not understand the white man's principles of ownership and exclusive use of land. The Indian would sow a patch of corn and the crop was his but not the land. Next year he would sow a patch somewhere else. There was plenty of land, even after the settlers began reaching out. Soon, however, the Indian began to feel hemmed in.

There was no real trouble while Massasoit was alive, but he died in 1661, three years after Bradford's death. Massasoit was succeeded by his eldest son, who died the following year, and his brother Philip became chief of the Wampanoags. Philip had long brooded over the encroachment of the settlers, he resented their attitude of superiority, and he resentd attempts to Christianize his people. Although the Pilgrims had never pursued their early ambition to spread the Word among the savages with anything approaching enthusiasm, by the

1660s missionary zealots were abroad in the colony; such people as John Cotton devoting most of their time to preaching to the Indians. To Philip, a praying Indian was a renegade. Relations between Plymouth and Philip were strained in spite of a new treaty between them, but actual war was a result of a murder in January 1674. A convert to Christianity, or "praying Indian" (he was also a preaching Indian), named John Sassamon, who could read and write, had for some years been Philip's adviser at Sowans. In that January he came to see Governor Winslow and told him that Chief, or King, Philip was preparing for war. On his way home, Sassamon was waylaid and murdered by some of Philip's braves, but the murder was observed by another Indian, who reported the crime and the names of the murderers. The three were rounded up, tried, and found guilty. Two were hanged in June, the rope broke over the third, and he was shot in July. Philip's reaction was to send the wives and children of his tribe to the Narragansetts, clearing his decks, as it were, for action. Plymouth sent out a force under pretty inept leadership, but Philip evaded them and swept around nearly to the palisades of Plymouth, attacking Dartmouth, Middleborough, Taunton, and other towns. More of the tribes joined Philip, and the Narragansetts were suspect. The colony towns each took action against their local Indians whether they were for Philip or not, driving them from their encampments and rounding others up to pen them on Clarke Island. Yet many Indians on the Cape remained faithful and useful friends to the settlers, some of them working with the militia, in which all the able-bodied settlers were enlisted.

The first effective English counterattack was a surprise move against the Narragansetts, who were building a large, palisaded encampment in a swamp. In December 1675 a combined force from Plymouth, Massachusetts, and Connecticut broke through the uncompleted palisade and killed hundreds of men, women, and children. Their food supplies captured or burned, the survivors scattered into the forest to die of starvation and exposure in the snow and freezing temperature of a New England winter. Seventy of the English were killed, but the Great Swamp Fight broke the power of the Narragansetts, and they were never afterward a serious threat. They had intended to join forces with Philip but delayed too long; had they taken to the warpath earlier, it is possible that the whole of Plymouth Colony would have been exterminated.

With the spring of 1676, Indian raiding parties began to appear, and an isolated garrison at Eel River was destroyed and eleven colonists killed; two weeks later, a company of militia under Captain William

Pierce pursued what they thought was a small band of raiders and ran into an ambush set by a thousand warriors. Fifty colonists were killed. Two days later, the Indians burned the town of Rehoboth and made hit, loot, burn, and run raids on other towns. The town of Scituate was looted and burned. All communications with Boston ceased, and alarming rumors were abroad in Massachusetts to the effect that Plymouth, Duxbury, and Bridgewater were destroyed, but by the summer of 1676 the worst was over. Philip's raiding bands had spread terror everywhere, and only toward the end did the English learn the arts of forest fighting. Military leadership, too, had been inept in the early days of the war, but the policy of fortifying part of each little town, denying food supplies to all but known Indian friends, harassing Philip's men with their own tactics now began to detach Philip's allies, who came in small groups to surrender. Philip's braves, much weakened in number and stamina, withdrew to their own homeland. Richard Church of Duxbury followed with a force of practiced Indian fighters. Church himself believed that only Indian tactics would defeat Indians, and that the Indian should also be matched in savagery. Within a short time, he and his men killed nearly six hundred. Philip was reduced to a few warriors and pursued from swamp to swamp. Finally, in July 1676, he was ambushed and shot dead, and apart from mopping-up operations the war was over. No mercy was shown to captured Indians; they were sold into slavery, usually to the West Indies, though a fair number of the settlers acquired slaves for their own households. All the remaining Wampanoag lands were confiscated and sold to provide for soldiers crippled or impoverished or both. The Wampanoag tribe ceased to exist.

The English deaths in the war were about one hundred, but that represented about seven per cent of the adult males. Three of the colony's fourteen towns were abandoned, and burned by Indians; three suffered heavy damage; two were raided but not badly damaged; six escaped altogether.

Roger Williams lived quietly among the Indians on Rhode Island throughout the war.

Select Bibliography

Rye, W. B.: *England as Seen by Foreigners in the Days of Elizabeth.* John Russell Smith 1865

Rowse, A. L.: *The Expansion of Elizabethan England.* Macmillan 1955

Stamp, Sir Dudley; and Beever, S. H.: *The British Isles.* Longmans Green & Co. 1950

Harrison, William: *A Description of England.* Ed. F. J. Furnivall, New Shakespeare Society 1877

Verney, Margaret: *Memoirs of the Verney Family.* Pub. in 1892

Ascham, Roger: *The Schoolmaster.* 1570

Brereton, Nicholas: *Fantastickes.* Pub. in 1626

Overbury, Sir Thomas: *Characters.* Pub. in 1614/16

Davies, J. G.: *The Making of the Church.* Skeffington 1966

Williams, C. H.: *William Tyndale.* Thomas Nelson & Son 1969

Parker, T. M.: *The English Reformation to 1558.* Oxford University Press 1963

Hart, A. Tindal: *The Country Clergy.* Phoenix 1958

White, B. R.: *The English Separatist Tradition.* Oxford University Press 1971

Rops, Henri Daniel: *The Church in the 17th century.* J. M. Dent & Sons 1963

Burrage, C.: *Early English Dissenters.* Cambridge University Press 1912 (Many early works on Dissenters including pamphlets available in the British Museum not listed here.)

Cowie, L. W. *Seventeenth Century Europe*. G. Bell & Sons Ltd. 1960

Clark, G. N.: *The 17th Century*. Oxford University Press 1966

Jones, I. Deane: *The English Revolution*. Heinemann 1966

Tawney, R. H.: *The Agrarian Problem in the 16th Century*. Longmans 1912

Trevelyan, G. M.: *English Social History*. Longmans Green & Co. 1942

Bridenbaugh, Carl: *Vexed and Troubled Englishmen*. Clarendon Press 1968

Notestein, Wallace: *The English People on the Eve of Colonization*. Harper & Row 1962

Morgan, Edmund S.: *The Puritan Dilemma*. Little Brown & Co. 1958

Smith, Capt. John: *Description of New England*. London 1616

The Pilgrim Fathers and the History of New Plimouth

Bradford, William: *Of Plimmoth Plantation*. Many editions but that published for the Massachusetts Historical Society by Houghton Mifflin Company in 1912 has voluminous notes and splendid maps and illustrations.

Morison, Samuel Eliot: *Of Plymouth Plantation*. Alfred A. Knopf, New York, 1952. An excellent edition of Bradford in modern English with an extremely informative introduction.

Masefield, John: *Chronicles of the Pilgrim Fathers*. Everyman's Library. John Dent & Sons 1910. Contains Morton's *New England's Memorial* and *Winslow's Relation & Brief Narration*.

Arber, Edward: *The Story of the Pilgrim Fathers*. London 1897. Includes *Mourt's Relation*. Mourt is published in many editions.

Young, Alexander: *Chronicles of the Pilgrim Fathers*. Charles C. Little & James Brown 1841

Burgess, Walter H.: *John Robinson*. Williams & Norgate 1920

Dexter, H. & M.: *The England & Holland of the Pilgrims*. Houghton Mifflin 1906

Harris, J. R.; and Jones, S.: *The Pilgrim Press*. Cambridge University Press 1922

Kitteridge, Henry C.: *Cape Cod*. Houghton Mifflin 2nd ed. 1968

Strahler, Arthur N.: *A Geologist's View of Cape Cod*. Natural History Press, 1966

Darrett, B. Rutman: *Husbandmen of Plymouth*. Beacon Press 1967

Usher, Roland: *The Pilgrims and their History*. McMillan, 1918

Langdon, George D., Jr.: *Pilgrim Colony*. Yale University Press 1966

Willison, George F.: *Saints and Strangers*. Reynal & Hitchcock, 1945.
(Very lively and full account of the Pilgrims, with illuminating
notes and a very complete bibliography)
Gill, Crispin: *Mayflower Remembered*. David & Charles 1970

There are a great many other books on and around the Pilgrims.
Plimouth Plantation and the Pilgrim Society publish numerous
pamphlets based on original research. Some examples are
Arms & Armor of the Pilgrims—Harold L. Peterson
Medicine at Plymouth Plantation—John J. Byrne
Notes on Life in Plymouth Colony—John Demos
Three Visitors to Early Plymouth—ed. Sydney V. James
Pilgrim Corn Planting—Arthur G. Pyle

The Massachusetts Historical Society Collection has published a vast
amount of material, all of it available in Pilgrim Hall, Plymouth, as
are the Plymouth Church Records (1620–1859) in two volumes,
Plymouth Colony Records in twelve volumes, and Plymouth Town
Records in three volumes.

Index

246   INDEX